The religion of Orange politics

Protestantism and fraternity in contemporary Scotland

Joseph Webster

Manchester University Press

The right of Joseph Webster to be identified as the author of this work has been asserted by him in accordance with the Copyright, Designs and Patents Act 1988.

Published by Manchester University Press
Oxford Road, Manchester M13 9PL
www.manchesteruniversitypress.co.uk

British Library Cataloguing-in-Publication Data
A catalogue record for this book is available from the British Library

ISBN 978 1 5261 1376 4 hardback
ISBN 978 1 5261 1377 1 paperback

First published 2020
Paperback published 2022

The publisher has no responsibility for the persistence or accuracy of URLs for any external or third-party internet websites referred to in this book, and does not guarantee that any content on such websites is, or will remain, accurate or appropriate.

Typeset
by Sunrise Setting Ltd, Brixham

The religion of Orange politics

Manchester University Press

New
Ethnographies

Series editor
Alexander Thomas T. Smith

Already published

In loving memory of John Bainbridge Webster

(1955–2016)

But you are a chosen people, a royal priesthood, a holy nation, God's special possession, that you may declare the praises of him who called you out of darkness into his wonderful light. Once you were not a people, but now you are the people of God.

(1 Peter 2: 9–10)

Contents

Figures

Unless otherwise indicated, figures are photographs taken by the author.

Acknowledgements

A great many people have helped in the production of this book. I am indebted to the Isaac Newton Trust and to Downing College, Cambridge, for funding and hosting my post-doctoral Research Fellowship, the second year of which was spent conducting fieldwork in Scotland. Without this extended time in the field, this book would simply not exist. Thanks are also due to colleagues in Downing College, as well as in the Department of Social Anthropology in Cambridge, and in the School of History, Anthropology, Philosophy, and Politics in Queen's University Belfast. My time spent within these communities of scholars has been invaluable and has done much to shape this book. In Cambridge, particular thanks go to Timothy Jenkins, Joel Robbins, Jay Stock, and Harald Wydra for being excellent conversation partners at different times during my research. At Queen's University Belfast, Veronique Altglas, Dominic Bryan, Crawford Gribben, David Livingstone, Justin Livingstone, and Tristan Sturm have all significantly shaped my thinking on religion, Orange or otherwise. Outside of these institutions, Jacob Hickman at Brigham Young University has proved to be an invaluable fellow traveller in the anthropology of religion, giving thoughtful and generous feedback at every stage of the development of this book, most especially by providing extensive commentary on a full draft of the manuscript. I have also incurred intellectual debts from a great many other colleagues – too many to name. My thanks to you all.

I would also like to thank Tom Dark, Senior Commissioning Editor at Manchester University Press, for waiting patiently for the completion of the book, and also the anonymous reviewers for their helpful comments on the draft manuscript.

Of course, profound thanks go to all those within the Orange Order who have shared their lives with me, 'warts and all', in the words of one particularly close informant. As above, naming everyone who has helped me along the way would be impossible. Additionally, the strictures of anonymity prevent me from naming names, so the initials of a 'chosen few' will have to suffice. Within Grand Lodge, I am particularly indebted to RM, DB, PD, and JJ. In Glencruix, JT and IM became my closest informants, and also my friends. In Edinburgh, JM was a generous gatekeeper and an insightful interlocutor. Without the help from these seven Orangemen, the narrative of this book would be truly threadbare. I hope you feel I have given a fair account of life in the Order, warts and all.

Finally, profound thanks go to my family for showing such forbearance throughout seven long years of fieldwork and writing. To my father, John, I miss you, and to my mother, Jane, always a sympathetic listener, I thank you. To my in-laws David and Rosemary, thank you for being such patient tutors in the ways and means of Ulster politics and religion, and for welcoming me so warmly into your family. Most of all, thanks are due to Judith and Luke for putting up with so very much. I love you both dearly.

Abbreviations

DUP	Democratic Unionist Party
EDL	English Defence League
GOLS	Grand Orange Lodge of Scotland
IRA	Irish Republican Army
MSP	Member of the Scottish Parliament
NWO	New World Order
RAP	Royal Arch Purple
RBI	Royal Black Institution
RBP	Royal Black Preceptory
SDL	Scottish Defence League
SNP	Scottish National Party
SUP	Scottish Unionist Party
UDA	Ulster Defence Association
UVF	Ulster Volunteer Force
UKIP	United Kingdom Independence Party

Series editor's foreword

When the *New Ethnographies* series was launched in 2011, its aim was to publish the best new ethnographic monographs that promoted interdisciplinary debate and methodological innovation in the qualitative social sciences. Manchester University Press was the logical home for such a series, given the historical role it played in securing the ethnographic legacy of the famous 'Manchester School' of anthropological and interdisciplinary ethnographic research, pioneered by Max Gluckman in the years following the Second World War.

New Ethnographies has now established an enviable critical and commercial reputation. We have published titles on a wide variety of ethnographic subjects, including English football fans, Scottish Conservatives, Chagos islanders, international seafarers, African migrants in Ireland, post-civil war Sri Lanka, Iraqi women in Denmark and the British in rural France, among others. Our list of forthcoming titles, which continues to grow, reflects some of the best scholarship based on fresh ethnographic research carried out all around the world. Our authors are both established and emerging scholars, including some of the most exciting and innovative up-and-coming ethnographers of the next generation. *New Ethnographies* continues to provide a platform for social scientists and others engaging with ethnographic methods in new and imaginative ways. We also publish the work of those grappling with the 'new' ethnographic objects to which globalisation, geopolitical instability, transnational migration and the growth of neoliberal markets have given rise in the twenty-first century. We will continue to promote interdisciplinary debate about ethnographic methods as the series grows. Most importantly, we will continue to champion ethnography as a valuable tool for apprehending a world in flux.

Alexander Thomas T. Smith
Department of Sociology, University of Warwick

Introduction: Orangeism, Protestantism, anthropology

When I arrived at the Glencruix Orange Hall, Dennis[1] was already standing behind the main bar at the far end of the building. He was serving members of the Thursday Pensioners Club, men and women in their seventies and eighties who came each week to drink, play bingo, and dance to swing music. Dennis saw me from across the hall and shouted over to say he would be with me in a minute. His movements were brisk, and he looked harassed. Dennis didn't have much time for these particular pensioners, he had told me previously. Most were not members of the Orange, he explained, and they sat for long periods without buying drinks, earning the hall a meagre income. Worse still, he said, two Roman Catholic women had recently started coming along; while the pensioners merely used the hall as a venue, and were thus technically nothing to do with the Orange Order – he found their presence galling. Waiting for him to finish, I stood in the smaller front bar where local Orangemen congregated to drink, and looked at the now familiar Orange iconography covering the walls – King Billy on his horse, Rangers Football Club at Ibrox, official images of the Queen, commemorations of the Battle of the Somme, and lodge portraits of members in their regalia.

Finishing serving the pensioners as soon as he could, Dennis joined me to deliver some news that had clearly infuriated him. Rigghill Orange Hall, he declared, had made the decision to lower their Union flag to half mast for a member of their social club who was a Roman Catholic. The more he told me, the more upset he became. Pulsating with anger, Dennis proclaimed with outrage 'Rigghill Orange Hall lowered their flag to half mast for a dirty fucking fenian bastard who never worked a day in his life! The only reason he drinks in the Orange social club is because he was barred from the only other pub in the village for passing dud fivers!' Red in the face, Dennis continued by explaining that as a result of this decision, taken by three men in the social club without wider consultation, a founding member of the Rigghill Lodge was now threatening to leave the Orange Institution in protest. 'He phoned me up to complain, and he was so angry he was actually greeting! He was actually greeting! He's a lifelong founding member who has never missed a meeting in his life, and now he's threatening to leave! I'm fucking raging! The more I speak about it, the more I have smoke coming out my ears!'

Dennis had considered issuing a complaint to the relevant Orange authority at County Lodge level, but explained that he had decided not to, not because the matter was not serious, but because he did not want the wider Orange Institution to know what had happened. 'Glencruix District would become a laughing stock!' he spat. With anger turning to disgust, Dennis further explained that when the mother of the complainant had died, the man had not even received a sympathy card from the Orange Order. 'If they [the Orange hierarchy] think they are going to let a lifelong member walk away, they have another thing coming!' he roared. After finishing his account, Dennis paced the floor in an apparent attempt to devise some kind of solution. His silence was broken when an Orangeman and his wife entered the bar, prompting Dennis to retell the story from the beginning, given with heightened emotion and additional swearing. This retelling, however, was suddenly cut short when Dennis received a brief but loud call on his mobile phone. 'Do you know what the latest is? The funeral is in St Joseph's or whatever it's called, *and then the purvey is in Rigghill Hall!* It's an utter fucking disgrace!' By this point, Dennis was so angry he was close to tears. 'Unbelievable!' he continued, 'What the fuck is going on?'

Puzzled by how the situation had arisen, I asked Dennis why the Catholic man in question had been given social club membership in the first place. Wasn't the Orange Order a Protestant-only organisation, I reasoned? Dennis replied by patiently explaining that the Orange *Social Club* was institutionally detached from the Orange *Lodge*, meaning that members of the public could join the former without needing to be a member of the latter. 'But *I* wouldn't do it!' he cautioned:

> I wouldn't even let them [Catholics] in the door! If they [Rigghill Orange Social Club] want to take money off Catholics, then fair enough, *but they dinna get to touch the flag!* This is wrong because it completely refutes the Orange Institution! You work your whole life [for the Orange Institution], and for what?! So those fenian bastards can take the piss out of you? We can't go to a Roman Catholic chapel, but they can come to us, to the Orange Hall, after a funeral?

Changing tack, Dennis began to formulate a longer-term solution. The situation, he reasoned, required a permanent change to the Laws and Constitutions of the Grand Orange Lodge of Scotland, and, to this end, he was planning to submit a motion for a law stating that the only person who could authorise the lowering of an Orange hall's Union flag was the Master of the Lodge. Once again, Dennis was cut off in mid flow, this time by the arrival of two Orangemen who had come to Glencruix for a meeting with him. The matter appeared urgent, so Dennis asked me to cover the bar.

Clumsily pulling pints and pouring whiskies for the Orange regulars while serving ginger and limes to the pensioners, all for the first time in my life, felt both reassuring and disconcerting; it was a mark of rapport, but also a reminder of how foreign the hall had felt at the beginning of my fieldwork. After joking about my poor skills as a barman, Sandy, another Orangeman present that afternoon, began to regale the group with stories about his recent holiday in Benidorm, describing how he spent most of his time drinking in one of two establishments, an Ibrox-themed Rangers bar, and an Ulster Volunteer Force (UVF) bar. Sandy was clearly in a good mood; as soon as Dennis returned from his meeting, he smiled and nodded to his audience, indicating a wind-up was imminent. 'What's this I hear about the flag being lowered for some *fenian* in Rigghill?' he boomed with mock seriousness, looking round and winking to the others. 'Don't you fucking *start!*' Dennis barked back, 'it's *nae* funny!' Perhaps noting my surprise at his willingness to turn the situation into a joke, Sandy turned to me and said 'Dennis just tends to get upset about these things'. Graham, another Orange regular at the social club seemed to agree that Dennis was overreacting, but, in contrast to Sandy's deliberately patronising tone, told me with a serious expression how, after all, the dead man was from a *mixed* Catholic/Protestant family.

As the afternoon wore on, the discussion moved from stories about boozing in Rangers bars on holiday, to reminiscing about drunken ferry journeys while travelling to Northern Ireland for 12 July. All the while, Dennis was making and receiving calls on his mobile in an attempt to resolve the crisis at Rigghill. At one point, the men began to discuss the contrasting ways in which pubs in 'Protestant' Glencruix and 'Catholic' Chapelgeddie had marked the murder of drummer Lee Rigby, with the former offering statements of condolence, and the latter said to have put up posters with the slogan 'Another British bastard dead'. When I expressed doubt as to whether any such posters had ever appeared in Chapelgeddie, I was told in no uncertain terms that they had. Asking what motivated their display, the answer I received was as short as it was assured; the posters were put up because Catholics in Chapelgeddie hated the army and everything British. Later, the Orangemen present began to argue about a person I had never met. Feeling this to be a good opportunity to make my excuses and leave, I began to say my goodbyes, my mind reeling from all that I had heard over the course of the afternoon. Seeing me head for the door, Dennis interrupted his latest phone call, and, with a fixed stare shouted across the bar to me: 'I'll let you know how it goes with Rigghill, *and you can put that in your book, warts and all,* Joe!'

Context and questions

The incident above occurred in June 2013, about six months after my first trip to Glencruix, and about nine months into what was to become a five-year ethnographic investigation into the Orange Order in Scotland. Forming in 1795 in Ireland and arriving in Scotland in 1799, the Scottish Order today claims an estimated (but not undisputed) membership of 50,000, making it the largest Protestant-only fraternity in the country. Dennis was one of many Orangemen I came to know during my fieldwork. A retired lorry driver, Dennis was in his early seventies when I met him, a stout but immensely energetic man with a red complexion and dark hair. Dennis was, moreover, a leading Orangeman in Glencruix, a town of 37,000 people. Located roughly halfway between Edinburgh and Glasgow, Glencruix became a key field site during my research. Built on coal and manufacturing during the industrial revolution, today Glencruix has a distinctly post-industrial feel.[2]

While the town had clearly seen better days, Glencruix still had a strong Orange tradition, a fact that Dennis, who fondly referred to the Order as his 'church', was very proud of. Further, not only was Dennis a proud Orangeman, but he was also a passionate and outspoken individual. Importantly, however, while he chose to express them more strongly than did some of his fellow brethren, Dennis's Orange views and commitments were not out of sync with the general convictions of many of the 'grass-roots' members I came to know during my fieldwork. What, then, are we to make of the encounter above, and the 'Orange culture' from which it emerged?

Why did Dennis take offence at two Catholic women attending their local pensioners social club on the basis that the venue was an Orange hall? And why would Dennis begrudgingly overlook this, but never allow Catholics to join the *Orange* social club, despite no such ban appearing in the Institution's own laws? Why, furthermore, did the lowering of an Orange hall's Union flag to mark the death of a local Catholic man represent the crossing of a red line, an act which, in Dennis's words, 'completely refuted' the Orange Institution? Why was the holding of a wake in the Orange hall seen as adding insult to injury? And why did Dennis repeatedly express his anger – to a researcher no less – in such strongly sectarian terms? Why did Sandy try and turn the situation into a joke, a humorous opportunity for banter? And why did Graham suggest that Dennis was overreacting on the basis of the entirely serious suggestion that the deceased man was somehow only *half* Catholic? Why did Dennis feel the Orange Institution was to blame, and why, in his mind, was the only possible solution a formal change to the Order's laws and constitutions? And why, finally, despite his fear of becoming a 'laughing stock', did Dennis implore me to include the incident, 'warts and all', when writing my book?

In asking questions such as these, this book will examine not only the ethnographic specificities of flags lowered, hate expressed, jokes made, and laws proposed, but will do so by placing such ethnographic phenomena within a wider historical, social, and political context. Here, a series of 'isms' familiar to those who have some knowledge of the Protestant world view of Central Scotland and Northern Ireland will necessarily take to the stage. Thus, throughout the pages that follow, mixed together in different combinations and concentrations, will be found not only the classic 'PUL' cocktail of 'Protestantism, unionism, and loyalism', but also the associated 'isms' of fraternalism, patriotism, conservativism, royalism and militarism, as well as that most hotly contested label, in Scotland at least, of sectarianism.

While the contestation is real, it remains true to say that the Order is ultra-Protestant, ultra-British, and, by extension, ultra-unionist, being dedicated to preserving the constitutional status quo of the United Kingdom as a fourfold family of nations made up of England, Scotland, Wales, and Northern Ireland. Yet, importantly, such context – made all the more acute by ongoing debates about Scottish independence and Brexit – will not be treated as mere backdrop, nor will it be regarded as determinative, but instead will be seen as co-constitutive of the actions and intentions of my Orange informants. Furthermore, while it may be fair to regard the 'isms' listed above as emic self-essentialisms, I will also argue throughout this book that these local ideal types may simultaneously be deployed as useful etic taxonomies with which to examine certain aspects of Scots-Orange sociality. As I describe below, most particularly in relation to my engagement with new debates within the anthropology of ethics and morality, using such emic concepts to engage in etic theory-building is a crucial step for those who seek to 'take seriously' the moral claims of others, for to do so allows our informants – in the truest sense of the word – to instruct us in such a way that we not only learn *about* those moral commitments, but also *from* them (Laidlaw 2014: 46. See also Robbins and Engelke 2010, da Col and Graeber 2011). Without wanting to pre-empt my argument too much, it seems worth noting at this stage that seeking to be instructed, corrected, and even rebuked by the moral commitments of Scots-Orangemen provides striking analytical insights, but also pointed ethical challenges. It is to the theoretical framing of these insights and challenges that I now wish to turn.

The anthropology of Christianity, morality, and ethics

While Scots-Orange sociality forms the empirical focus of this book, its broader conceptual focus is situated within both the anthropology of Christianity and the anthropology of ethics and morality.[3] Assessed critically, one could try and make the case that this dual focus is no focus at all, promising only to produce a kind of blurry double vision by conflating the foundational questions of these two intellectual projects, namely 'what difference does Christianity make?' (Cannell 2006: 1) and 'where is the ethical located?' (Lambek 2010: 39). Such an assessment, however, problematically assumes a basic incompatibility between the study of religion and the study of ethics and morality. Thus, while these questions should not be conflated by some ethnographic sleight of hand, it would be equally stultifying to pose religion on one hand and ethics and morality on the other, or indeed transcendence and immanence (Webster 2013), as entirely separate and incommensurable forces. Instead, then, by taking up the question 'what difference does Christianity make?', this book draws inspiration from Cannell's call to attend to the dual impetuses of 'Christianities as they are *lived*, in all their *imaginative* force' (Cannell 2006: 5. Emphasis added). Equally, by attending to both lived practice and imaginative belief, this book also takes up the question 'where is the ethical located?' Yet, in marked contrast to Lambek's wariness of the tendency of religion to intellectualise or transcendentalise ethics (2010: 3), this book finds ethics and morality not only within 'everyday comportment and understanding' (ibid.), but also within the 'reified abstractions' (ibid.: 4) of Orange belief, for example, in (intellectualised) British Israelite theology and (transcendentalised) Orange ritual. What such an observation suggests, I shall argue, is that, very often, the ostensible ordinariness of 'ordinary ethics' maintains a distinctly extraordinary character, despite its occurring as part of everyday Orange experience.

In reply, a differently critical assessment would be to regard such an approach not as 'double vision' but as more akin to bifocal lenses, producing two coexisting but still distinct optical planes. Thus, in asking 'what difference does Christianity make?', certain expressions of the anthropology of Christianity could be seen (perhaps somewhat counter-intuitively, given its ethnographic grounding) as suffering from a long-sightedness that comes as a consequence of an overly idealist attentive-ness to Christian meaning-making, belief, and theology (see Hann 2007). Conversely, in asking 'where is the ethical located?', certain expressions of the anthropology of ethics could be seen (again, somewhat counter-intuitively, given its philosophical grounding) as suffering from a short-sightedness that comes as a consequence of an overly materialist attentiveness to action, performance, and practice (see Robbins 2016). In this assessment, a dual conceptual focus on the anthropology of Christianity and the anthropology of ethics and morality act as bifocal glasses, producing two largely discrete and non-integrated perspectives, forcing the observer to toggle between 'transcendent' Christian hyperopia and 'ordinary' ethical myopia.

Yet, as above, this assessment seems to underestimate the extent to which extraordinary sacrality and everyday profanity are co-constitutive. In making this claim that transcendence and immanence, the sacred and the profane, and the extraordinary and the everyday necessarily co-constitute each other, I want to briefly set out a third possible assessment of the bringing together of the anthropology of Christianity and the anthropology of ethics. It is a more optimistic assessment than those outlined above, but it is not, I hope, a fanciful one. Readers will have to judge for themselves, of course; I only state it here, choosing instead to contend for it within the context of the ethnography that follows. Put simply, the position I have in mind would be to assess the different perspectives that the anthropology of Christianity and the anthropology of ethics offer the wider discipline as being broadly compatible. In this assessment, such a combination of perspectives would produce neither blurred double vision, nor unintegrated bifocal vision, but the kind of sight achievable when seeing the world through varifocal glasses. Such sight is dependent, it seems, upon clearly and convincingly integrating anthropologi-cal studies of religion, which take *belief* as a core concern, with anthropological studies of ethics and morality which take *practice* as their core concern. My suggestion is that this may best be achieved by refusing to regard religious belief as a metonym for disembodied transcendence, while also refusing to regard ordinary practice as a metonym for embodied action. Indeed, the very claiming of the word 'ordinary' by proponents of the ordinary ethics position is to render human experiences of transcendence as somehow 'out of the ordinary'. A varifocal view of religion and ethics (and indeed religion-*as*-ethics), would, in contrast, take human reflections upon religious beliefs to be 'ordinary' ethical acts with eminently practical conse-quences. Religious rumination is not opposed to the ordinary, since, for Orangemen at least, religious rumination *is* ordinary. It is part of the living of everyday life.

This is to put the matter crudely, yet, in doing so, we seem better able to grasp the extent to which the anthropology of Christianity and the anthropology of ethics and morality might address a single common question, namely, 'what should life be like?' The question is unavoidably normative and thus imaginative, addressing in the first instance not what life *is* like but focusing instead on what life *should* be like. Moreover, as a normative question, its being asked (and answered) seems to throw us back onto empirical studies of belief, of what is believed to be good or even 'evil' (Clough and Mitchell 2001, Csordas 2013, Olsen and Csordas 2019) and thus to be sought after or resisted, in the partial absence of its immanent presence in the here and now, like so many gods and spirits. Clearly, then, while beliefs may take many forms, in doing so they frequently retain a reflective and imaginative emphasis, as will be seen, for example, in the belief of many Orangemen that British Protestants are God's chosen people, or that Roman Catholicism conspires to rule the world. Yet, a key part of my argument here is that partially shifting focus away from immanent action and towards transcendent normativity is not tantamount to ignoring 'practice'. Seen from this vantage point, the question is thus also unavoidably *realist*: 'what should *life* be like?' Indeed, when taken as a kind of culturally framed moral realism (see Hickman 2019: 51–52), the question above can be seen as restating an emphasis on 'ordinary' ethical living, made manifest, for example, in the bureaucratic committee work of the Orange hierarchy as they process membership forms, collect lodge fees, or negotiate parade routes and traffic management plans with local councillors.

It is here, in a shared interest in what we might call *enacted moral normativity*, where the anthropology of Christianity and the anthropology of ethics meet, for it is this that both Christianity as religious 'values' (Robbins 2007) and ethics as 'practical judgement' (Lambek 2010: 61) strive for. And it is here, furthermore, precisely at the point where neither religion nor ethics is able to claim a monopoly over imaginative reflection or ordinary action, where we begin to ethnographically appreciate how belief may become a kind of practice, and how practice may become a kind of belief. As we shall see, this is the case among Scots-Orangemen insofar as religious transcendence is never *just* transcendence, but also finds itself indebted to the goings-on of ordinary everyday life. From this perspective, parading behind an open Bible topped with a plastic crown is not only a mystical enactment of the divine union between God and Queen Elizabeth II, but is also a decidedly routine and this-worldly statement of the right to freedom of assembly. Equally, ordinary ethics is never just ordinary, but also finds itself indebted to the goings-on of extraordinary transcendent religiosity. Thus, establishing parading routes not only involves navigating local government paperwork, but, from an Orange perspective, frequently requires one to resist the machinations of the Church of Rome and its dark spiritual efforts to bureaucratically debar loyal Protestant processions.

It is in this sense that 'the ordinary and the religious' (Robbins 2016: 6) coexist. Indeed, for Robbins:

> human beings really do sometimes stand back from the flow of their lives – it's the kind of thing that, as human beings, they can do, and often enough they resort to it. Such standing back, I want to suggest, is not less basic to people's ethical existence than their ability to participate in the flow of everyday life … For these reasons, I think the anthropological study of ethics would be impoverished if it were reduced to the study only of its ordinary, everyday forms, and in fact maybe the everyday itself does not make sense without some attention to the religious as well. (2016: 9)

The logic here seems clear. Standing back from ordinary, everyday life, to reflect upon the transcendent and the extraordinary is something that humans engage in; Orangemen ruminate on the mystical meanings of ritual initiation ceremonies, for example. In doing so, the transcendent, and belief in the transcendent, becomes a kind of practice, an action occurring within the everyday, while retaining its extraordinary character. The opposite is also true; everyday, ordinary life may be given an extraordinary character. In drinking pints of lager with fellow initiates, Orangemen create – they instantiate – mystical bonds of Protestant fraternal love, rendering 'normal' practice a kind of religious belief. Remaining within this ethnographic context of Scots-Orangeism, we now seem able to reformulate our earlier question ('what should life be like?') in such a way that the anthropology of Christianity and the anthropology of ethics may gain real, and simultaneous, purchase on the ways in which transcendent values and practical judgements co-constitute each other.

The question, reformulated in light of the above, is this: *what should a good Protestant life be like?* Framed in this way, the question inescapably addresses both religion and ethics, and, in doing so, requires that the transcendence of belief and the ordinariness of practice be examined not side by side (for to do so would return us to our bifocal critique) but by gradations, treating religious values and practical judgements as conjoined through a shared observational perspective of imagined normativity and realised action. Clearly, while the question is being posed in such a way as to produce a figurative varifocal theoretical lens, what is being looked at through this lens is ethnographic in form. So, according to Scottish Orangemen – according to their religious beliefs, their ordinary practices, their history, their ritual, their fraternal commitments, and their politics – what should a good Protestant life be like? It is this question that this book seeks to answer.

'The Good' of Protestant-Orange exceptionalism

Crucially, as the ethnography with which I opened this chapter indicates, some of the answers to this question may not fit standard definitions of 'Protestantism' or indeed 'The Good'. So important is this point, that failing to fully grasp it will lead the reader to misunderstand nearly everything in the chapters which follow. This being the case, it seems worthwhile taking some time to explain what I mean here, both in relation to the theoretical context of the anthropology of Christianity and ethics, and in relation to how such ethnography might challenge the reader to rethink what makes 'Protestantism' Protestant or 'The Good' good. Importantly, I am not asking the reader to undertake anything that I have not also imposed upon myself. Indeed, this task of 'rethinking' is one I have been undertaking since I began to spend time with Scottish Orangemen in 2012.

Very frequently, my assumptions about 'proper' Protestantism and 'genuine' goodness have been shown, through the process of doing the fieldwork, to be largely incompatible with the assumptions and behaviours of many of my Orange informants. Not being content to wallow in ethnocentric ignorance, I have sought instead to embrace the classic Weberian paradigm of *verstehen*, a mode of interpretation that can also be found at the heart of Geertz's (1984) famous essay 'Anti anti-relativism'. In practical terms, this has involved applying the basic principle of Weber's interpretative method to my own ethnographic data. Thus, where my assumptions about 'a good Protestant life' appeared at odds with the assumptions of my informants, it was *my* assumptions which were relinquished. The results have been insightful as well as unsettling – a process well known to anthropologists who emphasise the undertaking of fieldwork as centrally involving not only the adoption of new perspectives, but also a concomitant unlearning of previously held perspectives (see Jenkins 1994, Hastrup 2004). A few examples may be helpfully clarifying.

Prior fieldwork in Gamrie – a Brethren fishing village in north-east Scotland – had taught me that attending church, studying the Bible, and sharing one's 'born-again' testimony were all central to being a Protestant Christian (Webster 2013). My time among the Brethren also taught me that drinking in pubs, habitually swearing, and celebrating sectarian football rivalries would all disqualify a person from calling themselves a Christian, Protestant or otherwise. Gamrie's Christians, as a result, had given me a highly specific view of what normatively constituted 'a good Protestant life', and it was this view that I carried with me when embarking on new fieldwork among the Orange Order. I quickly realised, however, that this Brethren view of what a good Protestant life should look like left me ill-equipped to understand the kind of Protestantism my Orange informants were committed to. In the first instance, this was because the majority of Scots-Orangemen I met almost never attended church, only encountered the Bible when it was read aloud to them in lodge meetings, and had no experience whatever of born-again conversion as understood by the Brethren of Gamrie. Yet, my Orange informants not only regarded themselves as staunchly Protestant, but as the single most important voice of 'the Protestant people of Scotland'.

Intriguingly, it was often precisely those things the Brethren abhorred most that many of my Orange informants regarded as fundamental to their Protestant identity, namely supporting Rangers Football Club, drinking with fellow Orangemen, espousing sectarian views, embracing the politics of unionism, and performing secret Masonic-inspired rituals. Moreover, this way of life was, for my Orange informants, not only quintessentially Protestant, but also *good*. Contrary to what the Brethren of Gamrie believed, then, Old Firm matches were not sinful displays of drunkenness and hate, but, within the culture of Orangeism, were held to be opportunities for patriotic displays of national pride and Protestant fervour. Equally, campaigning against Scottish independence on religious grounds did not represent an evil attempt to pollute true Christianity with worldly politics (as the Brethren would see it), but was simply a fulfilment of one's religious duty to serve both God and Britain's anointed Protestant monarch. In the same way, taking part in Orange Masonic-style ritual was not a demonic act tantamount to devil worship, but a solemn spiritual re-enactment of ancient Biblical narratives and teachings. For my Scots-Orange informants, then, the Orange Institution defined and defended not only good Protestant *religiosity* but also, even more fundamentally, good Protestant *morality*. Importantly, as I argue throughout this book, far from justifying a kind of Durkheimian 'conflation of the moral and the cultural' (Robbins 2007: 294) whereby 'the moral ... does no distinctive conceptual work' (Laidlaw 2002: 313), such acts of defining and defending Protestantism appeared to take Orange religious and ecclesiastical adherence as a strikingly optional expression of the morality of Orange exceptionalism.

Yet, as will become clear in the chapters that follow, none of these emic claims go far enough, in and of themselves, if we want to fully grasp the kind of ethnographic and ethical re-evaluations that Scots-Orangeism seems to demand. In ethnographic terms, then, what if being a Scottish Protestant has little or nothing to do with regular church attendance, personal Bible study, or an 'inward experience' of 'born-again' conversion? What if, instead, the religiosity of Scots-Protestantism is defined by ethno-nationalism, fraternal bonds, footballing loyalties, political commitments, and Masonic-inspired ritual initiations? And what if, in moral terms, being a Scottish Protestant has little or nothing to do with personal piety, spiritual quietism, political non-participation, and strict teetotalism? What if, instead, the morality of Scots-Protestantism is defined by 'The Good' of ethno-nationalist exclusion, anti-Catholic bigotry, and, in extreme cases, alcohol-fuelled sectarian hate? Put another way, what if the ideal-type of a 'good Protestant' is not an elderly Brethren woman attending a prayer meeting, but an Orangeman parading with his lodge, drinking in his social club, and chanting 'The Billy Boys' at Ibrox? Are these latter images a viable place to start when seeking to interpret the ethnography with which I began, and might such images require us to redefine 'the Protestant good'? My claim is that they are, and they do.

By making this case, I follow Laidlaw in suggesting that 'the anthropological study of ethics is capable of being itself a form of ethical practice' (2014: 45). Yet, I cannot help but feel that making this case via an ethnographic study of Scottish Orangeism is going to be a 'harder sell' than if I were making the same case via a study of Jainism in India. My suspicion is that, while for many readers the strictures of Jain asceticism surely represents the carrying of a heavy moral burden, it also represents something that feels instinctively good, a valuing of all life in the highest possible terms, for example, or a critical attitude to avarice. In contrast, I suspect that many readers will see within Scots-Orangeism something that feels instinctively bad – contentious Orange parades which spark public disorder, or the fraternal celebration of casual anti-Catholic bigotry. Despite this challenge, I want to try and persevere in adopting this particular version of 'the ethnographic stance' (ibid.) which, according to Laidlaw, requires:

> in a specific sense *taking seriously* the forms of life we describe: regarding them – and therefore describing them – as something we learn from as well as about; and it involves learning to think with as well as about its concepts, such that they become resources in our own critical reflection and self-constitution. (2014: 46)

If Laidlaw is correct that allowing the forms of life we study to become part of our very self-constitution is 'a precondition … for anthropology as ethical practice' (ibid.) – and I am convinced that he is – then what might this mean for those of us who study the morality of hate directly, as opposed to studying its management by the State? (see Shoshan 2016). Must I become filled with sectarian hate as Rosaldo (1989), during a time of grief, found himself to be overtaken by rage? Happily, Laidlaw's answer is no, for this ethnographic stance does not require that the anthropologist of morality 'adopt its concepts and values as his or her own' (2014: 45). What then? How might I learn from a Scots-Orange morality built upon Protestant exceptionalism and anti-Catholic bigotry without fully adopting it as my own ethical subject-position? One answer, which falls short of full adoption, is to engage in a deliberate and considered refusal to reject or condemn this Orange morality. By drawing inspiration from Webb Keane's suggestion that 'we shouldn't decide in advance what ethics will look like' (2014: 444), I will argue, therefore, that Scots-Orangeism and Scots-Orange culture cannot be assumed to exist outside of established normative models of the Protestant good. If Keane is right, (and, as with Laidlaw, I am convinced that he is), then a startling implication of his proposal is that confrontational parading, fraternal drunkenness, and sectarian football chanting *can* be Protestant, that is, they *can* be understood within the anthropology of Christianity as part of certain human experiences of 'the religious'. Furthermore, if, as I have argued above, the moral cannot be subsumed under the religious, another, perhaps even more startling, implication of Keane's proposal is that exclusion, bigotry, and hate *can* be moral (see Shweder 2016), that is, they *can* be understood within the anthropology of ethics and morality as part of certain human experiences of 'The Good'.

As the reader progresses through the book, it will become clear how both of these arguments – that bigotry, for example, can be moral, or that drunkenness can be Protestant – rest upon a wider ethnographic and theoretical claim about the nature of exceptionalism. In ethnographic terms, my argument is that, for my informants, a good Protestant life is a life that affirms and protects Orange exceptionalism. The theme of exceptionalism permeated every aspect of my fieldwork. Many of my informants openly admitted that they believed British Protestants in general and Orange Protestants in particular to be historically, politically, ethnically and religiously special – a chosen people whose greatness stemmed from their being uniquely enlightened by the God of the Reformation. Moreover, for some of my informants, such a perspective meant that Orange triumphalism and anti-Catholic bigotry were both unavoidable and unassailable. Indeed, as one Orange informant explained to me, such sentiments were written into the very definition of the word 'bigot' – 'by God' – a phrase which he extended to mean 'by God I can do no more'.

In theoretical terms, my more general argument is that the Orange Order have no monopoly over exceptionalism. Indeed, I want to suggest that the promotion of such sentiments is remarkably widespread. In essence, my argument here will be that political, religious, and ethnic difference has the potential to erupt into social conflict because people like people like themselves. Put another way, people struggle with human difference, because they value human similarity, because they feel that their particular social group (however one defines it) is special. By drawing on Barth (1969) on ethnic boundaries, the end result of this pull towards similarity, is, I argue, that people desire to be surrounded by those they regard as like them, be they loyal Protestant Orangemen, or liberal cosmopolitan pluralists. As we shall see, while some members of these social groups define similarity and difference in ethnic terms (people who look like us), others may police the boundaries of belonging in ideological terms (people who believe the same as us), while still others may do both, drawing boundaries along ethno-nationalist and ethno-religious lines.

It needs to be stated at the outset that exploring the implications of these ethnographic and theoretical claims may take the reader to some uncomfortable places. Can bigotry really be moral, can it really be *good*? Do most people advocate, in some way, for their own exceptionalism? Regardless of my use of Laidlaw and Keane above, such pointed deployment of *verstehen* (or the 'ethnographic stance'), while arguably residing at the very heart of the anthropological quest for cross-cultural understanding, has the tendency to trigger accusations that not only has the ethnographer developed a methodological empathy with their informants, but also that they have developed (or perhaps always had) a personal sympathy for them (see Harding 1991 and Cannell 2005). This distinction is important to maintain, however, for where empathy involves a reflexive 'feeling into' the informant's world view, sympathy, by contrast, is about 'feeling with', and occurs largely uncritically and pre-reflexively, as if one had always cohabited within the informant's world and world view. Put another way, where empathy is a kind of 'reaching out', a fostering of new understandings, sympathy is a kind of 'digging in', or an affirming pre-established agreement. Within this framework, the words and arguments of this book may be read as an exercise in empathy, as I attempt to feel my way into the world of Scots-Orangeism, 'warts and all', as per my informants' demands.

What happens, then, if having understood the world and world view of the informant, the student of *verstehen* subsequently concludes that they do not particularly like that world and that they are not particularly sympathetic to it? (see Van Wyk 2013). One response might be to render the emic subordinate to the etic by super-imposing a second-level explanation on top of the first-level explanation already gained through *verstehen*. Reacting to the ethnography above, for example, Freudian theory might superimpose upon Dennis's words the notion of pathology (stating 'I understand what you are saying, but you are mentally unwell'). Equally, Marxist theory might superimpose the notion of false consciousness (stating 'I understand what you are saying, but you have been misled'). Yet, these accounts seem inadequate, for while their explanatory expressions may differ (clearly, I have oversimplified them for the sake of brevity), their shared final destination is still essentially reductionist, as seen in their refusal to countenance the analytical import of the actor's account of their own actions. A different response would be to persist in attempts to grasp the content of the emic, but then to proceed from there to some form of 'militant' ethical critique (Scheper-Hughes 1995) – a critique, for example, that understands Dennis's words, but condemns them (and, by extension, him). A researcher committed to an activist version of critical theory, for example, might simply conclude that Dennis's words are inherently sectarian, and therefore unacceptable and unjust. Yet this kind of critique, it would seem to me, still places a stranglehold on genuine *verstehen* insofar as it fails to heed Keane's warning that 'we shouldn't decide in advance what ethics will look like' (2014: 444). In this instance, then, the analysis is not conceptually reductionist but morally ethnocentric (see Kapferer and Gold 2018: 12), affirming and reproducing the ethical view of the researcher, by placing themselves within a kind of etic (and perhaps even anthropologically emic) echo chamber.

The obvious objection here is that I am calling for a suspension of critique. And in one sense this is fair, because this *is* what I am calling for, at least in the first instance. My contention is that really powerful ethnographic description and understanding require the ethnographer to hold in the back of their mind the nagging question 'what if they're right and I'm wrong?', that is, 'what if their world view accurately and legitimately disqualifies my own?' Here, the anthropologist does not confront poly-ontology (Scott 2007) but a singular world where my informants are correct, and I am mistaken. During my research among Scottish Brethren fishermen, this required asking myself 'what if the world really is about to end?'; 'what if the EU really is the anti-Christ?'; 'what if the vast majority of the population of the world really will be sent to hell?' Unpleasant as these questions were, they did not often require me to step into the same kind of ethno-religious bigotry that I encountered in the Glencruix Orange Social Club. The question 'what if Catholics and Protestants really should hate each other?' is almost impossible to ask, and for good reasons, as the history of Northern Ireland has taught us. Yet, it seems important to note that simply asking the question productively forces us into uncharted territory, not only methodologically, but also theoretically, as we struggle to come to terms with how, if at all, the anthropology of morality (see Robbins 2012, Mattingly and Throop 2018) can make sense of human experiences of bigotry and hate within its own (current) models of 'The Good'. My suspicion is that contemporary anthropology is ill equipped for such a task.

Yet, asking and then *not answering* a question can only take us so far. How, then, might we understand the morality of Scots-Orangeism anthropologically, without resorting to analytical reductionism, ethnocentric critique, or poly-ontology? The approach I take in the chapters that follow is one that seeks to examine and understand how my informants moralise their own beliefs and actions, and those of their Orange brethren, as good and proper and valuable. In doing so, my investigation into Scots-Orange morality is not uncritical, but attempts to hear (and listen to) the Orange critique of dominant models of 'The Good' as they are currently used within anthropology, asking what, if anything, can we learn from voices like Dennis's? This is not, in and of itself, a new anthropological approach; Margaret Mead (1928), for example, in her infamous account of the sexual lives of adolescent Samoans, had, as her target for critique, the social-sexual and educational mores of 'Western Civilisation'. Similarly, Sahlins' (1966) account of hunter-gatherers as the 'original affluent society' stands primarily as a critical account of Western capitalism. For Mead and Sahlins, then, one purpose of providing ethnographic accounts of exotic non-Western others is to allow these 'others' to offer up powerful ethical critique of Western values. Furthermore, such once-removed critiques are important insofar as they are not reductionist or ethnocentric, nor do they posit some form of poly-ontology, but instead offer the possibility of the emic correcting the etic.

My approach contains this same impulse to allow the emic to critique the etic but is also marked by some important differences. Mead, for example, offered her critique of Western sexual conservativism (via a sympathetic ethnography of Samoa) in order to advocate for the liberalisation of sexual politics. Similarly, Sahlins offered his critique of Western capitalism (via a sympathetic ethnography of hunter-gatherers) in order to advocate for a curtailment of neo-liberal avarice. My approach is different insofar as its final destination is a specific critique of anthropological models of morality, not, as I read in Mead and in Sahlins, a more general critique of Western ethics and social attitudes. Additionally, while the final destination of my critique is anthropological theory which refuses on principle to 'learn from' (Laidlaw 2014: 46) Orange morality, the pathway of my critique is an (empathetic) ethnographic account of the moral content of Scottish Orangeism. More specifically, what I have attempted to understand and empathise with are Orange critiques of popular political discourses within contemporary Scottish society which state that 'good' morality, like 'good' religion must, by definition, be liberal, tolerant, inclusive, and pluralist. In this sense, my Orange informants and I do share a common critique of the way in which liberal pluralism monopolises certain understandings of 'The Good'. Crucially, however, my critique is motivated by a desire to better equip anthropological theory to understand and thereby learn from 'non-liberal' (see Fader 2009) and non-pluralist cultures such as Orange exceptionalism, whereas the critique of my informants is, by their own admission, motivated by a desire to propagate Orange exceptionalism.

Thus, by using ethnography to show how my informants moralised themselves and wider Scottish society, I seek to place my informants in conversation with the kind of 'anti anti-relativist' anthropology that I find in the work of Clifford Geertz and Webb Keane, and, perhaps more fundamentally, at the heart of the Weberian project of *verstehen*. As described above, the conceptual basis of this conversation is found within the notion of exceptionalism. Exceptionalism, then, acts as the varifocal lens of this book – a lens through which the 'glorious' history, 'triumphal' parading, 'fraternal' belonging, 'patriotic' politics, and 'loyal' Protestantism of Scots-Orangeism will be viewed, in all its ideational and experiential complexity. Yet, of course, such complexity does not add up to a singular Orange reality, nor do Orangemen offer a unified emic account or monolithic 'native point of view'. Indeed, I found, very often, that the opposite was the case, whereby the Institution and its members appeared always to be doing more than one thing at once, and often in combinations that seemed contradictory. With this in mind, (and at the risk of engaging in just such a self-contradiction), I want to consider how any account of Scots-Orangeism must seek to empathise with and thereby integrate several different perspectives at the same time.

Scottish Orangeism as heterogeneous, homogenous, and dualist

Members of the Orange Order commonly describe the Institution to outsiders as a 'broad church', by which they mean that the Order is diverse, drawing into its ranks people with a range of different views, experiences, and priorities. Over the course of my ethnographic research among the Order in Scotland, I came to realise that this frequently offered description was simultaneously (and somewhat paradoxically) a significant understatement and a major exaggeration. In terms of being a significant understatement, my time among the Orange Order taught me that Scottish Orangemen commit themselves, as Orangemen, to a remarkably heterogeneous set of ideologies and practices. Indeed, described within the pages of this book are encounters with Orangemen who strongly maintain that the Order is, first and foremost, an evangelical Christian organisation which seeks to reclaim Scotland for Christ and 'the gospel'. Yet this book also describes encounters with Orangemen who openly admitted that they virtually never attended church and viewed public worship as almost entirely unimportant to the Institution as a Protestant organisation. For these members, the essence of Orangeism was, variously: its popular affiliation to Rangers Football Club; its close connection to the loyalist band scene; its support for the 'Protestant cause' in Ulster and; its defence of Britishness and the politics of unionism more generally.

Furthermore, contrary to the anti-ecumenicalism found among many conservative Protestants, a wide range of denominational backgrounds were represented within the Order, with Orangemen from the Church of Scotland, the United Reformed Church, the Episcopal Church, the Methodist Church, and those attending Congregationalist and independent evangelical churches. Equally, I met many Orangemen who were also Freemasons and who viewed the Order's similarities to Freemasonry – in structure, in ritual, and in symbol – as highly significant to their Orange identity (see Buckley 1985: 6–7, Cairns and Smyth 2002: 150, 152). I met other Orangemen who were strongly critical of the Masons, and virulently denied that there was any substantive or meaningful connection between the two organisations, either in style or in membership. In a similar manner, I met several Orangemen who, owing to their interpretation of Orange ritual, were avid British Israelites, while other members regarded the idea that British Protestants were biologically descended from the lost tribes of Israel as 'a bit heavy' and 'a lot to swallow'. I also met Orangemen from across the political spectrum, including trade union activists who self-identified as socialists, Labour Party members running for council, moderate Tory supporters, Scottish Unionist Party founders, UK Independence Party (UKIP) voters, and some with far-right sympathies. I even met an Orangeman who was a long-standing member of the Scottish National Party (SNP) and a supporter of Scottish independence, although as described in Chapter 5, this individual could be seen as the exception that proves the unionist rule.

As I built rapport with different members over time, several Orangemen I spoke with began to open up to me about their ongoing paramilitary sympathies. Indeed, a small number went as far as claiming active involvement in paramilitarism, some before and some after the signing of the Good Friday Agreement. I even interviewed one Scottish Orangeman who had served a custodial sentence for his involvement with the Ulster Defence Association (UDA). Yet I also met Orangemen, most often at Grand Lodge level, who not only condemned paramilitarism and paramilitary violence, but sought to expel from the Institution those who openly challenged this position. Moreover, and with a similar degree of variation, several of my key informants openly admitted to being (in their own words) 'bigots' who 'hated Roman Catholics'. Other Orangemen I met, however, were deeply uncomfortable with such sectarian attitudes, and sought to explain to me how their objections to Roman Catholic doctrine did not preclude them from being on good terms with

Roman Catholic individuals such as neighbours and colleagues, and, where 'mixed marriages' had taken place in the wider family, their Catholic sons-in-law, nieces, nephews and so on.

Another way to try and encapsulate this heterogeneity is to look beyond the immediate bounds of the Orange membership to include something of the variation within the other Loyal Orders, and among informal Orange sympathisers. Importantly, these other Orders and individuals were publicly recognised by Orange members as allies who were part of the wider 'Orange family', albeit to differing degrees. Such recognition was formally extended, for example, during platform speeches on parade days. Here my ethnography found an even wider ideological array among these 'loyal Protestant friends', as they were often called. Indeed, this array was inclusive of everything from the trenchant loyalism of 'Kick the Pope' bands, Rangers supporters clubs, and the Apprentice Boys of Derry, to the sterner Masonic-infused evangelicalism of the Royal Black Institution, a sister institution of the Orange Order. More than this, conducting fieldwork in the Greater Glasgow area around the time of both the Scottish independence referendum campaign and the flags dispute in Northern Ireland (see Nolan et al. 2014), I observed a further widening of the spectrum of 'Orange sympathisers'. Here, my fieldwork led me into contact with 'Maintain the Union', a loyalist campaign against Scottish independence, led by a key Orange informant of mine. The campaign had connections to the UVF-linked Progressive Unionist Party and the Rangers FC 'ultras' group, the Vanguard Bears. It was at a 'Maintain the Union' protest, furthermore, where I first came into direct contact with members of UKIP, as well as the hard-line loyalist group the Commonwealth Unionist Party (CUP), and the far-right street protest movement the Scottish Defence League (SDL). Such is the variety of Orangeism in Scotland.

But what are we to make of this variety – of Orangemen and Freemasons, of Rangers FC 'ultras' and Episcopalian ministers, of socialist trade unionists and far-right street protestors, of Bible-loving evangelicals and alcohol-fuelled bandsmen, of pro-establishment Conservative Party supporters and anti-establishment paramilitary ex-prisoners, of self-proclaimed Catholic-hating bigots and self-proclaimed Catholic-befriending progressives?

Given my stated theoretical aim to understand and learn from Orange morality in all its variety, answering this ethnographic question was one of the core challenges of this book, but it was not the only challenge. Another ethnographic challenge this book faced was describing and explaining how the remarkable ideological variety outlined above, is, within the Scottish Orange Order, framed by a no less remarkable sociological and demographic homogeneity. Importantly, according to Clawson's suggestion that fraternal associations have 'typically ... reached across boundaries, tending to unite men from a relatively wide social, economic, or religious spectrum' (1989: 11), this homogeneity renders the Orange Order as decidedly atypical. While most obviously and immediately marked by the Order being a Protestant-only institution, framing the homogeneity of Scottish Orangeism entirely by this religious criterion is to significantly underplay the extent of the sameness that unites members in other respects. Several of my informants, for example, when describing to me the differences between the Orange Order in Northern Ireland and Scotland explained that, in strong contrast to Northern Ireland, the Order in Scotland was almost entirely urban and almost exclusively working class. As described in Chapter 1, both of these claims are strikingly accurate. Clearly, the Order in Scotland is also a male-only institution, and while there is a Ladies Orange Association of Scotland, these women are only considered to be 'associate' members, and do not have voting rights at Grand Lodge (see Butcher 2014).

Other markers of social and demographic sameness are equally notable. The Orange Order in Scotland is not only contained within urban areas, but is largely confined to the Central Belt of Scotland, and particularly to its post-industrial West. As obvious as it may sound, the Orange Order in Scotland is also almost wholly Scottish. Indeed, while there are likely to be a few others, during my five years of fieldwork I personally met only two members who were not Scottish (one was Northern Irish, and one English). Following on from this, the Orange Order in Scotland is almost completely white and, again, while there may be others, I met only one member from an ethnic minority background, a Scots-born second-generation immigrant from Mauritius. Lastly, the Orange Order is by conviction and by official Grand Lodge pronouncement, exclusively and forthrightly unionist. As already indicated above, and as discussed further in Chapter 5, I met only one SNP member and Scottish independence supporter within the Order, whose political views were regarded by my other informants as, at best, deeply eccentric, and, at worst, a despicable betrayal of everything the Institution stood for. Such is the homogeneity of Orangeism in Scotland.

Reversing my earlier question, then, we might now ask what are we to make of this homogeneity – this Protestant, unionist, white, working-class, male, Scottish, urban, Central Belt sameness? My argument throughout this book will be that any adequate understanding of the Orange Order in Scotland needs to hold in tension these two seemingly contradictory realities, namely that Orange culture in Scotland is simultaneously a dramatically diverse and a strikingly homogenous phenomenon. Intriguingly, as I have observed it, this seeming paradox is made more puzzling still by the fact that, as well as being demographically mono-form and ideologically multi-form, the Orange Order is also something of a Janus-faced entity. Here, we must grapple with the fact that not only is the Order one and many, but it is also two.

I am not, importantly, the first to notice this particular double aspect of Scottish Orangeism. Elaine McFarland, in her foundational study of Orangeism in nineteenth-century Scotland, describes this dichotomy as 'the rough/respectable differentiation in Orangeism' (1990: 26). Here, McFarland is referring to a class-based division, between the Order's skilled and unskilled industrial-worker membership. Put very simply (see Chapter 1 for more detail) nineteenth-century Orangemen with a skilled trade were generally seen as inhabiting the ideal type of 'respectable' by virtue of their desire for upward mobility, whereas unskilled Orangemen, who did not want and/or could not achieve such mobility, were readily placed into the ideal type of 'rough'. McFarland further shows how this dichotomy was popularly imagined to be constituted by a whole series of associated social markers. Thus, 'respectable'

Orangemen were domesticated, took their leisure time at home, were engaged
with their families, were sober and peaceable, attended church, took a genuine
interest in theology, and were content at work. 'Rough' Orangemen, on the other
hand, were undomesticated, spent their leisure time in the pubs and streets, were
disengaged from family life, were drunkards and brawlers, attended football matches
instead of church, had no interest in theology, and were discontented at work
(1990: 139). Finally, her analysis also states that the 'rough' element of the Order
was mainly found among the Institution's rank-and-file membership, many of
whom were only fully involved with the organisation come its annual 12 July
parade. 'Respectable' Orangemen, on the other hand, were mostly found within
the hierarchy of the Orange Order and were involved in its activities, and those
of the Royal Black Institution, year-round (ibid.: 140).

It is my contention that the micro-dynamics of this dichotomy go to the very
heart of Scottish Orangeism, not only in the nineteenth century, but also in the
present day. This became clear to me by observing how different informants related
to each other during my five years of fieldwork, but also by experiencing how these
different informants related to me, particularly by making deliberate attempts to
direct my time and research focus towards what they regarded as 'real' Orangeism.
As I experienced it, this dichotomy largely followed McFarland's rough/respectable
'differentiation', as transposable onto the connected division between 'grass-roots'
members and the Orange 'hierarchy'. In contrast to the nineteenth-century case,
however, the source of this division within contemporary Scots-Orangeism was
not any acute difference in the material aspirations or occupational status of skilled
and unskilled workers, as post-industrial decline in Scotland had lessened this
cleavage between manual workers via an attendant expansion of the levelling
category of semi-skilled. In the contemporary context, then, what made one a
'respectable' or 'rough' Orangeman, it seemed, was the extent to which one valued
and courted (or scorned and rejected) the social and political approval of a (broadly)
liberal, pluralist, and non-Orange Scottish public. Put another way, as I experienced
it, this dividing line was not occupational, but ideological.

I came to realise the sharpness of this divide in ethnographic terms, when,
around the mid-point of my fieldwork, I began asking my informants what they
thought I should write about in my book. I was interested to hear how they would
answer such a question, hoping that it would reveal something of their foundational
assumptions about what 'real' Orangeism was. For the Orange hierarchy, whose
job was leading and directing the Order via internal Grand Lodge committee work
and external PR management, the 'real' Order was an eminently respectable Christian
organisation which sought to promote the ideals of their faith while fully supporting
the rights of others to hold different views. Indeed, for those I spoke to at Grand
Lodge, the Order was not only politically moderate and religiously tolerant but,
at its core, an articulate, sober-minded, and charitable grouping of committed
church-goers who joined together to celebrate Britishness, the Reformed faith,
and the monarchy. For many grass-roots members, however, this moderate and
tolerant image of Orangeism was an out-of-touch, aspirational, and condescending
fantasy. Moreover, for the great majority of Orangemen I came to know during

my time in Glencruix, it was not Grand Lodge but ordinary members who represented 'real' Scottish Orangeism – an Orangeism variously defined, as above, by fraternal drinking, footballing loyalties, support for Ulster Protestants, and a loathing of Catholics in general, and Irish Republicans in particular.

What, then, was I to write in my book? How could I do ethnographic justice to such diversity, such contradiction? In pushing my informants to help me ponder this question, obtaining a singular and definitive answer was not my aim. My aim, rather, was to try and ascertain what my informants hoped I would write about, and thus, what they would regard as a fair and honest account of 'real' Scots-Orangeism. In this sense, I am persuaded that neither group of informants were motivated by a cynical desire to manipulate my fieldwork experience with the aim of imparting a falsely 'respectable' or exaggeratedly 'rough' view of the Order. (I do recognise, however, that such contrasting efforts to shepherd me through my fieldwork, while sincere, were still intentional acts of shepherding, and thus selection). Bearing this in mind, then, what kind of account did my Grand Lodge and grass-roots informants want me to write? Perhaps unsurprisingly, both groups wanted me to give an account of Scots-Orangeism which defined their ('respectable' or 'rough') version of the Institution as encapsulating the 'real' Orange Order.

Thus, Dennis and many of my informants at Glencruix, while they didn't use the phrase 'rough', came close to doing so by pushing me to write a 'warts and all' account of their life in the Order – an account which did not ignore their anti-Catholic bigotry, eschew their fondness for drink, edit out their colourful language, or overlook their politically incorrect jokes. Such airbrushing, Dennis and others explained, would prevent me from representing 'real' Orangeism (*their* Orangeism), and would, they stated emphatically, make my research 'pointless'. Importantly, other informants outside of Glencruix agreed; one Orangeman from Edinburgh, for example, aware that I had been spending significant time among the hierarchy at Grand Lodge told me bluntly, 'you've *got* to get away from there – you are being fed the party line', explaining how most Grand Lodge office bearers would try and 'shield me' from any expression of Orangeism that was 'too radical' in its paramilitary sympathies or 'too critical' of the Order's leaders. From the perspective of my grass-roots informants, then, writing a 'warts and all' account meant representing their 'rough' Orangeism as 'real' Orangeism, in all its boozing, its bigotry, and its trenchant loyalism.

In marked (but perhaps now expected) contrast, my informants in Grand Lodge answered my question about what they wanted me to write about by stating that my book should make it clear that the Orange Order in Scotland is, by and large, a respectable and respectful Christian organisation. In the run-up to the 2014 Scottish independence referendum, for example, during an evening observing the Order's leafleting campaign, I asked an informant involved in the Institution's mid-level District leadership what *he* thought I should write. His answer was as unassuming as it was heartfelt; he wanted me to write that the Order was 'a broad church' and that their members were 'not animals, but people with families and normal concerns'. Another volunteer agreed, stating plainly that 'Orangemen are not bigots' and that 'the Orange Order is pro-Protestant, not "anti" anything'.

On other occasions, this same message of 'respectable Orangeism' was demonstrated practically as well as being asserted verbally. In early July 2013, for example, at the end of a day of parading, a fellow researcher and I were invited as special guests to a dinner hosted by the Grand Lodge hierarchy. As the evening came to a close, one leading Orangeman bid us farewell with the parting comment 'we're not all that bad, are we?' Two things struck me about his remark. First, heard within its immediate context, his suggestion seemed entirely reasonable, reflecting the tone of a civilised evening spent discussing theology and politics, and enjoying good food and wine. Second, this 'civility' was striking precisely because it contrasted so sharply with my experiences of Orangeism in Glencruix, where aggressive banter fuelled by rounds of lager and whisky were favoured over temperate conversation and formal dining. From the perspective of my Orange informants within the Institution's hierarchy, then, writing an account of Scots-Orangeism which showed its members were 'not all that bad' meant representing their 'respectable' Orangeism as 'real' Orangeism, in all its religiosity, gentility, and magnanimity. Such is the duality of Orangeism in Scotland.

Having surveyed something of the heterogeneity, homogeneity, and dualism of Scots-Orangeism, it also needs to be recognised that these similarities and differences are contained and given shape within the Order's own institutional structure. Indeed, it is difficult to overstate the extent to which life in the Order is governed by structure, by a set constitution, and by a system of laws, titles, ritual degrees, and so on. Central to this is a written codification of the Order as a rule-bound Protestant organisation which stands in opposition to the Catholic Church, as outlined, for example, in the 1986 version of the *Laws and Constitutions of the Loyal Orange Institution of Scotland*:

> An Orangeman, being necessarily a Protestant, must be a true Christian, as Protestantism is nothing less than pure and Scriptural Christianity. And by this it is to be understood that he is not merely one who professes hostility to the distinctive despotism of the Church of Rome; but that he holds the doctrines of the Reformation. (GOLS (Grand Orange Lodge of Scotland) 1986: 2)

Within the *Laws and Constitutions* are also found a whole host of regulations which govern nearly every conceivable aspect of life within the Order, including the (albeit largely theoretical) admission of converted Catholics, the suspension and expulsion of members, the governing of social clubs, the charging of membership fees, the wearing of regalia, the management of public processions, membership of political parties, the process of lodging a complaint, the management of improper conduct, and the painting of banners, as well as 244 other rules. The Orange Order being a Protestant-only organisation notwithstanding, in many respects the Institution is similar both in style and in structure to Freemasonry, especially in its use of symbolism (see Roberts 1971: 272, Cairns and Smyth 2002: 150). The Order is organised geographically into individual 'Private Lodges', local 'District Lodges', regional 'County Lodges', and a single national 'Grand Lodge'. Members of Private Lodges in Scotland progress through two Masonic-inspired ritual degrees – the Orange and the Royal Arch Purple, the first degree initiating candidates through a series of formal questions and vows, and the second 'higher' degree involving a dramatic re-enactment of the desert wanderings of Ancient Israel in the book of Exodus (known as 'the travel'). Fully initiated members may then fulfil one of over twenty office-bearer roles, ranging from the lowly Tyler who guards the outer door, to the highest office of Worthy Master, who runs the Lodge. Other Private Lodge office bearers include an inner door guard, two instructors, a Regaliast, two standard-bearers, a Bible-bearer, a chaplain, a treasurer, a secretary, a substitute Deputy Master, a Deputy Master, and the Past Master.

As in Masonry, the use of symbolism permeates all aspects of formal Orange activity. Each office bearer, for example, has an assigned emblem used to symbolise the practical task associated with that role; a sword for the Tyler who 'protects the outer lodge room door', two crossed swords for the inner door guard who makes 'doubly sure that nothing will disturb the assembled brethren', a key for the treasurer, crossed quills for the secretary, and so on. Taking on any such role involves a prescribed ceremonial process of election and installation, comprising a vote followed by the swearing of a formal obligation. Elected officers at District, County, and Grand Lodge level largely replicate these office-bearer roles, but membership is limited to those who have already received the Royal Arch Purple degree. As well as setting down the macro-structures of the entire Institution, the Order also sets down the content of regular lodge meetings. The Loyal Orange Institution of Scotland *Manual of Ritual and Ceremony for Lodges* outlines a set formula for the opening and closing of lodge meetings, as well as a series of prayers and Bible readings to be used by the chaplain during the course of the meeting. Prayers typically reaffirm the Order's Protestant and loyalist commitments, often with critical reference to Catholicism. Opening Prayer No. 1, for example, contains the following words:

> We bless Thee for the land of our birth; for the Protestant freedom we enjoy. We remember with gratitude Thy Victorious Servant, King William III, whom Thou didst raise up to deliver our land from the power of error and superstition. Bless all who seek to maintain our liberty, and may we, the members of our Loyal Orange Institution, ever dedicate our lives, body, soul and spirit, to the Precepts and Principles of the Order. Continue to Bless our Gracious Queen, Elizabeth, and all members of the Royal Family. Bless all Ministers of State. Direct their Counsels to Thy Honour and Glory, and the welfare of the people.

Here, the phrase 'power of error and superstition' acts as a kind of longhand for the Catholic Church. Similar sentiments are found throughout the phraseology of Orange ritual, with all six scripture readings outlined in the *Manual of Ritual* each followed by a commentary designed to directly refute Catholic doctrine. A reading from Jeremiah 17: 5–14, for example, gives the following brief explanation: 'This chapter speaks of God as the Judge of the heart of man. The Church of Rome empowers her priests to act as Judge at the Confessional, thus robbing God of his prerogative'. In addition to this formal codification of the Order's rejection of Catholic doctrine, the *Manual of Ritual* also positively outlines the formal procedures for opening a District Lodge and a new Lodge, as well as other 'special ceremonies' including banner unfurlings, the dedication of lodge furnishings, special prayers for Boyne demonstrations (including prayers at a cenotaph, and prayers for Northern Ireland), and a guide for Orange funerals. Such is the constitutional structure and ritual tenor of the Order.

But what does fieldwork among a rule-bound organisation as heterogeneous, homogenous and dualist as the Loyal Orange Institution of Scotland look like? How did I come to be interested in Scots-Orangeism in the first place? How did I negotiate access? How did I fill my time during fieldwork? In the micro-interactions of the 'daily round', how did I relate to my informants, and how did my informants relate to me? It is to questions such as these that I now wish to turn, not only as a way of providing a 'biography' of the fieldwork undertaken, but also as a route to exploring some wider issues surrounding the 'ethics' of ethnographic representation, or what might be described as the morality of the anthropological method.

Representing Scots-Orangeism: the morality of methodology

I first came to be interested in the possibility of undertaking an ethnographic study of Scots-Orangeism during the closing stages of my fieldwork in Gamrie, an Aberdeenshire fishing village of 700 people and six 'fundamentalist' churches (Webster 2013). These early reflections on Orangeism occurred as a result of discussions with a group of Gamrie Christians who were broadly supportive of the Institution's stated aims, a fact that now seems strange and incongruous, but only with the benefit of hindsight. Importantly, however, these informants were not 'local' Gamrics but Northern Irish 'incomers' – farmers who were active members of the village's newest church, a Free Presbyterian Church of Ulster (FPCU). Yet, the religiosity of these Ulstermen and women contained much that was familiar to the Brethrenism of local Gamrics: an urgent focus upon born-again conversion, a deep knowledge of the Bible, and an intense fascination with the 'end times'. On this religious register, these Northern Irish Free Presbyterian farmers were 'at home' among Gamrie's Brethren fishermen.

Their Ulster religiosity, however, also contained something that the Brethren of Gamrie worked hard to elide – party politics. Importantly, this was politics with a capital 'P' insofar as their interest in current events and electoral affairs were strongly focused upon the fortunes of the Democratic Unionist Party (DUP), established by FPCU founder, The Rev. Ian Paisley. Here, then, was an expression of Protestantism which combined ultra-conservative evangelicalism with the 'dirty politics' (Blom Hansen 2000) of electoral campaigning, yet did so in a way that denied any religious 'predicament' (ibid.) or worldly compromise. Very quickly, however, I became aware that my Ulster informants in Gamrie *did* perceive a sharp difference between the Protestant politics of Scotland and that of their rural North Antrim homeland. For what reasons, then, did these FPCU farmers view Ulster Orangeism as a broadly legitimate extension of evangelical unionism, while condemning Scottish Orangeism as defined by drunken disorder and sectarian football rivalries? And if they were right – if Scottish Orangemen were, on balance, more interested in alcohol and sectarianism than religious services and church parades – then what kind of Protestantism did Scots-Orangeism represent?

This reputation for impiety, in combination with what the Order in Scotland was said to *share* with the Order in Ireland – political lobbying, public parading, and ritual degree work – began to build a picture of a type of Protestantism significantly different to that which I had found among the Brethren. Thus, despite first 'discovering' the topic of Scots-Orangeism during my time in Gamrie, it was precisely its seeming contrast to Gamrie religiosity which drew my attention, for here was a form of ultra-Protestantism which sacralised not only the Bible, but also the sociality of fraternity, the politics of monarchy, and the ethnicity of nationality. Thus, having completed my main fieldwork in Gamrie, when the time came to embark upon a new ethnographic project, I sought access to the field in precisely the same way that I had previously, by writing formal letters to key gatekeepers – letters which attempted to explain in clear and straightforward terms who I was and what my research would involve. Writing to the Grand Master in June of 2012, this first letter explained how I was 'planning fieldwork research into the contemporary cultural identity of Protestant fraternities, with a special focus on the Loyal Orange Institution in Scotland'. The letter went on to explain that 'by looking at the different Orange Lodges in Scotland, the project hopes to gain insight into how the daily life of the Protestant Christian is experienced in Scotland today'.

With reference to my Christian commitment, my Protestant background, my upbringing in Canada, and my family connections to Northern Ireland, the letter continued: 'I am interested in the Order's belief system in the widest possible sense. The research would examine a broad range of issues including: the role of Orange Lodges in building community, the heritage of Orange Parades and Orange Bands, the politics of Scottish Unionism, the celebration of Protestant culture, the growth of the Ulster-Scots language, and the upholding of Britain's Christian traditions'. With my background declared and my research aims stated, the letter concluded with a request to meet to discuss my proposal. Before too long, I received a reply from the Executive Officer of the Grand Orange Lodge of Scotland inviting me to Olympia House in Bridgeton to do just that – a meeting which he said would primarily involve me talking with the Grand Lodge archivist. While I accepted this offer with enthusiasm, I was keenly aware that my being redirected to the archivist indicated that my research had likely been misunderstood as primarily concerned with historical documents and artefacts, as opposed to a contemporary study of the people and culture of the Order. As it turned out, I need not have worried.

Travelling from Edinburgh to Glasgow by train, I reviewed my notebook containing a long list of scribbled questions prepared for the archivist – questions which emphasised both the contemporary focus of my research, and the breadth of the 'Orange issues' I wanted to explore. Orange church life, Orange social clubs, royalism, Rangers Football Club, the Conservative Party, the Scottish independence referendum, the band scene, Orange regalia, ritual, and symbolism, and how best to investigate these topics, were all included on my list. Arriving into Queen Street station with time to spare, I decided to travel to Bridgeton on foot, rather than make the short journey by connecting train. As I walked, the cityscape morphed from the unremarkable iconography of late-capitalism – city centre shopping complexes and coffee outlets – to something that felt more distinctive to Glasgow's East End. The famous arch of the Barras Market, a string of independent jewellery and pawn shops advertising 'cash for gold', a greasy spoon cafe, a car modification shop, Scotland's oldest shellfish bar, a Catholic chapel and a sex shop sitting awkwardly opposite each other – all of this gave the district its own unique feel.

Coming into Bridgeton itself, I was struck by how this diversity was somewhat overturned by a strikingly consistent symbolic landscape, primarily brought about by a row of four loyalist pubs occupying one side of the main approach into Bridgeton Cross, the centre of the district. The first pub, the Crimson Star, flew three Union flags, with a fourth flag displaying a portrait of the Queen. Next was the Station Bar, which, as well as flying a Union flag, was also bedecked in Union bunting. Third was the Walkers Pub which flew a Union flag, an Ulster flag, and the Orange standard. The final pub was called the Seven Ways which was comparatively modest in its display which merely consisted of a long string of Union flag bunting. The pubs looked run-down but were obviously well used, with each already serving several mid-morning drinkers. A few buildings away sat Olympia House, a former Salvation Army Hall, and now the headquarters of the Loyal Orange Institution of Scotland. Built in 1927, this solid red-stone-fronted building dominated the smaller structures on either side of it, with its large blue-and-white sign, and even larger flagpole leaving passers-by in little doubt as to its ethno-nationalist proclivities.

Ringing the doorbell with some trepidation, I was met by a man in his early thirties whose stern expression and frosty reception did little to put me at ease. Explaining that I had an appointment to meet with Jonathan Henderson the Grand Lodge archivist, the man (who I later learned was called Alfie) simply said 'you do indeed' and turned to take me upstairs. Walking past a number of hanging displays of banners, flags, and regalia, Alfie knocked on the door of the archive, briefly introduced me to Jonathan Henderson, and quickly returned to the front desk downstairs. Jonathan's welcome was warm; he shook my hand (notably without the Orange 'grip' used between members) and introduced me to two other volunteer archivists, Derek and Andrew, who both greeted me somewhat more warily. Asked if my trip from Edinburgh had been smooth, I replied that it had, mentioning also how surprised I had been to see so many British and other flags flying through the centre of Bridgeton. Jonathan laughed in agreement, joking with obvious pleasure how Bridgeton could easily be mistaken for Belfast's Shankill Road. 'Now, we're going to do this the West of Scotland way' Jonathan continued, 'with the informal part before the formal part', before launching into a rather haphazard tour of the archive.

The archive room itself was tiny, and more closely resembled a rather jumbled social history museum than it did a formal research archive. Alongside and atop several filing cabinets and storage boxes were Orange objects of every conceivable type: drums, banners, sashes, medals and other regalia, ornamental walking sticks, gavels, presentation plaques, glass and silverware, commemorative ceramics and coins, as well as rows of shelves containing a small library of books on Orangeism and related topics, and various framed photographs. I had the sense that I had only been shown a fraction of the collection, and with each object being the occasion for telling the often-lengthy story of its history, it was Jonathan who did most of the talking.

After a briefer tour of the rooms beyond the archive – which involved viewing display boards filled with clippings from *The Orange Torch*, as well as a request that I signed a huge tome of a guest book (writing 'Downing College' below where all the other entries had listed their Lodge name and number) – we finally arrived at what appeared to be the 'formal' part of our meeting. The venue for this was a boardroom overlooked by a portrait of the Queen. Despite the setting, this too felt rather informal. Jonathan and I sat down, and, as before, Jonathan did most of the talking, moving from one story or reminiscence to the next, often without much context or explanation. The names of prominent high-ranking Orangemen were frequently mentioned, with Jonathan explaining their background and particular area of interest, ranging from the work of Grand Lodge chaplains, to the Institution's oral history project, to Orangeism in the West of Scotland, to Orangeism and the band scene, to Grand Lodge's campaign against Scottish independence. As Jonathan spoke, I dutifully scribbled down these names and other details in my notebook, yet did so with a growing sense of concern that the kind of access I required needed to amount to more than a list of names of people to interview.

Eventually, after what seemed like a long while, Jonathan asked me about my research and its specific focus. Glad of the chance to clarify, I explained that while I was interested both in Orange artefacts of the kind he had already showed me, and in speaking to high-ranking Orangemen, I was also interested in the everyday lives of ordinary members of the Institution. I emphasised how, as a result, it would be important for me to talk with, and spend time among, rank-and-file Orangemen. At this Jonathan paused, looking thoughtful, finally breaking his silence to explain that if I felt the named contacts he had already given me were selective, this was because they *were* selective, and deliberately so. His purpose, he elaborated, was to select for me contacts who were '*articulate*' (he stressed this word emphatically), and who would thus be able to put across their views 'clearly' and 'well'. Jonathan's smile was gone, he was now looking much more serious, the atmosphere feeling more awkward as a result. Not feeling able to push the point, I let the matter drop, choosing instead to ask a question about the fate of the Conservative Party in Scotland. This lightened the mood, with Jonathan proudly explaining how he was from a long line of both Church of Scotland members and Conservative Party voters, but that, in his opinion, the Scottish Conservative Party had changed, with people no longer knowing what they stood for. Labour was now the strongest unionist voice in Scottish politics, he exclaimed, in a tone that suggested he found his own words to be scandalous.

It was obvious from this first meeting, then, that while Jonathan's keen storytelling and wealth of contacts would make him a valuable informant, he would also be a shrewd and cautious gatekeeper whose priority would be to protect the image of the Institution by only assisting me in making contact with certain approved individuals. Fortunately, while the months that passed proved this latter observation correct, my time spent within Grand Lodge was still an ethnographically rich and informative experience. That first trip to Grand Lodge and to the archive quickly became a weekly appointment, mirroring the work schedule of Jonathan and the other volunteer archivists who came every Thursday to Olympia House to catalogue new artefacts, to document the history of particular lodges, and to discuss and debate Scottish Orangeism past and present. In this way, much of the early period of my fieldwork, during the autumn of 2012, was spent in that small, cluttered archive, as well as in the even smaller kitchenette at the end of the corridor, where the archivists and I took our coffee and lunch breaks.

So rich was this field site and the data gained there, that it forms much of Chapter 2, focusing on the social dynamics of the archive as a space where imaginations of the glorious past of Protestant history were recovered, and where Scotland's suffering under 'the menace of Rome', past and present, were exposed. My time at Olympia House also afforded me the opportunity to meet other Grand Lodge office bearers, including the Grand Master, the Grand Secretary, and others, as well as ordinary members who had business to conduct there. Importantly, such opportunities prompted other forms of contact with Orangemen outside Olympia House including annual Grand Lodge dinners and award ceremonies, national and district committee meetings, local loyalist band practices and parades, Rangers matches at Ibrox, and weekly Sunday services at Glasgow Evangelical Church, an independent church fondly referred to by members as the 'Orange Kirk'.

Over time, as these contacts snowballed further, I began to conduct fieldwork at other sites across the Central Belt, an important development due to the Grand Lodge-centric and Glasgow-centric focus of the first few months of my research. These sites included regular visits to Glencruix where I conducted my most intensive fieldwork, not only within the Orange Social Club, but also within the homes of members, as well as in the town's Protestant churches, Orange-friendly bars, and other public spaces. Moving east, I established regular connections with a Masonic Club and a Royal British Legion Social Club, both of which were frequented by Orangemen. Additionally, I followed a full Orange marching season, while also attending parades by the Apprentice Boys of Derry, the Royal Black Institution, and independent loyalist flute bands, events which took me to different districts in Glasgow and Edinburgh, as well as to several smaller towns across the Central Belt.

Importantly, I also forged other, more occasional, ethnographic opportunities, wherever such experiences could contribute to my broader understanding of the varieties of unionism and loyalism in Scotland. I joined with individual Orange lodges and loyalist bands as they distributed leaflets door-to-door calling for a 'No' vote in the Scottish referendum. I was taken on a tour of Scottish Covenanting sites in Hamilton by a leading Orangeman as a way of learning more about how the history of the Covenanters had been incorporated into the imagination of Scots-Protestant and Scots-Orange history. I visited and interviewed the elders of Zion Baptist Church, Glasgow's staunchly Protestant (and infamously anti-Catholic) congregation, founded by the late Pastor Jack Glass, a man dubbed by the media as 'Scotland's Ian Paisley'. I attended loyalist 'flag protests' in the west of Scotland and in Edinburgh, events which were organised on social media, and held in solidarity with loyalists in Ulster protesting about the removal of the Union flag from Belfast

City Hall. I observed and photographed Scottish Defence League marches protesting about the 'Islamification' of Britain. I conducted interviews, observations and a photo survey of the Lady Haig Poppy Factory in Edinburgh, talking with armed forces veterans (including some with Orange connections) about their experiences of serving in Northern Ireland during the Troubles, as well as their views on how and why the symbol of the poppy had been interpreted differently by different sides in that conflict.

Finally, to gain more detailed comparative data about Orangeism in Northern Ireland, I conducted twelve in-depth interviews with Orangemen in Belfast, ranging from the Grand Master, to an eighteen-year-old new recruit who, as well as being an Orangeman, was also an activist for the Traditional Unionist Voice, a hard-line breakaway from the DUP. Having since moved to Northern Ireland, I have also been able to observe and document Orange parades surrounding 12 July, as well as loyalist bonfire celebrations which occur each year on the eleventh night. Of course, as is far from unique to anthropologists interested in Orangeism, I have remained (along with much of the electorate) a close observer of Northern Irish debates about Brexit, Scottish independence, Irish unity, and the ongoing 'culture wars' between the Province's 'Orange' and 'Green' communities, which, as I write this, has continued to sustain an ongoing political crisis between the DUP and Sinn Fein, leading to the collapse of the Stormont Assembly (between January 2017 and January 2020), as well as the possible collapse of the DUP's confidence and supply arrangement with the Conservative Party as a result of disagreements about how to avoid a post-Brexit 'hard border' on the island of Ireland.

Given this breadth of access to such a diverse range of Orangemen and 'loyal Protestant friends', and given the depth of access I gained with smaller groups of Orangemen, both in the Glencruix Social Club and in the archive in Bridgeton, how did I relate to my informants, and how did my informants relate to me? I have already partially answered the first question above, in relation to my comments on *verstehen* and empathy, that is, I related to my informants as a researcher who was primarily interested in understanding Orangeism from their point of view. I thus embarked on the fieldwork with the assumption that my Orange informants found their Orangeism to be intellectually comprehensible and social and morally valuable, that is, I assumed Orangeism made sense to them and was something they found to be good. As such, I related to my informants as an apprentice would relate to their master (see Jenkins 1994); I treated them with respect, and, by and large, with deference. Intriguingly, the first Orangeman I ever met during my fieldwork, totally unprompted by me, took great delight in calling me his 'apprentice'. My desire was thus to empathetically 'step into' their world, without prejudice or prejudgement, with the aim of making Orangeism 'make sense' to me, just as it made sense to them, and thereby to see how Orangeism ('warts and all') could be experienced as good. In practice, while this was not always easy (what apprenticeship ever is?), this methodology often revolved around rather simple processes of watching what Orangemen did, listening to what they said, and, where appropriate and useful, asking questions to try and correct what I suspected were my frequent misunderstandings and misinterpretations.

How, then, did my informants relate to me? How did they make sense of who I was and what I was hoping to achieve by spending so much time among them? In answering this question, it is worth bearing in mind that I did not hide the fact that I was a practising Christian, nor that I was from a theologically conservative Calvinist background. Importantly, I could not have hidden this even had I wanted to, for many of my informants were expert in the process of 'telling' (Burton 1978), that is, in establishing a person's ethno-religious background by asking a few simple sideways questions about surname, place of residence, and so on. As with previous research among the Brethren, once my Orange informants had elicited this information from me, my Free Church affiliation was both a help and a hindrance, but for different reasons. It was a help insofar as, from an Orange point of view, my religious background marked me out as ethnically British and Protestant. Yet, it was a hindrance because the Scots-Calvinist tradition in general, and the Free Church of Scotland in particular, are known for being critical of the Order's relaxed attitude to the consumption of alcohol, and also of its insistence that members take vows of secrecy and perform Masonic-style ritual. In short, while I was the right ethnicity (bolstered by my upbringing in Canada and my in-laws being from Ulster), I was, in their view, a member of the wrong Protestant denomination.

While these helps and hindrances all provided useful talking points, none of them, it seems, had very much impact on the overall shape or extent of my access. Indeed several of my informants spoke to me of academics from Catholic backgrounds who had been given permission to study the Order in the past. By far the most significant barrier to full ethnographic access, then, was the simple fact that I was not a member of the Institution (something I discuss below, as well as in more detail in Chapter 3). As a non-member, not only was I not allowed to observe those rituals reserved for Private Lodge meetings, but I was also seen as someone who might, at least potentially, choose to present the Order in a negative light, as so many journalists and other commentators have, and continue to do. Interestingly, these suspicions were most marked among the Institution's hierarchy, who were generally more guarded around me than were ordinary rank-and-file members. When attending a Grand Lodge training meeting at Olympia House one evening, one of the office bearers introduced me to the assembled committee before adding (in an only half-joking manner) 'Just be careful what you say around him! Be careful what you say!' The response – nervous laughter – was just as telling, if not more so, than the comment which provoked it. The message was clear; as an observant non-member, I needed to be treated with caution.

This guarded attitude, and its being largely confined to the Order's top-level hierarchy, was confirmed to me as I attempted to develop access with Orange social clubs. Despite Jonathan's clear admission that he only wanted me to speak to a select few 'articulate' Orangemen, after a few weeks of visiting the archive, I asked him again for help in making contact with social clubs. Jonathan remained unenthusiastic but offered to make a few enquiries. The results were disappointing, with Jonathan explaining to me the following week that while he had reached out to a few clubs, all of those he had contacted were reluctant to entertain the idea of me hanging around: 'Oh, an *academic*' Jonathan mimicked, as he relayed the conversations back to me, 'I don't know if we want *him* around while we are trying to enjoy ourselves'. Wondering if I might have more success by representing myself to social clubs directly, I wrote a letter to Dennis, who ran the Glencruix Social Club, explaining who I was and what my research would involve. Within days I received a phone call from him inviting me to the club, and, in contrast to the aversion Jonathan had reported, I quickly established a friendly rapport with Dennis and the other club regulars, with Glencruix becoming one of the most important and revealing field sites of my ethnography.

Having been freed from the restrictions of Grand Lodge's cautious management of my time and attentions, my informants in Glencruix, as shown in the ethnography with which I began this Introduction, and as described in greater detail in Chapters 4 and 5, gave me a different perspective on Scots-Orangeism, one that was less preoccupied by the strict demands of Jonathan's desire for what he called 'articulate' expression. As such, I came to realise that what my gatekeepers at Grand Lodge were seeking to do was not so much protect the Orange Order from me (and my suspected academic misrepresentations), but rather protect *me* from the Orange Order (and its more outspoken grass-roots members). Indeed, Dennis and others clearly told me that this was the case. After an argument between Jonathan and Derek sparked by Derek's suggestion that I should interview a certain individual with significant paramilitary connections, Dennis said that he had received a phone call from Jonathan asking him to keep me away from Derek. Jonathan's aim, Dennis said, was to ensure that Derek's more hard-line Orangeism did not overly influence my research findings. What Jonathan wanted more generally, Dennis explained, was to give me a sanitised picture of the Order by ensuring I did not talk to anyone who was 'too militant'. 'But that's no good for the Orange Institution, and certainly no good for your research' Dennis asserted, restating his own view (as he often did) that what I should write instead was a 'warts and all' account of Orangeism in Scotland.

While I have already stated above that I was in agreement with Dennis that including this 'warts and all' perspective of grass-roots Orangeism had real merit, I also found myself sympathetic to Jonathan's view that the 'articulate' Orangeism of the Grand Lodge hierarchy be given serious ethnographic consideration. This is because the 'militant' Orangeism predominantly found among rank-and-file members, and the 'articulate' Orangeism predominantly found among the hierarchy are just as real as each other. Put another way, 'rough' and 'respectable' (McFarland 1990) Orangeism are *both* social facts despite being at odds with one another, with neither having a monopoly over 'true' Orangeism. Nor is the former obviously more representative than the latter, with some grass-roots members aspiring to more moderate and articulate forms of Orangeism, while various local and district leaders remain committed to more militant expressions of the same. To describe one perspective and not the other would thus be to present a picture of Scots-Orangeism that was fundamentally incomplete.

All of this is important to note here because the ideological heterogeneity, ethno-religious homogeneity, and rough–respectable dualism that made contemporary Scots-Orangeism what it was had a real and lasting impact upon how my informants related to me, as someone who could, variously, tell their proud history, communicate their tolerant views, and attest to their biblical practices, or, conversely, describe their political passions, understand their sporting rivalries, and contextualise their ethno-religious superiority. In essence, my informants related to me as someone who was there to tell their *particular* side of the story.

In ethnographically documenting these various 'sides', my aim has always been to try and piece them together or, where this proved impossible, to place them side-by-side, in an attempt to produce a coherent picture of what makes contemporary Scots-Orangeism what it is, why it makes logical sense, and why it seems morally good to its members. In doing so, in consistently and thoroughly attempting to 'step into' their Orangeism, some of my informants began to wonder aloud if I would ever join them by becoming a member of the Order. To some, my background spoke for itself; I was a church-attending 'Protestant', I was 'British', and I had certain reservations about the prospect of Scottish independence. Others concluded I would join the Order simply because I kept hanging around Orangemen. (It was also for both of these reasons, I think, that I was approached by another Glencruix informant about becoming a Freemason). Yet, for the most part, my Orange informants focused their attentions on converting me to Orangeism, not Masonry. Colin, for example (who was the oldest regular at the Glencruix Club and someone I had particular affection for), upon hearing I was attending an Apprentice Boys of Derry parade as part of my research jokingly piped up: 'He's abandoning us!' Then, fixing me in his stare, Colin's expression suddenly became more serious: 'Never mind the Apprentice Boys' he continued, 'when are you going to join the Lodge? I've been an Orangeman for sixty-seven years, and proud of it! We are Orangeman and that's it!' 'It's in your blood!' another man offered in loud agreement. 'No. It's in your heart!' Colin retorted more quietly, still locking me in his gaze with eyes full of tears.

Colin was not the only person to suggest I join the Orange Order. I'd had the same conversation months earlier, in a setting that could not have been more different from the Glencruix Social Club, in a spacious, high-ceilinged and well-decorated flat in an affluent part of South Edinburgh. I was sitting across from George Martin, a Past Grand Master of the Order, describing to him my research aims and methods, that I was interested in contemporary Scots-Orangeism in all its forms, and sought to understand it by spending as much time as I could with 'ordinary' members of the Institution. George looked thoughtful for a moment, and then said: 'Do you know what would be really cute? You could join. You could have on the front of your book "*A View of the Orange Order from Inside*"'. With a smile that seemed to contain more excitement than humour, George sat quietly awaiting my response. I replied by explaining that while I had thought long and hard about the possibility, I was still undecided. I added that I had received mixed advice from colleagues in anthropology on the matter, stating how, but not fully explaining *why*, the advice from Cambridge was that I should join, while the advice from Edinburgh was that I should not. It seems helpful now (in the way that it did not seem helpful then) to elaborate on some of these reasons.

Those in Cambridge seemed to regard the Orange Order in similar terms to an exotic Amazonian or Melanesian hunting cult – so removed from their own daily experience that the possibility of my becoming a member represented nothing beyond an intellectually intriguing (and thus politically harmless) ethnographic experiment. The advice from Cambridge, then, was to join because doing so would give me fuller access to the Institution's ritual and social life and would thus further my research. Those in Edinburgh took a rather different view, appearing alarmed that I had even countenanced the idea of joining. These colleagues seemed to be speaking from their own perceptions of the Order, that it was a belligerently anti-Catholic organisation whose members and supporters (they did not make the distinction) were, at best, overly fond of engaging in drunken disorder and, at worst, frequently implicated in bouts of serious sectarian violence. From this perspective, while Orangeism was perhaps no less exoticised, its infamy was both better known and much 'closer to home' on the urban streets of Central Scotland than it was in the Senior Combination Room of Downing College. The advice from Edinburgh, then, was emphatic; I should *not* join, for doing so would be politically, intellectually, and personally contaminating. Intriguingly, towards the end of the interview, while I still didn't feel comfortable fully spelling out all of these details, I did venture to raise with George the issue of how my work on the Order would be viewed if I became a member. George's reaction was quick, and a reversal of his earlier suggestion about my joining the Institution: 'No, you can't – no one would believe you were objective'.

As the early stages of my fieldwork progressed, word spread that I had been weighing up whether or not to join the Order. Alfie, the shop manager and receptionist at Olympia House cornered me on the issue as I was leaving the building after one of my regular trips to the archive. 'So I hear you are thinking of joining us?' he said in his usual matter-of-fact-cum-suspicious tone. Taken completely off guard by his question (I had only discussed the possibility with two or three people), I answered more openly than perhaps was prudent, explaining that while I *had* thought about it, this was primarily because I wanted to be able to observe the Order's degree work and other rituals. If I joined, I reasoned, I could finally see what Private Lodge meetings were like from the inside. It was immediately clear to me that Alfie was not impressed by my admission, and he stated in no uncertain terms that wanting to observe the Order's rituals to benefit my research was a bad reason to become a member, and that I should only join if I really agreed with the Order's principles of defending Protestantism and unionism in Scotland. Feeling embarrassed by this mild rebuke, I said goodbye, and made a quick exit.

In the end, I decided that George and Alfie were both correct, that is, my joining the Orange Order would be intellectually inexpedient *and* personally disingenuous. In terms of the former, it would, of course, be hard to defend my work against the charge that I had given up all critical distance by deciding to 'go native', for what Orangeman would (or even *could*) give an honest and accurate account of the Institution to which they had sworn such solemn loyalty. Perhaps more problematically, however, I also felt deeply uneasy on a personal level about joining the Institution. One reason for this was because I felt I lacked the necessary patriotic and ethno-religious passions required to be an Orangeman. This became most obvious when watching Old Firm matches, which I experienced both live in the stadium, and with Orangemen in the Glencruix Social Club. On all such occasions, many of my companions delighted in shouting vicious sectarian abuse at the Celtic players on the pitch. Having initially failed to 'take seriously' the moral worth of these performances, during my early ethnographic experiences of such matches, I found myself sitting in awkward and judgemental silence, ashamed to be in the company of those displaying such hate.

Similar ethnocentric reflexes seized me – perhaps less dramatically, but no less viscerally – during an early ethnographic moment in Glasgow Evangelical Church, when, in the context of an Orange worship service, the whole congregation began waving little Union flags as 'Land of Hope and Glory' was played on the organ. I still remember the feeling of indignation that washed over me as I bristled at the sight of what felt, at the time, to be an entirely improper melding of politics and religion. Equally, as a left-leaning resident of Northern Ireland, I also chose not to advertise the fact that I was an Alliance voter, not only because the party was widely disparaged as only attracting support from 'middle-class do-gooders' but also because the party was frequently accused by Orangemen of harbouring support for Sinn Fein's 'culture war' against Britishness in Ulster, an accusation that became particularly pointed during my fieldwork as a result of Alliance's role in triggering the Belfast City Hall 'flag dispute'[4] (Nolan et al. 2014). Given these marked differences in opinion between me and my informants, joining the Order seemed inappropriate, regardless of how sincerely I attempted to overcome my initial ethnographic failings and ethnocentricities.

Another reason for my unease stemmed from the fact that I did not want to cheapen or trivialise these same ethno-nationalist passions that Colin and my other close informants held so dear. Seen from this point of view, my joining the Order would have required I become a kind of ethnographic Peeping Tom, observing and recording ritual interactions that were intended to be seen only by Orangemen, not by an anthropologist play-acting at being an Orangeman, whatever their scholarly motives. At the risk of making a virtue out of a necessity, it seems to me, however, that the gaps in my ethnographic data produced by my non-member status (most notably, gaps about Orange ritual) are themselves ethnographically insightful. While I discuss this in more detail in Chapter 3, it seems helpful at this point merely to note that my non-membership of the Order, experienced by and among so many Orangemen as I conducted my fieldwork, was periodically revealing. Being asked to leave the room at a certain point in proceedings, receiving a fumbling handshake as the person I was greeting attempted to give an Orange grip that was not being reciprocated, observing the skill with which my questions about Orange belief and practice were answered in ways that avoided the breaking of a member's vows – all of these helped me understand where public Orangeism ended, and where the secrets of Orangeism began. Such experiences constantly required that I and my informants defined and redefined what made us the same and what made us different, religiously, politically, ethnically, and otherwise – efforts that were, I suggest, anthropologically instructive.

In undertaking this partial apprenticeship, I took confidence in the fact that my informants not only approved of my desire to understand contemporary

Scots-Orangeism, but went further, urging me to retell *their* Protestant history, describe *their* religious principles, and explain *their* political convictions. As I sought to do so, I found myself, even as a non-member, increasingly appropriated into the lives and works of my informants and Orange friends. This was true bureaucratically, as well as socially. In terms of the former, I quickly found myself absorbed into the Institution's own written record of itself and its dealings. Six months into my fieldwork, I was given what felt like unprecedented access to Glencruix District's minute books (including records of all their most recent meetings, some of which happened just days previously), and permission to make notes on anything I found. As I finished reading a section calling for Orangemen to resist 'Alex Salmond and his Nationalist cohorts', I was struck to see my name printed in the entry immediately below. In full, it read:

> We continue to get requests from academics and at present we have Dr Joe Webster from Cambridge University who is doing research on Protestant Fraternities in Scotland visiting us at Olympia House and our thanks to Brother Henderson for ensuring that the academics are pointed in the right direction to what we have in the archives and thanks also to the many members that we ask to give up their free time to meet these people.

While the minute itself did not contain any particular revelation about how my research was perceived, it was strange (although with hindsight, unsurprising) to see how I had been formally and thus permanently incorporated into the Order's own internal narrative and record. I was not, importantly, the only one taking notes. Be it fieldnotes or minutes, this seemed to matter less than the simple fact that some of my informants were observing me just as carefully as I was observing them, and that these observations, moreover, had begun to circulate in written form, for others to read and comment on.

At the same time that I found myself being absorbed into the bureaucratic life of the Order's hierarchy via their formal production of minutes, I also found myself increasingly drawn into the social and personal lives of ordinary 'grass-roots' Orangemen, some of whom became friends. As such, as well as talking politics and religion with the men in the Glencruix Orange Social Club, and following them out on parade, I also shared in other aspects of their lives. I joined with them for meals at their homes; I spent time with them at leisure; I shared with them in the ups and downs of working life, family life, and ill health; I sat alongside them at a funeral as they grieved the loss of an Orange brother. It was interesting, as a result, to see a narrowing of the gap between the hierarchy and the grass roots, insofar as my closest Orange informants – of all stripes, from the ultra-respectable to self-proclaimed bigots – seemed, almost without exception, to include me within the category of 'loyal Protestant friend', and, going further, to refer to me as 'almost a Brother', that is, almost an Orangeman, a designation that I took with a measure of unease and awkwardness, but nonetheless as a mark of trust and affection.

For better or for worse, the anthropological by-product of this trust and affection are the pages of this book, in all their ethnographic heterogeneity, homogeneity, and dualism. I have tried hard to do justice to all three of these elements, and thereby to the morality of the Orange lives that it describes. Before finally sitting down to write (a process which has itself taken several years), I was heartened, if a little daunted, by something Scot Symon, Grand Lodge Executive Officer[5] and one of Scotland's most prominent Orangeman, said to me during one of our last conversations before I left the field. With his characteristic frankness, he summarised his assessment of my research efforts by stating that 'unlike all the others who've written about Scottish Orangeism, your book will be based on facts, because you've been the only one into Grand Lodge to speak to people'. This was not, Scot stressed, because other researchers had not been permitted access – he repeatedly stated in media interviews that under his leadership the Orange Order in Scotland had an 'open door' policy – but because I had been the only one who had really taken him up on this offer. His exclusive focus on Grand Lodge notwithstanding (here again we find ourselves confronted by the dualism of Scots-Orangeism), I find myself heartened by Scot's words. This is not, importantly, because I am convinced that this book represents any kind of unchallengeable socio-scientific 'statement of fact', but rather because within Scot's statement is the reassuring affirmation that I 'spoke' to Orangemen. And insofar as 'speaking to Orangemen' can be taken as a metonym for the ethnographic enterprise, I can ask for no stronger words of endorsement. I only hope that Scot's fact-based approval is able to stand being buffeted by my decision to write what other Orange informants (well outside of Grand Lodge) demanded of me, namely a 'warts and all' account of life in the Order.

Before moving, in the next chapter, to consider how Scots-Orange morality and culture may be situated historically, as well as within contemporary Scottish society, it seems helpful to briefly summarise the ethnographic and theoretical importance of five interlocking themes, which, taken together, help us answer the central question of this book, namely, for Orangemen in Scotland, what should a good Protestant life be like? These themes are: religion, ritual, fraternalism, politics, and exceptionalism.

Religion

The theme of religion, which takes up almost the entirety of Chapter 2 but is also woven throughout the book, is presented in ways which attempt to avoid taking for granted what we mean by 'the religious'. Following an analytic of defamiliarisation, I present religion as both an ethnographic and theoretical puzzle. For Scottish Orangemen, is Protestantism a religion or a race? From the perspective of anthropology, if Protestantism *is* a race (even in part), then how might this change the way we think about religion, as a series of beliefs and practices, but also, possibly, as a substance, as an immutable essence, like blood, or bone? Here and elsewhere in the book, Orange imaginations of the spectre of Roman Catholicism necessarily take centre stage, as do human experiences of concealment and revelation, conspiracy and liberty, love and hate. Thus, if this book is about religion, this is because, for the Orange Order, the British Protestant religion *is* many things and *means* many things, just as its proffered opposite, Roman Catholicism, is and means many things too. Making sense of the interplay between this doubled religious multiplicity, as a series of enacted moral claims and counterclaims, is central to my argument about what a good (Orange) Protestant life looks like, and thus, more broadly, what we mean when we count something as religious.

Ritual

By examining Orange ritual, Chapter 3 asks how Protestant-unionist-loyalist life within the Order is dramatised, and who is meant to see what when these dramas are performed? Drawing on Simmel's (1950) classic sociological account of secrecy, I argue that Scots-Orange ritual practice offers new insights into the relationship between revelation and concealment. More specifically, I suggest that within the Orange rituals of public parading and private 'travel', revelation may be seen to function as a kind of concealment while, conversely, concealment may function as a kind of revelation. Central to this analysis is an understanding of the way in which Orangeism is indebted to Masonic epistemology. Here, participating in Orange parades (which are, in effect, mass acts of symbolic revelation), becomes a privileged and privileging way of concealing the world, keeping esoteric knowledge secret by (literally) hiding it in plain sight. In this quasi-Masonic purview, it is only those who are 'born free' who can 'see the signs'. Yet, just as public Orange parades may be interpreted as 'revelatory concealment', so too may private Orange initiation rituals be interpreted as a kind of 'concealing revelation'. As such, during the Order's second degree – the Royal Arch Purple – it is only by donning a blindfold that one is truly able to receive one's sight. What we find in Orange ritual, then, is a dialectic of revelation and concealment, of privileged blindness-giving-way-to-sight as set against undifferentiated sight-giving-way-to-blindness. It is the outworking of this dialectic that is the main subject of this chapter.

Fraternalism

In Chapter 4 I examine a different dialectic at the heart of Scottish Orangeism, namely the relationship between a love of British Protestantism and a hatred of Roman Catholicism. Based primarily on ethnographic data collected in an Orange social club, this chapter considers how Orangemen build fraternal bonds with each other, while also asking how these bonds create (and are created by) imaginations of and encounters with various anti-fraternal others. In the context of the Orange social club, Catholicism often comes to be conflated with Irish republicanism and Scottish nationalism in ways that allow performances of fraternal love and sectarian hate not only to run in parallel, but to run together, blending into one another in ways that make them inseparable and indistinguishable. By describing this co-constitution as a 'loving hatred' and a 'hateful love', new challenges may be posed to the emerging field of the anthropology of ethics, and particularly to what Robbins (2013) has called 'an anthropology of the good'. By arguing that religious hatred *can* be included within human experiences of 'The Good', this chapter contends that the sociality of 'the negative' (Burke 1966) needs to be re-theorised as a positive, that is, a culturally generative, force.

Politics

While this book is about Orange religion, it is also, by virtue of that very fact, a book about politics. Indeed, its title, *The Religion of Orange Politics,* is worded to raise questions about how Orangemen sacralise their politics, for example, through imaginations of Britain's status as a divinely established Protestant constitutional monarchy. As with the theme of Orange religion, while discussions of Orange politics are found throughout this book, they are also given a particularly focused treatment in a single chapter (Chapter 5). Ethnographically, this chapter addresses the Order's campaign against Scottish independence, first by examining the whys and wherefores of their exclusion from the mainstream political debate. Running parallel to this analysis of the exclusion of Orangeism by the political mainstream is an exploration of Orange attempts to create a Scots-unionist counter-politics which placed Protestantism centre stage. In the context of the independence referendum, I argue that my Orange informants came to experience the activities of the Scottish National Party as an ultramontane plot, that is, as a (partially hidden) proxy war between the British monarchy and the papacy. Furthermore, I suggest that my Orange informants made sense of their membership of the Order, in part, by imagining themselves as taking up different but complementary roles in this proxy war, either as latter-day Covenanters or as latter-day loyalists, and doing so in ways that always placed religious and ethnic boundaries at the centre of political discourse. What this chapter offers, then, is a critical reflection upon the limits of politics, where 'the political' comes to be defined as neither transparent nor secular, but instead as that which is driven by a veiled nefarious religious agenda.

Exceptionalism

If, in ethnographic terms, this book is about Scottish Orangeism, then, understood in broader theoretical terms, it may also be read as a book about exceptionalism. What does it mean to be special, and how might this specialness come to be expressed in religious and even racial terms? Having adopted the famous Rangers FC slogan, Orangemen would frequently proclaim 'We Are The People!' Similarly, Orange lodges and loyalist flute bands would often take the designation 'Chosen Few' as part of their name. The 'greatness' of Great Britain was also a common refrain, while Scotland, too, was spoken of as specially blessed by God, second only to Israel according to some of my informants. Taking such ethnographic observations as a final point of departure, this book concludes by suggesting that Scots-Orangeism is best understood as a grand exercise in the imagination, construction, and reimagination of Protestant exceptionalism. Being exceptional, I argue, comes to be experienced by my Orange informants as both an imparted status and an inalienable essence – an external light shone by God upon His people (The People), who, by virtue of being the 'Chosen Few', are also already possessors of a special inward state of being. This imparted-yet-inherent exceptionalism is not only religious and political, but also understood to be material in nature. Here, the substance of

Orangeism is articulated in terms of being a member of the British Protestant 'family of nations' – kith and kin who inherit their exceptionalism (at least in part) simply by virtue of sharing in that 'bloodline'. It is this blood-bought and blood-secured membership of the Order, and thus to Protestantism as a 'race apart', which comes to define Orangemen as truly exceptional.

Notes

1 Wherever possible, the names of people and places have been changed.
2 Only 2 per cent of jobs in the town remain within the manufacturing sector, less than a quarter of the national average. As a result, unemployment is a third higher than the national average, with 6.3 per cent claiming Jobseekers Allowance. The Glencruix work-force is also less well qualified, with only 29 per cent having a degree (national average 34 per cent) and 19 per cent having no qualifications at all (national average 13 per cent) (Scottish Government 2011).
3 I follow Laidlaw (2014: 116–118) in not treating ethics and morality as fundamentally different phenomena.
4 The flag dispute developed in response to a debate within Belfast City Council in December 2012 regarding when to fly the Union flag over City Hall. Unionist councillors wanted the flag to remain in place over City Hall 365 days a year, while nationalist councillors wanted to remove it altogether. Alliance, who at that time held the balance of power within Belfast City Council, chose not to vote down the motion to remove the flag altogether, but instead offered what they felt to be a compromise, namely flying the Union flag on eighteen designated days per year. This compromise motion was resisted by unionists but passed with support from nationalists, triggering a unionist backlash against Alliance. Forty thousand leaflets were jointly distributed by the DUP and the Ulster Unionist Party in loyalist areas, blaming Alliance for the removal of the flag. It was in this context that loyalist protests occurred across the Province, with prominent Alliance politicians receiving threats of violence. In addition to the homes of two Alliance politicians being attacked, one Alliance Party office was destroyed.
5 Scot has since stepped down from this particular role, and is no longer Executive Officer.

1

Situating Scottish Orangeism

During my earliest fieldwork conversations with Orangemen, I was often struck by how consistently these informants assumed that I was there to study their history. Intriguingly, these assumptions often persisted well after I had explained that I was an anthropologist, and that, as such, I was primarily interested in the lives of Scots-Orangemen in the present. As the tally of such conversations grew, I began to realise that my being endlessly redirected towards books and pamphlets about Orange history, and to Orangemen knowledgeable about the Order's past, was not so much a misunderstanding of my ethnographic project, as it was a counterclaim my informants were making about what they thought my research on Orangeism *should* be about. Importantly, I was seldom left with the sense that such efforts of redirection were insincere or a kind of decoy. Indeed, not many of my informants could be accused of shrinking away from the anthropological spotlight, and as it will become clear in the chapters that follow, most shared their present-day Orange experiences with me generously, even forthrightly. Instead, as I came to know more Scots-Orangemen, and came to know them better, I learned to recognise the immense importance that Orangemen placed on Orange history, not only as something that stood as the backdrop for their present-day Orange experiences, but as its very substance.

As obvious as it surely sounds to seasoned members of the Order, what those early conversations taught me was that when Orangemen live out their contemporary Orangeism, what they are claiming to live out is their history. Crucially, this statement is not only true with reference to the Order's famous annual public processions, which every 12 July (and on several occasions besides) commemorate the Battle of the Boyne in 1690. Private Lodge rituals and degree work, for example, are also understood as akin to acts of ancestral conjuring, whereby the Orange brethren of today, both neophyte and veteran, convene with the actions and memories of departed brethren who also 'travelled' the Exodus wilderness by perambulating their Orange hall (see Chapter 3). So, too, when Orangemen share with each other books of remembrance which list deceased members of a particular lodge, or when they sit and drink in their social clubs, the walls of which are covered with old lodge portraits, discoloured with age. Here, the names and faces of the Orange past are made ever-present. Even the fight against Scottish independence can be interpreted as a convening with and a conjuring of history, as Orangemen transform themselves into latter-day Covenanters and latter-day loyalists, refighting (variously) the battles of their Presbyterian and paramilitary forebears (see Chapter 5). Equally, as I describe in Chapter 2, my Orange informants were acutely sensitive to the ways in which the past was being repeated within their present. According to these informants, for example, 'the menace of Rome' was not only an ancient foe, but a real and present danger which sought to manipulate Scotland into conforming to the hidden will of a papacy determined to eradicate British Protestantism. Here too, in these moments of reflection upon the *longue durée* of 'Romish influence', the present was explained with reference to a past that was said to haunt modern Scotland in uncanny and malevolent ways.

I am not the first to notice this privileging of history as an explanatory trump card. Dominic Bryan, writing on the different but related context of historical commemorations of the Battle of the Somme and the Easter Rising, both in 1916, states that:

> As an explanatory tool for understanding 'who we are', history is predominant. Thus, in popular culture, the examination of group identities is usually undertaken by narrative histories. [...] I have always been struck by the claim, particularly amongst people in working-class Protestant groups in Northern Ireland, that young people need to learn their history so that they can know their identity. (Bryan 2016: 24, 38)

Bryan's argument is a pointedly critical one, since he argues that, in reality, 'the construction of the past is present orientated' (2016: 27), and is undertaken by 'nations and states that legitimise themselves through historical narrative' (ibid.: 38). In this view, historical commemoration is often 'used to disguise what is really taking place' (ibid.: 29), namely an inherently political justification of power relations, which, via a (no less political) deployment of a diachronic view of the past, seeks to transform eminently contestable narratives into incontestable truth claims. For Bryan, then, 'commemorations are a way of capturing the sacrifices of the past for the legitimation of the political present and the imagined political future' (ibid.: 24).

What Bryan's argument helps us see is that, by seeking to redirect my attentions from an anthropological concern with the present to a historical concern with the past, my informants were (I think, implicitly) reproducing this privileging of history, and particularly its popular diachronic narrative form. By doing so, my Orange informants were reproducing the kinds of efforts that State political leaders engage in when they seek to legitimise 'the nation' through various acts of commemoration, by, for example, laying wreaths at a cenotaph. Similarly, through an emphasis on 'learning their history', my Orange informants sought to justify the present existence of their fraternal organisation, just as politicians seek to justify the power relations which undergird the nationalist narratives of the nations they lead. By commemorating a battle that happened over three centuries ago, for example, the Order's Boyne commemorations are thus merely a difference in degree (not in kind), when compared to the Irish government's commemoration of the Easter Rising, or to EU leaders' commemorations of the centenary of the end of the First World War. As above, all of these examples are, in Bryan's words, 'a way of capturing the sacrifices of the past for the legitimation of the political present' (ibid.).

It is for this reason, then, that my informants responded to my emphatic emphasis on 'contemporary' Orangeism with a no less emphatic emphasis of their own, that sought to conflate present (political) happenings with past (historical) events by claiming the latter as the explanatory framework for, and justification of, the former. As a result, I found myself cast in similar terms to the working-class Protestant youth Bryan describes above, that is, I was told that if I wanted to understand contemporary Orange identity, I would need to learn Orange history. Again (and here I suspect that I am somewhat at odds with Bryan), I am convinced that there was no subterfuge or 'will to power' sleight of hand going on here; my Orange informants were not trying to fool me, but were simply telling me what they believed to be true, namely that Orange history (and the history of British Protestant-ism more generally) contained the answers to the questions I was asking about contemporary Scots-Orange identity. Of course, their doing so may have been a result of the way in which, at a societal level, 'popular history lies at the core of nationalist ideological constructions' (Bryan 2016: 38), but there is no clear way of telling, and, in any case, such an argument stands outside of my current focus on emic understandings of the importance of Orange history. Simply put, my primary interest is in how, and with what effects, Orangemen deploy Orange history as a route to making sense of their present. I am less interested, as a result, in trying to second-guess what power interests such constructions may serve, and even less interested in questioning whether or not the histories they construct are historically accurate.

Thus, instead of trying to unearth hidden or unconscious political motivations in the minds and lives of my history-obsessed informants, what I offer in this chapter is a series of brief sketches of different aspects of Scottish Orangeism, some of which are more directly historical, and some of which are more contemporary, but all of which contain (at least) a little of both. The topics I have chosen to draw together are diverse, but all aim to offer something particular about the multiple meanings and contexts of Scottish Orangeism, past and present. The account I give is roughly chronological, although not straightforwardly so, starting with the totemisation of 'King Billy' and his mythic clash with James II at the Boyne, before examining the birth of Irish and Scottish Orangeism, its ritual and institutional structure, its often (but not always) unifying treatment of 'Ulster's Cause' in the context of 'The Troubles', its relations with other Loyal Orders and 'loyal Protestant friends', before concluding with some reflections on how Scots-Orangemen are perceived by non-members, as well as how Scots-Orangemen of different positions and persuasions regard each other.

Taken as a whole, these sketches may be overlaid upon each other to build up a situated sense of who my informants were, and where they were coming from, both as individual Orangemen, and as fellow Orange brethren. Yet, such sketches, despite their emphasis on situatedness and context, should not be read as providing any kind of direct causality or reductionist explanatory logic. Dennis did not rail against Catholic pensioners drinking in the Glencruix Orange Social Club (simply) because of his political support for Protestant/unionist politics in Northern Ireland, just as teenage loyalist bandsmen did not choose to parade with the Orange Order (simply) because they wanted to commemorate King Billy's victory over James II at the Battle of the Boyne in 1690. The context that follows below, then, should be read as indicative but not determinative. With this stated, it seems appropriate to start at the point where most of my Orange informants chose to begin my Orange education, that is, with the totem of King Billy, and his mythic defence of the Protestant people of Britain.

Of myths and totems: the defeat of James II by 'King Billy' Prince of Orange

A brief (and thus necessarily selective) survey of the monarchical arm-wrestle between James II and William III provides an apt introduction to how the Orange Order, both in Ireland and in Scotland, makes sense of its history, the celebration of which they regard to be one of the chief reasons for their existence as a Protestant fraternity. This selective story, as my Orange informants would demand, places James's Catholicism and William's Protestantism centre stage. To be clear, in deliberately framing the history of these two monarchs in this way, I am not making any claim about the truthfulness of the account itself, despite my referencing scholarly historians whose work corroborates that the events described below 'really did' happen. This is because, despite my giving a diachronic narrative account (as Bryan would describe it) of the 'Glorious Revolution', my interest is not so much in the individual events themselves, but in how these may be pieced together in such a way as to form, from an Orange perspective, a compelling story about the primordial conflict between Roman Catholicism and British Protestantism. Whether or not the sketch I present below offers a balanced view of religion as a political driving force of late seventeenth-century England is thus beside the point. The point is rather that this is precisely the kind of historical sketch that my informants shared with me, and, believing it to be true, used as the basis for their vigilance against and hostility towards the contemporary Roman Catholic Church, both in Scotland, and globally.

The narrative may be told as follows. In 1669 James the Duke of York, whose brother Charles II was then King of England, converted to Roman Catholicism (Miller 1977: 58). His long-suspected conversion, which was not at all welcomed by the Anglican establishment of his day, who had enjoyed over a century of power rooted in the English Reformation of the 1530s, was finally exposed by the Test Act of 1673, used to prevent Roman Catholics from taking public office (Speck 2002: 2). Undeterred, soon after being widowed, James was remarried to Mary Beatrice of Modena, an Italian Princess, via a Roman Catholic proxy wedding (Miller 1977: 73). With Charles II having no heir, fears grew that the King would die, passing the throne to his Catholic brother James. In what would turn out to be an ironic twist, James's own Protestant daughter Mary (born from his first marriage to Anne Hyde) married James's ultra-Protestant nephew William of Orange in 1677 (Troost 2005: 139–140).

Meanwhile, with Charles II still without an heir, Parliament sought to prevent James from becoming King by attempting (on no less than three separate occasions) to pass the Exclusion Bill. Charles II did not approve of the Bill, and responded by repeatedly dissolving Parliament, an act which damaged his popularity and that of his brother, as well as provoking a period of political turbulence known as the 'Exclusion Crisis' (Jones 1985). However, with the failure of the Rye House Plot of 1683 which attempted to assassinate both Charles II and James, the brothers were returned to favour (Miller 1977: 115–117). Then, with the death of Charles II in April of 1685, James II was crowned King (Speck 2002: 36–37). Two months later, James II survived two rebellions designed to overthrow him, and responded by enlarging the size of his standing army 'which increased to almost nineteen thousand officers and men' (Miller 1977: 142), including 'nearly a hundred Catholic officers' (ibid.: 143) who were not subjected to the Test Act. A year later, in 1686, James initiated a violent suppression of Scottish Presbyterian Covenanters whom he suspected of harbouring political as well as religious dissent – a period which came to be known as the 'Killing Time' (Cowan 1968: 50). In this same year, the King's Secretary of State advised 'a purge of office-holders in order to fill the court, the administration and the armed forces with … Catholic allies' (ibid.: 151), a move which greatly worried the English Protestant establishment. Their fears were compounded, when, by 1688, James II and Queen Consort Mary had produced a Roman Catholic son, offering the prospect of the English throne permanently coming under the control of a royal Catholic lineage. That James himself clearly desired this religious transformation seems undeniable, as revealed by his letter to the Pope announcing the birth: 'this so much wished for pledge of a succession to our kingdoms has been granted to us by the Benevolent Being' (Speck 2002: 62).

The birth of James Francis Edward – nicknamed 'the Old Pretender' – was a tipping point for the King's opponents. That same year, a group of Protestant noblemen – the 'Immortal Seven' – petitioned William of Orange to 'restrain' James (Cruickshanks 2000: 23). Following that invitation, in November 1688, The Glorious Revolution had begun, with William landing his army in Torbay (Childs 1980: 169), stepping ashore to announce, as Orange myth would have it, the famous words 'the liberties of England and the Protestant religion I will maintain'. This move quickly led James II to flee to France (Miller 1977: 205, Speck 2002: 80), leading to a declaration that he had abdicated, thereby allowing his daughter Mary to jointly take the throne with her Protestant husband William III (Miller 1977: 209). A year later, in 1689, James landed in Kinsale, Ireland, to ready himself for an attack on England in order to regain the throne (ibid.: 221). William responded by meeting him in Ireland, landing at Carrickfergus, before attacking and defeating James's army near Drogheda, at the Battle of the Boyne in 1690 (ibid.: 231–232). James again fled to France, never to return (ibid.: 233).

William III and Mary II jointly held the throne from 1689 to 1694, with William ruling alone after Mary's death, until his own death in 1702 (Keates 2015). Because William and Mary had produced no children, following William's death, Mary's sister Anne was crowned Queen. A Protestant line of succession was still not secure, however, because Anne had no surviving children, a situation which again raised the prospect of the return of James II's Catholic line. To prevent this claim to the throne from being mounted, Parliament passed the Act of Settlement in 1701, which 'provided explicitly for the crown to "descend to and be enjoyed by such person or persons being Protestants as should have inherited" in the event that at any time the next in blood were disqualified for being a Catholic and were therefore to be treated as if "naturally dead"' (Nenner 1995: 229–230). The Act placed Sophia of Hanover as next in line to the throne, but Anne outlived her by fifty-four days, meaning that Sophia's son George became King (Blanning 2017). Regardless, William of Orange, in conjunction with Parliament, had successfully 'maintained' the English throne as Protestant (first militarily and then constitutionally) by excluding the possibility of the return of James II and his Catholic lineage. The Glorious Revolution had not only been won, but had been secured, as had the future of British Protestant ascendancy – and it is *this* which the Orange Order has celebrated every 12 July, up to the present day.

To the extent that William of Orange is (literally) the totem of the Orange Order, it also seems fair to say that James II may be seen as the Order's anti-totem – a historical bogey man, not unlike Guy Fawkes, but backed with royal power – who comes to represent 'the menace of Rome' (see Chapter 2), in all its religious and political ambition. As we will see, particularly in Chapters 2 and 5, the story of the Glorious Revolution provides the Order with a neat template for understanding both the recent past and the present of British, Scottish, and Irish Protestantism – as well as the threat said to be posed to it by the papacy. Orange interpretations of the different facets of the seventeenth-century narrative outlined above may thus be seen as offering a series of unflattering like-for-like comparisons with contemporary Catholicism, in Scotland, Britain, and globally. Consider the following comparative claims, many of which I heard my Orange informants make.

Just as James initially practised his Catholic faith in secret, so too are many political leaders today secretly guided by Catholic doctrine, and thereby the political influence of the Vatican. Just as Charles II sought to thwart the will of Parliament during the Exclusion Crisis in order to allow his Catholic brother to become King, so too is Catholicism today essentially anti-democratic, driven by dictatorial impulses to gain and maintain power by whatever means necessary. Just as James II sought to bolster his position by amassing a large standing army led by Catholic officers, so too has the papacy of the recent past agitated for war as a route to extending its global dominance. Just as James II persecuted Presbyterian Covenanters during the 'Killing Time', so too does contemporary Catholicism seek to wipe out British Protestantism, and most especially those Protestants who remain strongly committed to the founding principles of the Reformation. Just as James II sought to purge his Royal Court of Protestants, so too do powerful Catholics in Scotland today seek to exclude Protestants from positions of influence in all areas of public life. Finally, and most worryingly for my Orange informants, just as James II received help from Catholic France and Catholic Ireland in his attempt to defeat William at the Boyne, so too do European Catholic countries today form a hidden political coalition against Britain and British Protestant interests, as evidenced most recently by the hostility shown to the Conservative Party (and their Democratic Unionist Party allies) during Brexit negotiations. Such, for my Orange informants, is the contemporary relevance of the 'cautionary tale' of James II and his attempted Roman Catholic takeover of the English and Scottish Crowns.

Many of the details of these Orange claims, as well as how they are lived out in the lives of my informants, are described in the chapters that follow. What I offer in the next section of this chapter, then, is the story of the birth of the Orange Order, as the Institution which claims to be the last real guardian of King Billy's Glorious Revolution.

The birth of Orangeism: warring peasants and the revival of the Williamite tradition

Following William's victory at the Boyne, a series of Irish Penal Laws, or 'popery laws' (O'Loughlin in Connolly 2007: 462), were introduced in an attempt to cement Protestant gains – gains which later became known as the Protestant ascendancy. More specifically, this involved 'the enactment from the 1690s of a series of discriminatory measures directed against Catholic clergy and laity [which] reflected the hardening of Irish Protestant attitudes following their experiences under James II' (ibid.). For almost a century, 'the code excluded [Catholics in Ireland] from political office, the liberal professions, and the more profitable economic activities, as well as prohibiting their possession of firearms' (Senior 1966: 3). So effective were these laws at achieving their aim, that, 'by the last quarter of the eighteenth century, most upper and middle class Protestants had come to take the subordination of Catholics for granted, and were inclined to take a more moderate view of the ascendancy' (ibid.: 4). However, the Irish Protestant peasantry, whose position was, by definition, far more precarious, did not share this new spirit of ecumenical generosity. Indeed, unlike their social and economic 'betters', these 'lower orders' of Protestants faced real material losses if legal changes were introduced, since, 'as a result of the penal code [they] had become a kind of plebeian aristocracy' (ibid.).

Yet, if the term 'plebeian aristocracy' may accurately reflect the *religious* supremacy of Irish Protestant peasants over their Catholic counterparts in the eighteenth century, it certainly cannot be said to reflect their *economic* position, for Protestant peasants, too, existed within a land tenure system which virtually guaranteed their poverty. Indeed, 'these staunch "King's men" were caught in a continuing spiral of economic rivalry and sectarian bitterness with their Catholic neighbours, and had not forgotten that … their forefathers had … participated in William's campaigns' (Haddick-Flynn 1999: 11–12). The situation was particularly tense in the border counties of Ulster, where Protestant and Catholic peasants were forced to compete for short-term land leases controlled by a series of middlemen who acted as brokers for (often absentee) landlords. Since both landlords and brokers were primarily interested in maximising their own incomes, tenancy agreements were set for short periods of time, and would be transferred to the highest bidder upon their expiration, with little regard for the ruinous consequences any changeover would have on the existing tenant. Such problems were compounded by chronic 'land hunger', caused by a high rural population density in religiously mixed mid-Ulster, which ensured that when tenancies came up for auction, competition was fierce, and often occurred along sectarian lines. From the perspective of the Protestant peasantry, such a state of affairs was made worse still with the relaxation of the Penal Laws, as this meant that Catholics became relatively more prosperous, and were thus better able to bid against their Protestant neighbours, who had long felt that access to the best land was theirs by a divine right secured for them by William at the Boyne.

The result was that 'long-standing feuds and economic rivalries kept denominational strife alive among the lower classes [which] consequently made the poorer Protestants sensitive to any rise in the status of Catholics' (Senior 1966: 2). Crucially, some within the peasantry (on both sides of the 'sectarian divide') chose to act upon this sensitivity by banding together into agrarian secret societies designed to secure their (seemingly zero-sum) economic and religious interests. 'Such societies, once organized, could normally neutralize the power of the landlord-magistrates by intimidating witnesses and juries, and could penalize unpopular landlords by houghing and slashing their cattle in nightly raids' (ibid.: 4). Within the context of the formation of the Orange Order, the most important secret society was the Peep O' Day Boys who made it their business not only to violently resist their exploitation under the land tenure system, but also to take it upon themselves to enforce the Penal Laws. Such acts of 'enforcement' often took the form of early morning raids (hence 'Peep O' Day') on Catholic farmsteads, where properties were ransacked, ostensibly in the search for illegal firearms. Catholic peasants who had entered the (Protestant dominated) weaving industry as a way to supplement their meagre farming incomes also had their looms smashed and webs cut by the Peep O'Day Boys during these raids. Such acts of proto-industrial sabotage merely heightened sectarian tensions further.

Co. Armagh's Catholic peasantry reacted in kind by creating their own secret society, The Defenders, who 'were formed with the evident object of preventing the growth of [Protestant] denominational bands' (Senior 1966: 8). By definition, The Defenders sought to protect themselves against the Peep O' Day Boys by obtaining firearms, a situation which further challenged the Penal Laws and encouraged yet more Peep O'Day searches and raids. Predictably, it was 'under the pressure of such raids [that] the Defender organisation grew ... and became more purely Catholic in character' (ibid.: 9). Equally predictable was the fact that such a situation 'was unacceptable to the Protestant peasantry and [that] the Peep O' Day Boy elements were prepared to oppose it by force' (ibid.: 8). A downward spiral of Protestant–Catholic violence ensued; 'imbued with their inbred hatreds, [each] looked to their own strengths. For years the tense relationship between them had been deteriorating and, in mid-Ulster, had reached boiling point' (Haddick-Flynn 1999: 127).

Aptly for an anthropological audience, this boiling point was reached because of a cockfight. Staged at Dan Winter's pub, at the Diamond crossroads near Loughgall, Co. Antrim, in May 1795, the cockfight attracted the attention of a passing Catholic spectator, who, being 'foolhardy enough to loiter too long in this Protestant heartland' (ibid.: 135), was beaten up by a group of Peep O' Day Boys:

> Later, as he painfully limped home, he swore vengeance on his assailants. Soon it was reported that Dan Winter's pub had been earmarked for a Defender attack, and within a few days shots were fired at the premises by galloping horsemen. (ibid.)

Winter was a Freemason and, very likely, a Peep O' Day Boy, with his pub serving as the venue for local Peep O' Day Boy meetings, as well as being used by a similar Protestant secret society, the Orange Boys (ibid.: 134). The Orange Boys were created the previous year, in 1794, by Winter's relative James Wilson, of the village of Dyan. Wilson, who, like Winter and many other founding Orangemen was also a Freemason (see also Roberts 1971: 272), formed the Orange Boys after helping to lead a successful counter-attack against a group of Defenders who were smashing and burning Protestant homes in the village of Bendurb. According to Haddick-Flynn, Wilson 'had pleaded with his Masonic brethren to join him in getting rid of the mob, but they steadfastly refused. As he mounted his horse for home, he shook his fist at his timorous friends and swore that 'he would light a star in the Dyan which would eclipse them forever" (ibid.: 133). The Orange Boys were established the very next day, and, 'in imitation of the Prince of Orange, [swore] to act as protectors of the Protestant people' (ibid.). In the three months following the Defender shooting of Winter's premises, violent clashes between the Peep O' Day Boys and the Defenders escalated, leading Winter to call on the aid of Wilson and his Orange Boys in anticipation of a full-blown Defender assault on his pub.

On 14 September, and in the week following, the anticipated assault finally came, with large numbers of Defenders assembling north of the Diamond. In response, the Peep O' Day Boys and the Orange Boys gathered, 'and were joined by other Protestant groups' (ibid.: 136). Winter and his sons barricaded themselves into their pub, and successfully repelled a number of Defender attacks, but were eventually burnt out by Defenders with torches, and were forced to flee. Once Winter had regrouped with the Orange Boys, an ambush was set for the Defenders while they were occupied with looting the pub. The ambush was a success, and around thirty Defenders were killed by several volleys of rifle fire and a subsequent bayonet charge (ibid.: 137–138).

> The victory was total. The Protestants – Peep O' Day Boys, Orange Boys and others – had driven off their opponents and frustrated what they saw as a Defender plan to drive them from the area … The victors assembled in a field opposite the smoking ruins of Dan Winter's pub and, with their faces still blackened from gunshot powder … they clasped their hands and … vowed a solemn oath to form a greater and more effective brotherhood than hitherto, and to take measures for their mutual protection. (ibid.: 138–139)

Retiring to Winter's farmhouse, James Sloan, James Wilson, and Dan Winter 'discussed the project in outline' (ibid.: 139), and met again that night in Sloan's tavern in Loughgall, where 'an early decision was taken that the new brotherhood should be called after the Royal House of "The Great Deliverer" [William III], and that those initiated should be known as Orangemen' (ibid.: 140). New waves of sectarian violence followed this establishment of what later became known as the Orange Order. 'The Protestant peasantry went on the offensive and began a series of night raids against Catholics ... known as the "Armagh Outrages"' (ibid.: 147) – a situation which Orangemen blamed on 'uncontrollable Peep O' Day Boy elements, who were not members of the Order' (ibid.: 148). As the embryonic Order developed, power struggles ensued as these early Orangemen sought to cultivate the level of social respectability required to entice Protestant landowners and other gentry into joining the Institution. As a result, James Wilson, with his long history of sectarian violence, found himself sidelined (ibid.: 142–143), as did others with clear Peep O' Day Boy connections. Yet, while 'it cannot be established that Orangemen, acting as such, were responsible for the terror, it is likely that a number wore two hats: one, as upright citizens when acting as Orangemen, and another when engaged in moonlight activities against Catholics' (ibid.: 148), an accusation that is still levelled at the Order by its contemporary critics today.

Notably, the proffered solution to this eighteenth-century Orange problem with sectarian thuggishness was the expansion of its Masonic-style system of ritual. The solution was enacted through the introduction of 'a new degree or second level of membership ... [which] would place more onerous obligations on their wilder spirits and bring greater control' (ibid.: 152) to Orange leaders. As well as deliberately setting membership dues at a level above that which most Peep O' Day Boys could afford, this second degree sought to place Biblical piety at the centre of Orangeism. Of crucial importance for my wider argument about Orange chosenness and exceptionalism, this new ritual was based on 'a number of Exodus passages ... such as the giving of the Law on Mount Sinai and the wandering in the Wilderness, [with] these themes acted out in episodic ritual dramas to give a sense of association with the Chosen People' (ibid.: 153–154). As Haddick-Flynn rightly observes, 'it was a winning formula that would stand the test of time' (ibid.: 154).

Consequently, in the years immediately following the aftermath of the Battle of the Diamond, with the backing and assistance of a growing number in the Irish Protestant gentry, who were concerned about revolutionary events in France reaching Ireland in the form of the United Irishmen (McFarland 1990: 34), James Sloan began rapidly signing 'warrants' giving formal written permission for the formation of new lodges across Co. Antrim and further afield, each, as in Masonry, with its own number. MacRaild, another important historian of Orangeism, gives this assessment of the early period of the Institution:

> Having grown from a weak base, Orangeism attained a position from which its members could bargain. In later 1797 and early 1798 ... the organisation grew rapidly to around 40,000 members. From this point it had a settled purpose: to be a movement to add structure and gravity to the task of subjugating Catholics, mixing loud declarations of loyalty with a willingness to sometimes do violence. Maintaining ascendancy in this sectarian competition was a key concern of the Order. (2005: 2)

With the Battle of the Diamond taking its place within the Irish Protestant mythos alongside the Battle of Boyne, 'a new confidence arose as the faded fabric of the

Orange tradition was taken out and refurbished; [within this] new atmosphere the Order grew beyond all expectations' (ibid.), and not just within Ireland. It is to this growth, and specifically to the arrival of Orangeism in Scotland, that I now want to turn.

Early Scottish Orangeism: migrating Ulstermen and the quest for respectability

Orangeism reached Scotland at the close of the eighteenth century, when Scottish soldiers first encountered the Order while posted in Ireland. According to Haddick-Flynn, 'following the founding of the Order and the advent of military lodges, a number of Scottish regiments were granted warrants. In 1798 the Dumbarton Fusiliers returned from Ireland with warrant No. 573' (1999: 398). Importantly, this military connection did not lead to a replication in Scotland of the large-scale violence of early Irish Orangeism. Indeed:

> The advent or Orangeism in Scotland was much less dramatic and auspicious than in Ireland, with no equivalent of the battle of the Diamond and its associated folklore. The Scottish Institution seems to have arrived without eliciting significant comment from any quarter for, as in the North of England, the original lodges seem to have functioned mainly as private ex-servicemen's clubs, with an additional role as benefit societies. (McFarland 1990: 50)

According to McFarland, moreover, unlike in Ireland, the growth of the Orange Order in Scotland was slowed by a lack of revolutionary threat (ibid.). Still, by 1813 the Order had reached Glasgow, and by 1824 it had spread to Airdrie, with 'the first attempt at a full ceremonial twelfth of July parade' occurring in 1821 (ibid.: 51). Yet, as in Ireland, the spectre of sectarian disturbance was never far away. In 1822, for example, the Order's annual 12 July parade ended with Irish Catholics besieging the marchers within their hall. 'Police and even military intervention was required and 127 Orangemen were taken into safekeeping, returning home ignominiously "with their sashes in their pockets"' (ibid.). Such Protestant–Catholic conflicts in Scotland may be partly understood as a product of the demographic and economic make-up of a second wave of members joining the Order. These were not Scottish soldiers returning from Ireland, but Protestant-Irish weavers coming to Scotland in search of work (ibid.). Importantly, the arrival of these Irish Protestant workers 'reinforce[d] the sense in which Orangeism in Scotland was an adjunct to already existing bitterness towards Roman Catholics' (ibid.) originating in religious and economic conflicts in mid-Ulster. Crucially, by carrying this stigma of imported sectarianism, as well as by demonstrating some willingness to enact it in violent confrontations on the streets (ibid.: 66), Orangemen in Scotland failed to attract 'any upper class involvement in the Order ... in the 1820s' (ibid.: 54). In this context, the notion of Protestant ascendancy took on a more populist and bellicose feel among the Institution's new urban proletariat members:

> While fuelled by a virulent hatred of Roman Catholicism this was paradoxically not without some 'democratic' input ... The key to the anti-Catholic hostility was

found in a representation of that religion as an absolutism that had been overthrown by some form of Protestant democratic alliance – so preserving 'the freedom of individual consciousness' and 'civil and religious liberty'... For the rank and file Orangemen then 'Protestant Ascendancy' could frequently mean not aristocratic dominance, but the ascendancy of the people over 'Popish' influence. (McFarland 1990: 60–61)

By the mid-point of the nineteenth century, with the Great Famine in Ireland acting as a major push factor – in combination with the pull of new economic opportunities in Scotland as a result of rapid industrialisation – further waves of Catholic and Protestant migrants crossed the Irish Sea to settle and work in Scotland. As Ulster-identifying Protestant migrants to Scotland sought to differentiate themselves from Irish-identifying Catholics, (with the former also benefitting from their longer-established industrial skill base), the Order became a key venue for the assertion of such identity politics. The impact on the size of the Order's membership was marked. In 1872, Scotland's annual 12 July march comprised 1,500 Orangemen; the following year that number had risen to at least 15,000 (ibid.: 70–71). Thirteen years later, with the proposal of the First Home Rule Bill, the Order's membership in Scotland rose again, as unionists of all stripes feared loss of British control over Ireland (ibid.: 71). By 1892, the Order in Scotland had 25,000 members, 8,000 of whom were in Glasgow (ibid.: 72), and this despite the fact that 'it was still over-whelmingly an organisation of the industrial working class' (ibid.: 78). Crucially, as was the case among the Irish peasantry of the eighteenth century who were clashing over the enforcement of the Penal Laws, for nineteenth-century Irish industrial workers in Scotland:

> The dynamics of sectarianism ... were not simply reducible to the workplace, and may indeed have drawn more on ideological and political factors than the economic level. The question perhaps was more one of territoriality or intercommunal relations than production, with the entry of Roman Catholics into the workplace being seen as an unfavourable shift in the overall balance of forces. (ibid.: 87–88)

Thus, as well as the very tangible *economic* advantages of membership of a benefit society, there were other factors motivating those Protestants who decided to throw their lot in with the Order in Scotland. Indeed, beyond boosting professional identity and opportunity (ibid.: 88–89), membership of the Order afforded the brethren a greatly enhanced *religious* identity, namely 'the sense of belonging to some form of elite or vanguard' (ibid.: 89) community marked by special divine approval and thus worth. Importantly, 'whether a genuine or bastard religiosity animated the ordinary member is rather missing the point. For to subscribe to 'The Protestant Religion' had much wider resonances than church attendance, being intertwined precisely with claims for political and territorial ascendancy' (ibid.). Thus, as in Ireland, the theological and material dynamics of Scottish sectarianism were difficult to separate.

Yet, as attractive as this proletarian Protestant ascendancy was to those who joined the Orange Order in Scotland, it cannot be said to have matched the Order's religious, political, and economic attractiveness in Ireland, for, as McFarland points out, by 1900 the Order in Ulster had managed to build a membership of 100,000 from a population of just 1.5 million, whereas the Order in Scotland had only achieved a membership of 25,000 from a population of 4.5 million (ibid.: 106). Connected to this relative demographic weakness was a striking absence of clergy within the ranks of the Scottish Orange Order, with only nine (or less than 1 per cent) Church of Scotland ministers publicly identifying as members in 1900, six of whom were Ulstermen (ibid.: 124). As a result, with no obvious Orange-friendly denomination in Scotland, many members simply chose not to attend any place of worship – an impious decision which meant that 'the Order's unsavoury reputation, which itself had contributed to its marginalisation in Scottish religious life, was again reinforced' (ibid.: 136).

Perfectly capturing how negatively Orangeism was perceived by late nineteenth and early twentieth century Scottish bourgeois society, McFarland quotes an editorial in the *Glasgow News* from 1878, which described the Order and its membership as follows:

> They disgrace society and originate evils of a particularly far reaching kind. They pander to ignorance and intolerance and excite political animosity and sectarian hate. They are at best a mischievous anachronism alike degrading and disgraceful – a splendid testimony to our perfect freedom but a sad example of the way even freedom can be abused. (1990: 147)

The question remains, then, how much has changed since this editorial was penned almost 150 years ago? What happened to Orangeism in Scotland over the twentieth century and into the twenty-first? Stepping back to take in the global picture of twentieth century Orangeism is helpful in better understanding both the relative weakness of the Order in Scotland at this time, as well as its stubborn persistence into the contemporary period. According to Kaufmann:

> By the year 1900 ... the Imperial Grand Council of the World reported that there were 5,000 Orange lodges worldwide, including some 1,700 in Canada, 1,600 in Ireland, and 800 in the United States. The key figure, however, is not the number of lodges reported, but the dues paid – which reflects total membership. [...] In making sense of these trends, one must always be mindful of the target population of British-origin Protestants. On this basis, we can calculate the per capita strength, or 'density' of Orangeism among the Protestant male adults of each of the major jurisdictions. (2007: 42, 45)

Following this method, Kaufmann goes on to report that in the 1920s, while 20 per cent of Protestant males in Northern Ireland were members, the figure stood at only 2 per cent for Scotland (ibid.: 45). By 1951, furthermore, the figure for Glasgow had not budged, with 4,000 Orangemen in membership representing 'about 2% of that city's population' (ibid.: 52). With the arrival of the 1960s, as associational life began to collapse across the North Atlantic context (Putnam 2000), Scottish Orangeism 'appears to buck the trend' possibly as a result of 'the way Rangers–Celtic matches "translated" sectarianism into the postmodern age. Thus, even as religion declined, the ubiquity of Premiership football may have endowed Orangeism with relevance for many young Scots' (Kaufmann 2007: 55), a suggestion which my own ethnographic research supports, as discussed below.

Yet the 1950s and early 1960s were not without their challenges for the Order in Scotland, since, as McFarland (1990: 215) notes, the beginnings of secularisation and the attendant liberal enthusiasm within the Church of Scotland for ecumenical links with the Catholic Church further alienated many Orangemen from the national Kirk, and vice versa. The flourishing of licensed Orange social clubs during this period did little to offset this widening gap, reinforcing the Order's 'reputation for paying lipservice to temperance and sabbatarianism' (ibid.).

At the same time as the Order in Scotland found itself increasingly estranged from mainline Presbyterianism, it was also suffering the effects of nationwide social and economic turmoil which came in the form of urban regeneration and deindustrialisation. According to Marshall:

> Loss of political influence and lack of clerical support were serious enough blows to the confidence and vitality of the Orange Order, but the most potentially damaging threat to its continued survival were the changes which took place in the socio-economic structures of industrial Scotland during the 1950s and the 1960s. Entire communities were disrupted as massive urban regeneration and slum clearance programmes were enacted in a number of the country's largest towns and cities. This was occurring at the same time as the traditional heavy industries of coal mining, iron and steel and shipbuilding continued their steady decline ... Such upheavals within the urban working class communities of the Central Lowlands posed great difficulties to the stability and future prospects of the Orange movement, for it was in precisely these communities that it had developed and entrenched itself. (1996: 156. See also Bruce 1985: 167)

Importantly, the Order in Scotland has proved largely unable (and possibly also disinclined) to expand beyond the familiarity of this particular social and economic trench. Indeed, despite the potential benefits of such an expansion, from this mid-twentieth-century period to today, Scottish Orangeism has remained almost entirely working class, and almost entirely confined to the urban west-central region, facts which continue to closely mirror the class profile and settlement patterns of Protestant industrial workers migrating from Ulster from the famine onward (Marshall 1996: 46, 57). Walker, too, confirms this analysis in his insightful commentary on the cultural interaction between Ulster and Scotland during this period:

> The Protestant Irish [were]... a distinct group in Scottish society until well into the 20th century ... In the realm of heavy industry, the possession of skills often learned back in Ireland served the Protestant migrant workers well in the job market. In the case of certain Scottish firms ... there was a positive effort made to recruit Protestant workers from Ulster, and it is likely that an Orange Order network operated for this purpose. (1995: 8–9)

Yet again, we see here how the material realities of industrial life cannot be understood in isolation from their ethno-religious context, for as Walker also points out:

> The Orange Order ... remained essentially an Ulster Protestant immigration organisation in Scotland, a central part of a community network which was spiritually ministered to by evangelical preachers characterised by Lord Rosebery as 'carrying the Shorter Catechism in one hand and a revolver in the other'. (1995: 33)

Given this Orange emphasis on militant Protestantism (in the activist sense, as well as doctrinally), as described below, it is easy to understand why the late 1960s, with the outbreak of 'the Troubles' in Ulster, offered the Order in Scotland a renewed sense of political and ethno-religious urgency. It was during the decade which followed that many of my closest informants 'came of age' as adult Orangemen, just as the sectarian violence of the conflict in Ireland peaked in 1972, with almost 500 killed, half of whom were civilians (McKittrick 1999). It is in this context, then, that some Scottish Orangemen began to develop greater sympathy for loyalist paramilitarism. Yet, as Bruce points out, it is important to remember that, in Scotland, whenever such sympathies tipped over into practical action, this normally concentrated on fundraising as opposed to active involvement in UVF or UDA violence (1998: 112).

The Scottish Orange Order's commitment to a certain brand of politically militant Protestantism also helps explain why Kaufmann identifies 'the Pope's first visit to Scotland' in 1982 as a key date when explaining the slow decline of Scottish Orangeism in the modern period, as the resounding success of the visit in the minds of most Scots represented 'a major setback for Orange political aspirations' (2007: 55). Kaufmann's macro-analysis on this point also makes ethnographic sense. While several of my Scots-Orange informants spoke to me of their efforts to publicly protest against this Papal visit, they also readily admitted that, in comparison to the adoring crowds turning out to see John Paul II, their own numbers were small and their critical voices seldom heard. On this point, according to Bruce, as few as 1,000 people attended the Order's official anti-papal rally, many of whom were not Orangemen but 'Scottish Loyalists whom the leadership of the Orange Order had condemned as "young drunk rowdies"' (1998: 114). For Walker moreover, 'this perception of Ulster Protestant militants importing sectarian quarrels to Scotland ... was a significant one in prejudicing much political opinion which considered itself progressive, tolerant and rational' (1995: 33). As I have already argued in the Introduction (an argument I develop in Chapter 4), this 'mainstream' Scottish self and civic identification was itself dependent upon the identification of an (often Orange) 'other' that was understood to be regressive, intolerant, and irrational.

This final point seems critical for understanding the demographic and socio-political marginalisation of the Orange Order in contemporary Scotland, as well as its internal social and ethno-religious dynamics. Among many of my grass-roots Orange informants, the relationship here is co-constitutive, with experiences of social marginalisation and expressions of ethno-religious bigotry feeding off each other in a 'nobody likes us and we don't care' self-fulfilling logic of mutual loathing. Thus, by the start of the 2000s, having witnessed mainstream Scottish civic society embrace both John Paul II's visit to Scotland, and Sinn Fein's entry into a power-sharing government in Northern Ireland, Scots-Orangemen found themselves uniquely out on a limb, railing against a papacy many seemed to revere, and a Irish Republican party many seemed now willing to trust.

Yet, while Orangeism has found itself to be an increasingly niche product in contemporary Scotland, it would be wrong to conclude that *nobody* is buying. Indeed, for many Orangemen and Orange sympathisers (even if not for many within Scotland as a whole), it remains imperative to maintain 'eternal vigilance [against]... disloyal Catholics working to undermine state and society' (Walker 1995: 69). As described in the chapters which follow, such vigilance takes many different forms, from historical revisionism, to ritual initiation, to public parading, to sectarian storytelling, to fraternal binge drinking, to football fandom, to constitutional campaigning. Of particular relevance to the wider contextual account presented in this chapter, however, is the way this message of Scots-Orange vigilance against globalist ultramontanism draws inspiration from the milieu of militant Protestantism, unionism, and loyalism in Troubles and post-Troubles Northern Ireland. It is to this subject that I now want to turn.

Hands across the water: contemporary Scottish Orangeism and 'Ulster's cause'

Early on in my fieldwork in the Glencruix Orange Social Club, I was given access to a storage room containing several filing cabinets, each filled with what appeared to be a rather random assortment of bundles of papers, booklets, newsletters, and magazines. I was told by one of the leading Orangemen at the club that some of it might be of interest to my research, and was instructed to look through the materials and take away whatever I wanted. The opportunity seemed too good to pass up, so I abandoned my normal plans of chatting with the Orange regulars who were drinking in the bar next door and instead busied myself with combing through this rich textual dumping ground. What I discovered was rather eye-opening, the filing cabinets containing, as they did, a large collection of militantly anti-Catholic, loyalist, and in some cases paramilitary publications. In addition to piles of old programmes from many years of Boyne parades, as well as folders full of outdated Orange Order 'Laws and Constitutions' books, were a wide range of other (less official) documents. These included leaflets with titles such as 'Commemoration of Ulster's Solemn League and Covenant', 'Ten reasons why the Pope should not visit Britain', 'Who and what Martin Luther was', 'An urgent appeal to all true Christians: Are you praying for Northern Ireland?', 'The Falklands versus Northern Ireland', 'Justice for the UDR Four', 'The deathless story of the Somme', 'No Surrender', and 'A True Protestant'.

In addition to these short leaflets were several longer booklets. One, entitled 'Discrimination: The Truth', sought to outline the ways in which Protestants in Northern Ireland were disadvantaged in comparison to Catholics when accessing employment and public services. Another, 'Ulster – The Prey', by Peter Robinson MP, outlined unionist opposition to the Anglo-Irish Agreement. A third, a copy of the 'The Red Hand', was the official publication of the Loyalist Prisoners Welfare Association Scotland, a UVF-backed organisation which raised money to support the families of those convicted of involvement in paramilitarism. A fourth, 'Combat' magazine, was the official organ of the UVF in Northern Ireland. A fifth, simply titled 'Ulster', was the magazine of the UDA-backed Ulster Loyalist Democratic Party. Other documents included a catalogue from the Scottish Protestant Union, a DUP leaflet arguing against a united Ireland, and a booklet published by the

Shankill Historical Society commemorating the seventy-fifth anniversary of the original UVF.

While I think it doubtful that my Orange informant intended for me to discover these long-forgotten loyalist and paramilitary publications, I also do not think that he, or any of the other club regulars, would have been at all concerned by being associated with them or the organisations which published them. Indeed, the walls of the Glencruix club were covered in images and snippets of text very similar to those I discovered in the storeroom. While some of these depicted generic Orange and loyalist themes – King Billy on his horse, the thirty-sixth Ulster Division at the Somme, the Scottish Covenanters, Rangers Football Club – others were more pointedly associated with the Troubles in Northern Ireland. As well as images depicting the conflict at Drumcree, there were paintings of British soldiers on patrol in Northern Ireland, a commemorative image of three Scottish soldiers killed by the Provisional Irish Republican Army (IRA) in 1971, and further clippings from the UVF 'Red Hand' Loyalist Prisoners Welfare Association Scotland magazine. For Walker, these (at times rather unsubtle) hints of Scots-Orange sympathies for radical Ulster loyalism and paramilitarism are unsurprising, and can be explained as part of the cumulative effect of larger social and economic changes occurring within working-class communities across Scotland's Central Belt from the 1960s:

> To a long history of Catholic grievances were added those of some Protestants who felt marginalised in a rapidly changing society in which the Catholic community profile enlarged. In terms of identity, the Catholics could appear to have maintained a coherence and vigour in the midst of social, economic and demographic changes which had weakened to a large extent the Protestant self-image, particularly among the working class. Resentments over loss of identity, or feelings of insecurity about identity in the context of a powerful Catholic presence, could draw some towards the militant Protestantism of Loyalist flute bands and paramilitary style groups (discountenanced by the Official Orange Order) which took their inspiration from Northern Ireland. (Walker 1995: 182–183)

To this we might want to add *officially* discountenanced by some within the official Orange Order, particularly within its hierarchy. As discussed in Chapter 4, for Orangemen and Orange-sympathisers in Glencruix, local experiences of a socially, educationally, and economically confident Catholic community did indeed seem to add further challenge (and often resentment) to their own difficult post-industrial circumstances. For many of my closest Orange informants, the response was, as Walker suggests, the fostering of an ethno-religious identity based on militant – and in some cases, paramilitary – loyalist convictions.

In reality, such convictions formed something of a spectrum, as reflected in the wide variety of documents listed above. Some of my informants delved into the relatively more distant past to give shape to their loyalism by teaching themselves and their fellow Orangemen the stories of the Protestant Covenanters, martyred for their Reformed faith. Others kept abreast of political events in Northern Ireland, and spoke at length about the threat of a resurgent Sinn Fein to the future of the Union. Others lambasted the Democratic Unionist Party for not doing enough to hold Irish republicanism to account. Some focused their energies on building bridges between the Order and loyalist flute bands, praising the fact that bandsmen were able to embrace more trenchant forms of loyalism due to their semi-detached connection to official Orangeism. While spectating at Orange parades, it was often approvingly pointed out to me by such Orangemen that some bands did their best to flout the Grand Lodge code of conduct by carrying flags or wearing uniforms which made strategically oblique references to their support for various Northern Irish loyalist paramilitary groups. Still others turned to football, performing their support for Rangers in ways that sought to emphasise the club's association with radical Ulster Protestantism, often through sectarian chanting, but also by fostering links with certain Northern Irish Rangers supporters clubs, such as the Vanguard Bears, known to have hard-line loyalist sympathies.

To these specific cases of how Scots-Orangemen performed support for Ulster loyalism could be added other more diffuse examples of the same. On the periphery of most large Orange parades were usually found a series of fancy-goods stalls selling a huge range of souvenirs, including dozens of different lapel badges with loyalist and paramilitary symbolism, tables of CDs containing recordings of loyalist bands, as well as flags and football scarves which blended Ulster and Rangers iconography. While many of these symbols were purchased and worn by my Orange informants as a kind of clothing on parade days, with flags draped over the shoulders, or lapel badges pinned to collarettes, many also had such iconography inked directly onto their bodies in the form of tattoos. While the tattoos on display at Orange parades were diverse, combinations of Ulster and Saltire flags were especially popular, as were more explicitly paramilitary tattoos, sometimes worn alongside official Orange emblems (see Figures 1.1 and 1.2).

Among the very small number of my Scots-Orange informants who had been actively involved in loyalist paramilitarism, it was common to hear accusations that others were guilty of adopting paramilitary symbolism as little more than a fashion accessory or game. 'Someone has sold them a badge, and they think they are in the UVF!' one man said. 'They want to be tin soldiers!' another jeered. The majority of my grass-roots Orange informants, in contrast, were content to express a more casual sympathy for loyalist paramilitarism. Songs glorifying the UVF and the UDA were a mainstay of Orange social club jukeboxes and concert nights, and similar slogans were often chanted during screenings of Old Firm matches. Equally, as described in Chapter 4, while the letters UVF and UDA were worn (often literally) as badges of honour, the converse was also true, with the acronym IRA being used as shorthand for anti-Catholic and anti-republican abuse, typically 'IRA bastard'. Much of this support for 'Ulster's cause' generally, and for loyalist paramilitarism specifically, was performed by reminiscing about past parades in Northern Ireland, with such stories often focusing on contentious marches which ended in sectarian disturbance. One Orange informant, for example, described to me with relish how he had been involved in the Drumcree riots in Portadown in the mid-1990s, while another often frequently talked about his annual parading trips to the Shankill Road, not only to take part in Orange marches, but also to reconnect with old friends in the UVF.

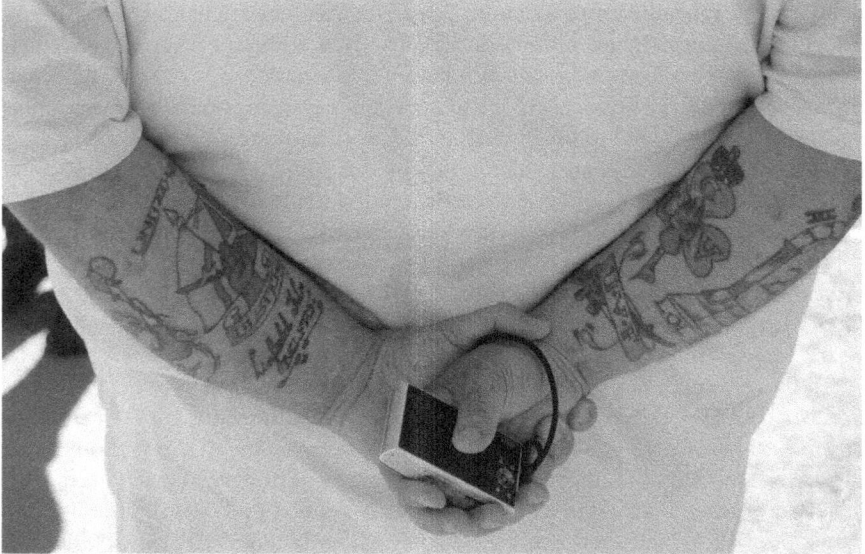

1.1 Loyalist tattoos 1
Showing: Ulster and Saltire flags conjoined by a Red Hand; 'Linfield FC Belfast' (the city's
'Protestant club'); YCV emblem (Young Citizen Volunteers – youth wing of the UVF);
UVF initials with assault rifle; Orange arch with the Order's mystical number of 2½ and
LOL (lodge number not shown).

Just outside the immediate confines of the Order, the loyalist band scene was
known to attract men with even stronger paramilitary sympathies, a fact I discovered
for myself early on in my fieldwork. Having attended a Grand Lodge evening event,
I was offered a lift home in a minibus being shared by an Orange lodge and
members of two loyalist flute bands, all of whom had been invited guests at the
same event. Before I got on the bus, some of the bandsmen, mostly in their early
twenties and all clearly drunk, crowded around me. 'Do you drink? Do you smoke?'
one asked. 'A bit?' scoffed another in response to my reply. 'What good is that?'
he said, shaking his head. 'Well the party starts on the bus, and we'll have you
smoking by the end of the night!' shouted another, provoking raucous cheering
from the group. As several of the bandsmen began boarding the bus, one of the
company stood in front of me, pointing to a deep and relatively fresh-looking gash
which ran across his cheek. 'Oh!' I said, in a show of pain, 'What happened?' 'Don't
worry about that – that's nothing' he said perhaps rather too matter-of-factly, 'that's
just the life we lead'.
    As the bus pulled away from the hotel, cans of beer were opened and a bottle
of port began to circulate. The port was quickly drained and replaced (rather
incongruously) by a bottle of peach schnapps, which also did the rounds. With
the exception of myself and the driver, and, to a lesser extent the band sergeant,

1.2 Loyalist tattoos 2
Showing: King Billy on his horse; Ulster flag within map of Ulster; 12th July;
UVF; RFC; Maze (paramilitary prison); Orange star with Red Hand;
PAF (Protestant Action Force); UVF crest.

who had clearly been designated my chaperone, everyone on board was extremely intoxicated. As the bus made its way along the motorway, the stereo blared loyalist tunes, with 'Fuck the Pope and the IRA!' being a favourite refrain, trumped only in popularity by 'Stand up if you hate Celtic!', the chanting of which caused most of the bandsmen to rise out of their seats to hammer on the roof of the bus in time with the music.

While the band sergeant was still cogent, it was clear he too had had a lot to drink. In between swigs of schnapps, he began to explain to me how, contrary to popular stereotypes, Orange culture outside of Glasgow was more militant than in Glasgow itself because those who entered the Glasgow loyalist scene often did so by default, not out of true conviction. He also explained that the loyalist band scene across Scotland had active connections with the UVF and UDA, and conducted fundraising on their behalf. At points, the sectarian bravado on the bus seemed to descend into humourless fantasy, with one man claiming to have personally met with senior loyalist paramilitary leaders in Northern Ireland to suggest that, as a better alternative to single random killings of Catholics, napalm be dropped from planes onto Catholic neighbourhoods. At other points, however, the group's Ulster-inspired sectarianism was more subtle, with one bandsman giving a quiet and strikingly emotional rendition of 'Daddy's Uniform' – a well-known loyalist song about a father imploring his son to take up arms and join the UVF – which stunned the other bandsmen into admiring silence.

What such ethnography provides is an account of the kinds of lived experiences which, taken as a whole, come together to allow some Orangemen and bandsmen to transform themselves into fellow protagonists of Ulster's 'Troubles' which, regardless of the signing of the Good Friday Agreement in 1998, many of my informants refused to consign to the past. As with Orange celebrations of the Boyne, then, so too do we find in Scots-Orange engagement with Ulster's Troubles a dwelling within history in a way that draws the past into the present. In this sense, the (past and present) ethno-nationalist conflict in Northern Ireland was replayed, more or less in proxy, by these Scots-Orangemen and bandsmen who chose to make sense of their Protestant identity primarily as a mode of engagement with fellow loyalists across the Irish Sea, whom they proudly described as their 'kith and kin'. Here, feelings of sharing a common history (and often a common conflict) was that which substantiated feelings of common ethno-religious ancestry, or 'blood'.

Yet, whether or not these local artefacts and performances of imagined kinship described in the ethnography above may be primarily explained with reference to the declining social and economic fortunes of working-class Protestant unionists in Glencruix is not central to my argument here. As such, rather than speculating on the role of macro-demographic changes in fostering Scots-Orange affective ties with Ulster loyalism and paramilitarism, I instead want to focus on the impact of such ties. Put another way, I want to focus not on demographic causes, but on moral effects. This focus, moreover, seems a particularly important element of what Laidlaw describes as 'the ethnographic stance' (2014: 45), for it is by attending to the immanent consequences of the moral imaginations described above that anthropology may not only learn about but learn *from* Orange models of 'The Good'.

From this perspective, certain Orangemen yearn to bring the paramilitary past into the present not primarily because they are members of a disaffected white working class, but because the violence of loyalist paramilitarism is 'good' insofar as it seeks to uphold the exceptional historical, constitutional, and spiritual qualities of the British Protestant people at all costs. Conversely, by turning away from the imaginative force of such claims, and towards (counter) claims about demographic causality, what the social scientist offers is essentially deprivation theory, with all of its reductionist impulses. The result here is not explanation, but an *explaining away*, a dissolving of 'moral world building' (Hickman and Webster In Press) into a (no less invented) claim about the socio-economic status and materialist motivation for religious beliefs and ethical commitments. In contrast to this singularising deprivation narrative, the effects of this moral world-building were not only diverse, but divisive.

A house divided: 'rough' grass-roots and 'respectable' hierarchies

Though alcohol and hyper-masculine bravado clearly played an important role in some performances of paramilitary affinity, in more sober moments too, the spectre of paramilitarism was never far from the loyalist band scene, or from the sentiments of many of my grass-roots Orange informants. Yet it would be wrong to suggest that support for loyalist paramilitarism formed an uncontested narrative within Scots-Orangeism. Indeed, some of my Orange informants worked hard to distance themselves and their organisation from the militancy of the loyalist band scene, and from the drunken disturbances that were routinely the focus of post-parade newspaper reports. The result was a strongly felt divide between those members of the Institution who knew the Order in Scotland had a reputation for sectarian thuggery and viewed this as a problematic stereotype which needed to be addressed, and those members who knew the Order had a reputation for sectarian thuggery and viewed this as a reality to be embraced.

As already described in the Introduction, those in the former category were mostly confined to the Grand Lodge hierarchy, while those in the latter category were more often 'ordinary' members found within the Order's 'rank and file'. However, given that the Order in Scotland was almost entirely urban and working class across *all* its levels, this rough/respectable divide cannot easily be explained as a by-product of differences in members' socio-economic status, as it generally is in Ulster, where stereotypes of upstanding Orange middle-class farmers from North Antrim are frequently contrasted with equally stereotypical images of militant Orangemen from deprived loyalist estates in Belfast. Instead, the divide, as I observed it during my fieldwork, appeared to be ideological as opposed to economic in nature. For those attracted to serve within the upper echelons of the Order's hierarchy, being an Orangeman came to focus upon celebrating Scotland's Protestant heritage, while defending 'civil and religious liberty' for all. As such, while my informants in Grand Lodge were often sharply critical of Roman Catholicism as a 'system', they were at pains to point out that they bore no ill will to Roman Catholics as individuals.

Maintaining this officially anti-sectarian line presented clear challenges to those within Grand Lodge, who knew only too well that their position of non-aggression towards Catholics was not always embraced by their own 'rank-and-file' members, let alone by those within the loyalist band scene, or by the large crowds of 'loyal Protestant friends' who regularly turned out to spectate at parades. Because parades were the main occasion where the non-Orange public encountered the Order, the majority of Grand Lodge's efforts to improve the image of the Institution were focused here. The use of an 'approved bands list' was one method deployed by Grand Lodge to this effect. In reality, it functioned more as a blacklist, with those bands that lost their 'approved' status being banned from parading with any lodge. While such bands were still free to parade with other Loyal Orders, (notably the Apprentice Boys of Derry, who had no such approved list), being banned from parading with the Order represented a major blow to the economic viability of a band, since many depended on Orange lodges being willing to hire them to cover their costs. In practice, there were only two reasons for a band to be removed from the list, either for displaying paramilitary symbolism on uniforms and flags, or for engaging in disorderly conduct, normally public drunkenness and/or street brawling. As such, all bands parading with the Order were required to sign a lengthy contract proscribing various behaviours 'of a manner likely to bring discredit to the Orange Order, while on parade', and to submit photos of all band regalia, a requirement designed to allow Grand Lodge officials to check that approved bands were not displaying paramilitary symbolism.

The training and deployment of marshals to manage the movement of lodges and bands as they paraded through the streets was another method devised by Grand Lodge to try and better control marches, with marshals used not only as a way to meet government recommendations related to safe crowd control as set out in the Orr Report (2005), but also as a further method of PR-driven self-surveillance. Marshals were thus expected to monitor the attire and conduct of bands, and, where contracts were being infringed, to inform Grand Lodge. Perhaps more obviously, as their title suggests, marshals were tasked with facilitating the orderly progression of a parade by keeping lodges and bands in their correct formations, while also assisting members of the public to cross the parade route at appropriate points and times. Taken as a whole, the aim of the marshals programme was to improve relations with local government officials and the police, who were jointly faced with the challenge of managing Orange parades. In addition, Grand Lodge hoped that better-marshalled parades would improve relations with local business owners who resented any disruption to usual trading conditions, as well as with members of the public, many of whom viewed Orange parades as a public nuisance at best, and a sectarian anachronism at worst.

With all lodges on parade required to provide enough marshals to cover a minimum quota (one marshal for every ten marchers), fulfilling this became an unwelcome burden for many rank-and-file Orangemen who found themselves unwillingly pressed into the role. Attending a Grand Lodge training committee meeting early on in my fieldwork revealed that the Order's top hierarchy were well aware of the problem. 'The pressure is on to get as many people through the marshals training. They might not *want* it, but they *need* it' said one Grand Lodge official earnestly. Another agreed, adding that ordinary members saw the training as little more than a formal box-ticking exercise: 'As soon as they go out that door, it's a shrug of the shoulders, unfortunately'. What these comments do not make clear, however, is the fact that some Orangemen also resented the largely implicit requirement that marshals monitor the behaviour and symbolic displays of bands, especially where those Orangemen felt a closer affinity to the local band than they did with Grand Lodge, a common occurrence given that many Orangemen are also bandsmen.

One solution discussed at the committee meeting was to admit bandsmen onto the Order's marshal training programme in an attempt to bring their behaviour into greater alignment with Grand Lodge standards. Tellingly, however, this idea was rejected on the basis that any such official sanctioning of bands might backfire, bringing the Order into further disrepute: 'The last thing we need is for something to kick off at a flute band parade, and then half a dozen [bandsmen] start waving Orange marshal certificates at the police for some incident that's happened at a flute band parade that's got nothing to do with our Institution whatsoever!' To be clear, the kind of 'kick off' in question, normally an alcohol-fuelled physical altercation, was not a figment of Grand Lodge's imagination, nor was it confined to independent band parades. At the very end of the Order's East of Scotland Boyne Parade in Edinburgh in 2013, for example, a number of police officers suddenly ran past me, making their way towards a line of private hire coaches where dozens of bandsmen were congregating. The incident was little more than a scuffle between two bands with a history of rivalry but had clearly spoiled the day for some in Grand Lodge. 'Bands! Who needs them?' was the clearly frustrated response from one leading Grand Lodge marshal when I asked him about the event the following day.

Of course, that the Order does indeed need loyalist flute bands to provide the music and pageantry of Orange parades is beyond dispute, hence the frustration of my informant above – a frustration surely made worse by Grand Lodge's inability to curb both the trenchant loyalism and the penchant for street violence that some 'Kick the Pope' bands continued to display. Yet, while Grand Lodge did appear preoccupied by the challenge of reining in what they regarded as the problematic behaviour of these bands, this task did not seem to preclude them from also seeking to change the behaviour of their own members, albeit in more subtle ways. Indeed, while Grand Lodge viewed many bandsmen as overly militant in their expressions of loyalism, when it came to members of their own institution, Grand Lodge tended to view many in the rank and file as insufficiently pious in their expressions of Protestantism. As with band militancy, assumptions about this deficit of Orange piety seemed to have been formulated by Grand Lodge in reaction to popular critiques of the same. Such popular critiques, found in the media and public debate, drew heavily on anti-Orange stereotypes, namely that while Orangemen claimed to be Protestant, they knew little about Reformed theology, seldom went to church, and chose instead to spend their time parading and drinking.

That certain figures within Grand Lodge accepted aspects of this stereotype as true is difficult to deny. During a Grand Lodge annual divine service, for example, Grand Chaplain Bro. Alex Forsyth stood to preach on the theme of 'Scotland's Protestant vision'. As the sermon reached its final climax, Forsyth loudly declared that:

> Within our ranks there is a terrible famine – there is a famine of hearing the Word of God! We must become again a distinct and determined people of God in our life of righteousness and holiness. An Orange people! A Protestant people who will pray, cry, and plead for Scotland's Protestant vision! We are the people of the Protestant Christian vision, and we ask for it to return! Oh that Almighty God would rend the Heavens and come down, granting us a second chance to be His people.

Despite the irony that these words were spoken to a congregation of Orangemen who had just spent the last hour singing hymns and listening to the Bible being read from and preached, Forsyth's sentiments nonetheless echoed those of other leading Orangemen who often bemoaned the lack of spiritual interest shown by their grass-roots membership. Lower than desired attendance at annual divine services was not the only complaint, with several of my informants in the Orange hierarchy also complaining to me that few Orangemen took part in open-air worship services or stood to listen to Orange platform speeches on parade days. The appeal of returning to their District to drink in their Orange social club, was, I was told with regret, simply too great for many. It was for these reasons, then, that Forsyth's claim about 'a terrible famine' within 'our ranks' resonated powerfully with the assembled hierarchy. Perhaps unsurprisingly, given its far stronger association with evangelicalism, it was Northern Ireland's Royal Black Institution (and not Scotland's Orange Order) that was seen by Grand Lodge as offering the most credible solution.

In essence, this 'solution' was a religious education campaign, called 'Take Five!', which focused on the doctrinal content of the 'Five Solas', used to summarise the theology of the early Protestant Reformers.[1] Launched in advance of 2017 within the context of the five-hundredth anniversary of the posting of Luther's ninety-five theses, the campaign sought to position the Royal Black Institution and the Orange Order as the contemporary guardians of historic Protestantism. Yet, in addition to this attempt at an institutional revivification of Protestantism was a message that was designed to be pointedly personal. This intent can clearly be seen within the 'Take Five!' campaign booklet – titled *A New Look at Old Truths*. Here, towards the end of the booklet, printed over a drawing of Luther at Wittenburg, hammer in hand, was the following summary and question: 'This is what the Bible says. This is what Reformed Protestants believe. DO YOU?' (Imperial Grand Black Chapter 2013: n.p.). Taken as a rhetorical question, the challenge it posed was unambiguous, namely that if the reader was a Sir Knight – that is, a member of the Royal Black Institution (RBI) – or an Orangeman who did not affirm these 'five basics of the Protestant faith', then something was badly amiss. Of course, those in Scotland's Grand Black Chapter and Grand Orange Lodge who advocated for the campaign hoped that it would serve as a way to reveal to their rank-and-file membership this individual piety problem, 'so that those whose Protestantism has been merely nominal in its nature may return to the faith of their fathers' (ibid.). Indeed, just as some hoped that training bandsmen in certain 'correct' modes of parading decorum would rein in their disorderly conduct, so too was it hoped that the 'Take Five!' campaign could be used to educate Scotland's Sir Knights and Orangemen away from a view of Protestantism defined by fraternal drinking and football rivalries, and towards an emphasis on scripture, grace, and faith in Christ.

Despite the implicit condemnation of Catholic theology contained within the campaign, it appeared to provoke little interest among Scotland's grass-roots Sir Knights and Orangemen. At the Royal Black Institution's annual parade in 2013 in Renfrew, the 'Take Five!' campaign was promoted heavily, with leaflets being widely distributed and large standing banners used as the backdrop for platform speeches by the hierarchy, the first of which was essentially a sermon outlining the merits of the campaign. Yet, as I had also repeatedly observed at Orange parades, here too the numbers of Sir Knights standing to listen to the speeches were far outweighed by the hundreds of marchers who took no interest in these more formal religious proceedings. What's more, at the end of the event, the ground was strewn with 'Take Five!' leaflets that had been distributed and then promptly dropped by their recipients. Among my Orange informants from Glencruix, the explanation for this lack of interest in the campaign was clear, namely that the

Royal Black Institution was trying too hard to be spiritual, and, in the process, succeeded only in making ordinary Orangemen feel looked down upon. In addition to the usual complaints from Orangemen that Sir Knights wrongly thought of themselves as an 'elite' (see Buckley 1985: 8), the 'Take Five!' campaign provoked within some of my closest Orange informants further indignation at being accused of having a 'merely nominal' Protestantism. When a prominent Sir Knight was invited to speak at an anniversary service in Glencruix, Dennis said that his speech was 'typical of the man's holier-than-thou stance', adding angrily that 'he had no business telling Orangemen how to live their faith'. As Dennis spoke, he grew more irate; 'At the end of the day, the individual knows what his faith is!' 'And that's the truth!' Colin piped up in heated agreement. 'And that's the *whole* truth!' bellowed Dennis in response.

Other examples of this gulf between the preferences and priorities of the hierarchy and those of the grass roots are equally insightful. In 2006, a BBC television documentary *21st Century Orange Man* followed Scotland's then Grand Master George Martin as he attempted to modernise and liberalise aspects of the Order's practice. Revealingly, a proposal to allow Scots-Orangemen to attend Roman Catholic Mass without fear of expulsion, designed so that members with religiously mixed extended families could attend their funerals, did not receive support from a majority of the rank and file. In a recorded mock-up of a Private Lodge meeting at which George Martin was present, after an Orangemen was shown describing the Catholic Mass as a form of cannibalism, the documentary shows another ordinary member of the lodge standing to ask Martin the rather pointed question: 'Why should we change to suit the politically correct brigade?' The question, and Martin's reply – that 'it has to concern any organisation how it's viewed in the public sphere' – neatly encapsulates the divide I have been describing. The point is that while the hierarchy of Scotland's Order is indeed deeply concerned about how the Institution is viewed by the non-Orange public, the Order's grass-roots members, by and large, are not.

Indeed, as the ethnography presented in the following chapters demonstrates, the majority of my Orange informants outside Grand Lodge viewed the hierarchy as too concerned with courting public approval, an approval which they often told me was both unobtainable and undesirable. Be it in the 'blood and thunder' culture of flute band parades, the alcohol-fuelled fraternalism of the social club scene, the sectarian chanting associated with the Old Firm, or the deliberate rejection of moderate unionism in favour of a more hard-line campaign against Scottish independence, what I repeatedly encountered during five years of fieldwork among Orangemen across Scotland's Central Belt was an institution divided. Importantly, while these divides produced multiple fault lines running across the religiosity, politics, and social life of the Order, they also converged, in spite of their multiplicity, to produce two broadly distinct groups, the 'rough' grass roots and the 'respectable' hierarchy. While these two groups existed within the same institution and often had much in common, they also often viewed each other with suspicion and a measure of resentment, as, variously, an irreligious loyalist rabble needing to be reined in, or a sanctimonious and politically weak elite to be tolerated when necessary but largely ignored where possible.

Conclusions: liberal critiques and illiberal prejudices

Perhaps unsurprisingly, public, political, and journalistic debates about the Orange Order in Scotland largely ignore (or are ignorant of) these internal cleavages. Indeed, in the minds of many Central Belt Scots, the Order is as simple as it is sectarian, a bigoted anachronism marked by little more than a universal loathing of Roman Catholics and Roman Catholicism. More than this, in the imagination of these same Scots, membership of 'the Orange' is assumed to extend well beyond those marching in collarettes and includes both bandsmen and spectators. This understandable, if inaccurate, conflation of Orangemen, bandsmen, and spectators presents the Order with a further challenge, namely their being implicitly associated with (and often explicitly blamed for) the bad behaviour of a small minority of Orange sympathisers who are not themselves Orange members.

I observed several such instances during my own fieldwork, with each one serving as a reminder of the sheer diversity of people who associate themselves with the Order, and of the lazy tendency to ignore this diversity by focusing only on the apparently anti-social. Two such examples stand out in my mind, both of which occurred in a mixed crowd of Orangemen and Orange spectators during large parades. The first instance took place late on in my fieldwork, as I stood talking with a young Orange Grand Chaplain who was asking about my research while earnestly detailing to me the evangelical commitments and general spiritual ethos of the Order in Scotland. Dressed in a dark suit and clerical collar with Bible in hand, the chaplain appeared to be the very embodiment of the pious Orange community he was describing. In seeming contrast, less than ten feet away were two very skinny topless men, their shoulders draped in loyalist flags, who stood smoking joints and swigging from bottles of Buckfast as they watched the bands march past. With the unmistakable sour scent of cannabis wafting over us, the chaplain continued to detail how biblical Protestantism existed as the very foundation of the Order, ignoring these two loyalist spectators with a determination that betrayed the awkwardness and incongruity of the moment.

A second instance occurred just a week later, at the height of the July marching season, during the speeches at the Central Scotland Annual Boyne Celebration. As one of the Orange dignitaries stood to issue formal words of welcome from the platform, a spectator in the centre of the gathering, swaying slightly under the influence of alcohol, suddenly bellowed out 'Fuck the Pope!' at the top of his voice. The reaction from the crowd was critical if muted: 'Now *come on*' came the frustrated rebuke from one Orangeman, while others in the crowd simply murmured disapprovingly. The reaction from the platform was marked by its absence, in the form of stony silence and resolutely expressionless faces. With the sectarian sloganeer duly ignored, the ritual of welcome continued as if nothing had happened. Yet not all incidents of disorder could be contained by simply ignoring them, a reality the Order faced on a semi-regular basis when the misbehaviour of Orange spectators got badly out of hand.

During the Order's campaign against Scottish independence, for example, an altercation in 2014 between two unidentified groups on Glasgow Green led to a girl being struck in the face by a stray glass bottle. Images of the twelve-year-old, her face covered in blood, were widely circulated in the media, provoking renewed calls for Orange marches to be banned in Scotland, and intensifying the already marked criticism levelled by the mainstream 'Better Together' campaign against the Orange Order (see also Chapter 5). Two days after the incident, a representative from Grand Lodge appeared on a BBC Radio Scotland programme to make clear they did not support anti-social behaviour, stating that the Order was a 'democratic, law-abiding organisation' exercising its right to 'celebrate and promote our Protestant culture'.

More recently, when a group of young men spectating at an Orange parade in Glasgow in July 2018 attacked a Catholic priest (spitting on him, and calling him a 'fenian bastard' and a 'paedo') as he stood at the door of St Alphonsus Church bidding his parishioners farewell after Mass, the ensuing public outcry again led to calls for Orange marches to be banned. In this case, such efforts were more organised, with the circulation of an online petition demanding that Glasgow City Council 'stop this outdated and repressive display [by] call[ing] time on the Orange Order marching on our streets'. With the petition attracting more than 84,000 signatures, and with politicians from across the political spectrum condemning the attack, the Grand Orange Lodge of Scotland was forced to release a statement making clear that 'no members of the parade were involved' in the 'vile and disgusting' attack, adding 'we hope those involved are brought to justice'. Following a Police Scotland investigation, one of the attackers, Bradley Wallace (who was not an Orangeman, but who was associated with a Rangers supporters club in Bridgeton) was arrested, tried, and sentenced to ten months in prison for spitting on Canon White.

Of course, no matter how explicitly Grand Lodge condemned such attacks, the reputational damage could not be undone, with Wallace's actions, and those of other parade spectators engaged in disorder irrevocably associated in the minds of the public with the Orange Institution. Tabloid characterisations of Wallace as the 'Orange walk bigot', complete with a photo of the scowling accused superimposed upon a background of dozens of Orange banners, merely reinforced the association. So too did media reports of the sheriff's suggestion that Wallace had been emboldened by the assumption that he acted 'under the cover of this aggressive and threatening crowd', quoted in the context of estimations of the size of the march, with 4,000 Orangemen on parade, and an equal number of spectators. That the petition called for an end to Orange marches despite the fact that Wallace himself was not a member seemed to trouble few outside the ranks of the Order. Indeed, in the public con- sciousness, Wallace's behaviour formed an integral part of Orange culture, and, on that basis, while his actions were judged to be shamefully bigoted, they were also regarded as entirely in keeping with the real ethos of Scotland's Orange Institution, regardless of the protestations of Grand Lodge to the contrary.

The difficult question that emerges here is not so much *who* to believe, for neither Grand Lodge nor their media critics can be accused of serving up pure falsehoods. For Grand Lodge's part, it is undeniably true that outbreaks of violence and anti-social behaviour associated with Orange parades in Scotland are almost always perpetrated by a very small minority of spectators, not by members of the

Orange Order. From this perspective, it seems unreasonable to directly blame the Order for actions carried out by those they have no formal affiliation with, or control over. And, as the Order is quick to point out, the right of free assembly is protected by law.[2] Yet, seen from the perspective of the Order's critics in the media and elsewhere, it is also true that Orange parades consistently attract an anti-social element who, while spectating, engage in binge drinking, public displays of anti-Catholic bigotry, and in some cases actual violence. As such, it also seems unreasonable to absolve the Order of all responsibility for the behaviour of non-members, who, in other circumstances, the Order refers to as 'loyal Protestant friends'. If the Order is guilty of anything in relation to the behaviour of non-member spectators, then, it is for creating an atmosphere conducive to outbreaks of anti-Catholic bigotry, a situation surely not helped by the displaying of Orange banners with captions such as 'No Popery' which are paraded through the streets to the booming musical accompaniment of (accurately titled) 'blood and thunder' and 'Kick the Pope' bands.

If both sides of this debate are genuinely 'onto something', the difficult question, as above, is not so much *who* to believe, but rather *why* someone might come to believe one 'side' over the other. The answer, I suggest, has more to do with politics and aesthetics, and specifically with one's vision of 'The Good' and 'good taste', than it does with any a priori truth claim. The irony which repeatedly emerges in the chapters of this book is that, on this basis, that is, on the basis of political aesthetics, the Orange Order in Scotland has no monopoly over fostering the conditions necessary for bigotry and a condemnation of 'the other' to thrive. This is a similar irony to that which I have written about elsewhere, in my analysis of strong types of pluralism which, I argue, stand as a (deeply oxymoronic) rejection of everything which rejects anything (Webster 2018). Often then, the Orange Order in Scotland finds itself to be the subject of critique because it is deemed by those critics to be insufficiently pluralist. Indeed, petitions calling for Orange marches to be banned are made on the basis that such displays are 'outdated and repressive', and, as such, are guilty of 'spreading bigotry and division'. Orangemen are well aware that this is what they stand accused of, and while some embrace this moniker (see Chapter 4), others choose to resist it, especially at the level of Grand Lodge. A poem titled 'A Word to Our Critics', written by an Orangeman and published in *The Orange Torch* in September 2014, neatly captures this latter spirit of resistance:

> You do not even know my name
> But call me a 'knuckle dragger',
> 'Drunken bigot', 'Neanderthal',
> A '17th century bragger'.
>
> Now that you have had your turn,
> I'll knock the wind right out your sail.
> So come with me on a journey
> And I'll tell you quite a tale!
> Did you know we believe in freedom,
> For all to have their say? [...]

You slag us off and call us names,
And halfway you won't meet us. [...]
We trust the Lord, honour the Queen,
Believe in civil and religious liberty,
So why is it, when we think this way
You won't show us the same courtesy?

The poet's question, it seems, is a plea for acceptance, a desire to be recognised as tolerant and respectable by their eminently respectable critics, who, as members of mainstream civic society, appear to permanently occupy the moral high ground over the Order's (rather un-pluralist) exclusively Protestant membership. But what if the direction of travel were shown to move in the opposite direction? Could it be the case that, while the Order is indeed guilty of encouraging a certain anti-pluralist bigotry, so too are its enemies? If true, this would see not the Order joining the ranks of the tolerant and respectable, but the (ostensibly) tolerant and respectable joining the ranks of the intolerant and bigoted. Far from being implausible, such a reversal would perfectly explain why those whom Orangemen frequently refer to as 'the chattering classes' choose to display their liberal credentials by expressing deeply prejudiced opinions about the Orange Order. Camilla Long, for example, covering the Order's flagship anti-independence rally in Edinburgh for the *Sunday Times* described the event thus:

> On a small square of emerald behind Edinburgh Castle a furious Hobbit army gathers. Nearly 15,000 Orangemen and women – none more than 5ft 6in – pour into the park, clutching fancy caps, braids, straps, pompoms, feathers, actual flutes of war and swag upon swag of militant polyester. Even the mobility scooters seem ready for battle, pimped with 'naw' slogans and fluttering Union flags. The vast meeting, including members of Orange lodges from all over Scotland [is] a boiling river of rampant Protestant 'nos'[;] a deafening, unbridled, wildly tasselly rally. The Orange march is the nearest I have ever been to a military assault featuring toy soldiers and children dressed as William and Mary. It is hysterical, occultish and oddly prancing. When it comes to political loons, Scotland is clearly up there. (*Sunday Times*, 14 September 2014)

Using fewer words, but deploying similarly prejudiced sentiments, Ruth Dudley Edwards, in her generally sympathetic account of the Order in Northern Ireland, seems to reserve special revulsion for a group of working-class Scots attending the Order's 12 July celebrations in Belfast, describing them as 'a contingent of five or six nasty-looking young men with tattoos, militaristic haircuts and rasping Glaswegian accents ... carrying cartons of beer' (Dudley Edwards 1999: 14). That Long and Dudley Edwards are able to publish such comments without imperilling their (generally implicit) claim to being moderate voices of liberal tolerance – that is, without imperilling their membership of the 'chattering classes', as my Orange informants would have it – is surely part of the reason for the feeling of injustice expressed by the poet in *The Orange Torch*. Indeed, 'You slag us off and call us names / And halfway you won't meet us'.

My point is not to affirm such feelings of injustice, or even to critique the prejudices being expressed by Dudley Edwards and Long, but rather to simply point out that there is a gulf here – a gulf, crucially, that is not only political, but also aesthetic in nature. The former point, of course, is readily admitted to by most ethnographers who spend time getting close to what Esseveld and Eyerman call '"distasteful" social movements' (1992: 217), which, in the first instance, they define as 'social movements which thwart or work against "progressive" social change' (ibid.: 218). That the Orange Order works against 'progressive social change' as defined by the majority of modern Scots is difficult to deny. Indeed, to this day, the Order remains dedicated to professing 'hostility to the distinctive despotism of the Church of Rome', and to expelling its own members who attend a Catholic Mass, including the funeral Mass of a family member. Here, the gulf between the Order and its critics is primarily political and ethical, caused by a disagreement over whether a good life requires showing hostility or welcoming acceptance towards Catholicism.

Yet, possibly by simple virtue of the fact that such a political and ethical disagreement exists, those who feel themselves to be on the progressive side of the debate may also feel themselves to have some licence to express antipathy of a different kind, especially when directed against those whom they regard to be regressive. Here, the charge levelled at the Order does not concern their being *politically* distasteful, but aesthetically, of offending 'good taste' as opposed to good morals. As such, members of the Orange Order come to be criticised not only for their illiberal views on Roman Catholicism, but also for being 'nasty looking' and Hobbit-like, for having 'rasping Glaswegian accents', for wearing pompoms and polyester, for having tattoos and 'militaristic haircuts', and for being 'occultish and oddly prancing'. What are we to make of this? Regardless of whether or not it is justifiable for political and moral critiques of Orangeism to slide inexorably into condescending aesthetic revulsion (my instinct is that it is not), the question remains, how might anthropology bridge this gulf? Put another way, in the context of studying a 'distasteful' social group who are themselves subject to distasteful (that is, prejudiced and illiberal) forms of critique, how might anthropology seek to make sense of the 'moods and motivations' of that social group, rather than simply condemning or lampooning them?

While Esseveld and Eyerman are surely correct here in emphasising the 'need to overcome distance, to create sufficient closeness in order to attempt to understand its members' thoughts and actions' (1992: 232), my own commitment to *verstehen* as methodological empathy-building pushes this further. Indeed, rather than warning against 'the trap of trying too hard to make actions and actors understandable' (ibid.: 233) for fear of giving distasteful groups 'intellectual as well as political legitimacy' (ibid.), my concern is primarily with the consequences of not trying hard enough in this regard – a trap that Long and Dudley Edwards, when read from an anthropological perspective, seem to fall into. This is a concern that Omelchenko and Pilkington seem to share, as articulated in the closing comments of their documentary film *Loud and Proud: Listening to the English Defence League*:

> Our aim in conducting this research has been neither to support, nor to condemn the views expressed by the EDL [English Defence League]. It has been rather to listen to voices of individual members within the movement and to seek to understand rather than to judge the meanings they attach to their own activism.

For some, this very act of listening will still feel like a legitimation of these views. […] So what is the role of the academic here? I think it is not to use the knowledge gained either to support or condemn any particular political position but to encourage society to engage in critical reflection. To do that we must first be self-critical and challenge our own positionalities, something which ethnography forces us to do on a daily basis. Does this somehow evade the responsibility of the researcher to take up a stance in relation to his or her research subject? I would argue, on the contrary, that this critical reflection itself constitutes such a stance because the people we are addressing is not the EDL per se but a political system that fails to engage in a listening practice and whose only response to unwelcome voices is, to quote, 'to smash the fash'. The stance taken here therefore is one of resistance to the replacement of explanation by condemnation. (Omelchenko and Pilkington 2015: n.p.)

In my own analysis of the Orange Order – a group which, like the English Defence League, is readily identified as 'distasteful' by its critics – I too seek to resist replacing explanation with condemnation. Yet, in doing so, my aim in the chapters which follow is not to impart external intellectual and political legitimacy to Scottish Orangeism, but instead to show how and why, internally, its own members believe it *already* had such legitimacy well before it drew the attention of a curious anthropologist. Clearly however, what I offer is not an unmediated ethnographic 'view from the inside', but a descriptive analysis drawn from five years of listening to and watching Orangemen live their lives as members of the Order. As all acts of listening and watching are mediated (at the very least) by the person undertaking these tasks, it seems necessary to ask what was it, more precisely, that I was listening to and watching? It is here that my approach differs somewhat from Pilkington's, since, in her written ethnographic account of the EDL, she states 'that the object of analysis was the individual, not the organisation or the ideology of the movement' (2016: 10). For my part, I take all three of these facets as the subjects of my analysis, namely, individuals who are members of the Orange Order in Scotland, which, as an institution, is driven by an ideology which fuses ethno-nationalist Protestantism with ethno-religious unionism (and vice versa). I do so, in the next chapter, by considering how my Scots-Orange informants sought to live good Protestant lives by recovering the glories of their religious history while at the same time exposing those Catholic forces which, they believe, seek to destroy everything the Order holds to be sacred.

Notes

1 *Sola scriptura* (by scripture alone); *sola gratia* (by grace alone); *sola fide* (by faith alone); *solus Christus* (through Christ alone); *soli Deo gloria* (for the glory of God alone). Of course, each 'sola' can also be seen as a contradistinction to Catholic teaching via a rejection of, variously, Catholic Church tradition, indulgences, rituals of merit, the mediatory role of priests, and veneration of the Virgin Mary.
2 However, in the context of the attack on Canon White, as well as other incidences of loyalist/republican disorder in Govan in September 2019, Glasgow City Council and the SNP Government considered banning loyalist and republican marches, before concluding that there was 'no legal basis' for such a ban.

2

The menace of Rome

I stepped into Olympia House from the pouring rain, completely soaked, but excited about the morning ahead. It was here, in the centre of Bridgeton, within the headquarters of the Grand Orange Lodge of Scotland, that the Orange archive was housed. The archive itself was a tiny room overflowing with crumbling minute books, several filing cabinets, a small library, a pile of rolled-up banners, and several glass-fronted cabinets filled with various artefacts and framed pictures. Most of the floor space was taken up by two tables pushed together, making the room feel like a workspace, as well as a place to browse, as if one was visiting a small gallery, or local museum. By that point in my fieldwork – late January 2013 – I had been visiting the archive for several months and had come to know the three volunteer archivists fairly well.

Jonathan, who was in his late seventies or early eighties, was a retired office manager, past Grand Secretary, Church of Scotland elder, and accomplished amateur historian. As well as having self-published several books on Scots-Orange history, Jonathan was also a leading figure within the Scottish Covenanter Memorials Association. Unlike many of my Scots-Orange informants, as an ardent traditionalist, Jonathan had never turned his back on the Scottish Conservatives, remaining a faithful (if beleaguered) Tory, even after Margaret Thatcher signed the Anglo-Irish Agreement in 1985, and throughout their electoral struggles during the early devolution years (see Smith 2011). Jonathan's moderate politics and generally restrained personality contrasted strongly with Derek, a powerfully built and outspoken retired coal miner in his early seventies. As well as being vocal about his socialist leanings, Derek also enjoyed talking about his passion for the Scottish loyalist band scene, within which he and his sons were well known. Derek was also a convinced British Israelite, as well as being open about his sympathies for (and past connections with) Protestant paramilitaries in Northern Ireland. Also in his early seventies, Andrew, the third archivist, was a retired tradesman, ex-weightlifter, opera fan, and wine buff. Perhaps most controversially, Andrew was also a committed supporter of the SNP and their campaign for Scottish independence. As different as these three men were, what drew them together was their shared passion for Orangeism, and particularly Scots-Orange history.

As the months passed and the Orange archive grew in importance as an ethnographic field site, much of my time at Olympia House was spent discussing

Orange history with these three men, as well as with frequent visitors to the archive, generally Orangemen, and some Orangewomen, who came to research the history of their Private Lodge. On that particular Thursday morning, Derek was attending a funeral, and Andrew was in the boardroom next door conducting an oral history interview, meaning that Jonathan and I were alone in the archive. At one point, Jonathan stepped out to discuss something with one of the other members of the Grand Lodge hierarchy. To fill the time in Jonathan's absence, I browsed the archive's small library of books which stood on open shelves. As I scanned the titles, one in particular caught my eye – an old coffee-table book called *This is Rome*, which was full of large colour photographs of Italian rural life, famous Catholic churches, and other prominent landmarks. The book itself seemed relatively uninteresting, and I was puzzled by its inclusion within the archive, especially given how it sat alongside books on the Reformation, Orange history, and the British monarchy. Just before I put it back on the shelf, however, I noticed something I had missed initially, a handwritten inscription on the inside front cover, which read:

> This book may be 30 years out of print – but the menace of Rome is still the same! She has not changed! She cannot change! For were she to relent or change one iota, she would cease to be Rome. The price of freedom is eternal vigilance.
>
> *Grand Lodge Hierarchy*

The longer I spent with Jonathan, Derek, and Andrew in the archive, as we catalogued donations of Orange artefacts, combed through old lodge minute books, and sat together over coffee and lunch breaks, the more I came to realise that this inscription, and particularly its emphasis on 'menace' and 'vigilance', encapsulated a major theme within the social life of Orangeism. Equally, the theme of papal intransigence is also important to bear in mind, a theme neatly encapsulated in the pages of a short booklet written by senior Orangeman David Bryce entitled *The Irredeemable Papacy* which details 'the long established depravity of the Popes' (2018: 1) from 955 to the present day. That such themes of opposition between Protestantism and Catholicism emerged through ethnographic research on Orangeism is unsurprising. Indeed, as discussed in Chapter 3, a key initiation vow of the Order is to 'resist by all lawful means, the extension and encroachment of that Church', that is, 'the Church of Rome' (GOLS 1983: 26). What struck me as less expected, however, was how this menace came to be conceptualised so comprehensively among many of my Orange informants, and in such a 'joined up' manner. This chapter, then, attempts to make sense of this menace, and the vigilance it demanded. More specifically, it examines how Scots-Orangemen of all stripes (from grass-roots members to those in the hierarchy) came to experience Scottish history and contemporary society as framed by a multifarious menace driven by a single purpose.

As such, what this chapter analyses is the imagination of conspiracy, or Scots-Orange imaginations of the machinations of Rome within Scottish society (see also McFarland 1990: 90). Importantly, while it seems fair to refer to this type of conspiracism as an 'imagination' (insofar as I examine how these machinations are conceptualised, observed, narrated, connected, and believed), I deliberately want to avoid referring to them as 'conspiracy theories'. This is because to do so would carry with it such a weight of scepticism and implied mockery that the resultant analysis would be undermined (see Robertson 2016: 39). Instead, as outlined in the Introduction, my aim here is to pursue a kind of *verstehen* which places empathy at the centre of my method of interpretation – a method which involves, in this framing of 'the ethnographic stance' (Laidlaw 2014: 45), *feeling my way into* a world of Scots-Orangeism dominated by the menace and machinations of the Church of Rome. I will do so by describing my ethnographic encounters with Orangemen within the Grand Lodge archive and elsewhere. These descriptions, and the analysis which follows, will journey through Orange accounts of different Scottish institutions, from local and national politics, to the media, to the education system, to public memorialisations of history.

Importantly, it will be shown how, from the perspective of my Orange informants, these diverse institutions can be seen as acting in concert, directed towards a single aim, namely the undermining (and eventual destruction) of Scotland as part of a British Protestant constitutional monarchy. In this sense, while the manifestations of menace may be plural, the agentive force, Roman Catholicism, remains, within Scots-Orange imaginations, to be both singular and unchanging, or else 'she would cease to be Rome'. In order to better explain these machinations, that is, their multiple workings and singular design, I want to return to the Grand Orange Lodge archive.

Lunchtime in the Orange archive

During the early stages of my fieldwork, about four months prior to finding the handwritten inscription quoted above, I had already begun to recognise just how central Catholicism was to Orange cosmology. Indeed, although not expressed to me in precisely those terms, 'the menace of Rome' seemed to follow me wherever I went in search of ethnographic opportunities among Scottish Orangemen, and this was true no more so than within the Orange archive. As the busyness of a morning spent scrutinising, cataloguing, and reorganising various papers and artefacts came to an end, I would join Jonathan, Derek, and Andrew for a lunch break, which we would take in the tiny kitchenette down the hall from the archive. As the men drank coffee and ate sandwiches, the conversation would frequently turn to politics and current affairs, and it was here, almost without exception, that Catholics and Roman Catholicism took centre stage.

It was only my second trip to the archive, in October 2012, but the men already seemed notably more relaxed in my company. As I sipped instant coffee from a blue commemorative mug adorned with the totemic image of William on his horse, the group that afternoon, which included Andy Cooper, a prominent Glasgow Orangeman and co-founder of the Scottish Unionist Party (SUP), began to discuss Scotland's education system. Andy explained how, in the early days of the SUP, a key policy of the party had been to end government funding for Roman Catholic schools, and to replace them with non-denominational schools. As Andy talked, he became animated. It was outrageous, he argued, that Scottish taxpayers' money was funding Catholic schools which were permitted, regardless of this public subsidy, to only hire Catholic teachers. The policy, Andy said, was blatantly sectarian.

Andy continued by explaining that Fred Morrow, the leader of the SUP, had appeared before the Scottish Parliament Petitions Committee to demand an overturning of the ruling which permitted Catholic schools to discriminate in this way. As the petition hearing concluded, what Andy found most egregious was the betrayal shown by a Scottish Conservative Member of Scottish Parliament (MSP) on the matter who, far from supporting the petition as Andy had expected any Tory politician to do, stood to declare 'If Morrow's petition is upheld, this will mean the *end* of Roman Catholic schools in Scotland; it *must* be rejected on that basis!', which, needless to say, it was. Staring at each of us in turn, Andy stood open-mouthed and with astonishment on his face. As the men grumbled at the injustice, Andy ended the story by describing how a lawyer in the audience had approached Morrow to inform him that European law made the Scottish government's policy illegal, and that he would have a strong case to appeal to the European Court. When I asked Andy if the SUP had pursued the case, he admitted with frustration that because the party could not afford the legal costs, they were forced to let the matter drop.

The issue of public funding for Catholic schools clearly still vexed Andy, who described what he saw as underhand methods used by these schools to bolster both their funding and influence within the community. For example, Andy described how Catholic schools kept their roll artificially high by including all those attending evening classes within their total number of 'pupils'– 'Spanish, ballet, swimming, you name it!' A further consequence of this dishonesty, Andy claimed, was a consolidation of resources into these schools, which, over time, came to have far better buildings and facilities than non-denominational schools. To make matters worse, Andy explained, Catholic schools were also guilty of taking children from outside their areas by bussing them in from other districts, thereby further inflating their roll. 'If you look outside a Catholic school at the beginning and end of the day, there are always *loads* of buses outside – *that's why!*' he said, with a real sense of scandal.

Andy's story led Jonathan to share one of his own, about a Protestant mother who wanted to baptise her daughter as a Roman Catholic to enable her to attend a local Catholic primary school which was believed to have superior educational outcomes. The woman's husband came to Jonathan for advice, and Jonathan explained that while *officially* the Education Act stated that children did not need to be a baptised Catholic to attend a Catholic school, *in reality* places were allocated to Catholics first. Andy, who was nodding in agreement, chipped in 'there are two myths about Roman Catholic schools – that they have better educational achievement and better discipline'. Jonathan continued, explaining how, in the end, the mother had prevailed, with the decision taken to baptise their daughter as a Catholic. When invited to the baptism, Jonathan had refused, he said, because he could not celebrate the girl's entry into the Roman Catholic Church. Jonathan was keen to point out that he did not bear the child any ill will, but, as he had explained to her father at the time, he fundamentally disagreed with the Roman

Catholic 'system' and 'religion'. 'After all that', Jonathan scoffed, 'she went to a non-denominational school!'

As the lunch break continued, so did the discussion of Catholicism. Andy announced to the group that a new piece of research had shown that 37 per cent of Scotland's prison population was Roman Catholic, despite making up only 16 per cent of the general population. The Catholic Church had responded by claiming that Scotland's judicial system was anti-Catholic. The absurdity of the claim was revealed, according to Andy, by the fact that many prominent legal positions in Scotland were occupied by Catholics, including the Lord Advocate: 'they've got every powerful job going, and they say the judicial system is anti-Roman Catholic!' he remarked with anger and disbelief. According to Andy, Catholic infiltration of powerful British institutions went far beyond the judicial system. Reflecting on the situation as he saw it in 2012, Andy listed several other influential positions which were occupied by Catholics: 'The Director General of the BBC, the head of the Civil Service, the head of the Bank of England, the Secretary of State for Scotland!' came the list, 'and nobody points this out! The press have covered this up! They [Catholics] are the minority, and they wallow in victimhood!'

On a different occasion, Andy discussed various crime statistics he had written into a notebook to make the same point. Flicking through the pages like a police officer recounting an interview, Andy stated that while there had been over 4,000 reported race hate crimes, there had been only 693 sectarian hate crimes within the same period. 'It's nothing! It's nothing!' Andy concluded of the latter. Andy also rejected claims about the seriousness of the fact that Scotland's Catholics (who he said made up 15 per cent of the population) had experienced 58 per cent of sectarian crime. Instead, Andy inverted the injustice by offering some statistical analysis of his own, 'Protestants have experienced 40 per cent of the sectarian crime at the hands of 15 per cent of the population! So 15 per cent of the population are committing 40 per cent of the hate crimes!' he said triumphantly. From Andy's perspective, the reality was inescapable, Catholics were over-represented within Scotland's prison population because Catholics committed more crimes than Protestants, and this, despite the fact that, far from being anti-Catholic, Scotland's legal system was run by Catholics.

By this point, Andy was red in the face and his thick fists trembled slightly as he paced the tiny floor of the kitchenette. 'Glasgow hasn't had a Protestant Lord Provost since 1975! The press are aware of it, but aren't talking about it! Since 1975! Think if that was true of the Roman Catholics!' Such dominance, Andy said, was the result of Roman Catholic control over the Scottish media, backed by a highly developed system of lobbying and PR designed to manipulate public opinion. Giving the example of 'Catholic Voices', set up around the time of the Pope's visit to the UK in 2010, and working at that point under the tag-line 'Putting the Church's case in the public square', Andy detailed how this group would always make sure that a Catholic perspective was represented in the media. It was clear that Andy was both impressed and incensed by their level of organisation, lamenting the fact that Protestants in Scotland did not have the same public presence. '*Every* radio phone-in, they have someone putting across their views!' he bellowed.

Importantly, Andy's claims about Catholic control over the Scottish media went beyond public relations. Referring to recent media reports about child abuse by Catholic clergy, Andy recounted that while the case had been headline news on an 11 a.m. radio news bulletin, by 12 noon the story was no longer being reported. 'And they [the Catholic Church] do this *all* the time! They just *control* the media, burying the bad news. And we never, never, never get Protestant voices on the media; nobody from the Kirk from a Protestant perspective!'

Next, Andy returned to attacking the Scottish Conservative Party by recounting a conversation with a Tory politician who, despite being from a Protestant back-ground, supported state funding for Catholic schools, as well as a change to the Act of Settlement. This latter position was particularly dangerous from an Orange perspective, since it would allow any future monarch to marry a Catholic, thereby allowing 'Rome' to seize the British throne and reverse the victories of both the Battle of the Boyne, and the Reformation. Yet, what seemed to rankle with Andy the most was the explanation this politician gave as to why, *as a Protestant*, she had adopted these pro-Catholic positions. 'Because I'm a *Christian*', came the answer, mimicked by Andy in a mockingly haughty tone. Jonathan echoed Andy's exaspera-tion, bemoaning the fact that while Catholics were still confident enough to refer to themselves as Catholics, the term 'Protestant' was no longer acceptable in 'polite society' having become somehow 'politically incorrect'. 'And they wonder why they [the Scottish Conservatives] lost the vote of the Protestant working people!' Andy said with incredulity.

When I asked who most working-class Protestants in Scotland vote for today, Andy's reply was that the majority were politically apathetic, and had adopted what he called 'a curse on both your houses' attitude. While this apathy clearly frustrated Andy, he also seemed to understand it, commenting how during a local cross-party election debate for Orangemen, an SNP candidate publicly stated 'we will do nothing to upset the Roman Catholic Church because the Catholics are united, and you're no!' 'He said that, to a hall of Orangemen!' Andy exclaimed.

Importantly, the conversations described above were not the product of any idiosyncratic interest shared between Andy and Jonathan alone, but were central to many of the interactions – in gossip, storytelling, reminiscing, and debating – between Orangemen within Olympia House and elsewhere. Indeed, the following week in the archive, it was not Jonathan and Andy, but Derek and Andrew who spent much of their morning discussing Catholicism. Andrew began by stating that whenever he was asked by friends why he was a member of the Orange Order, he would reply 'Because I love the Lord Jesus Christ, and because I want to defend my civil liberties', an answer which, as will become clear below, echoes broader Orange claims that Catholicism is both anti-Christian and anti-democratic. An Orange visitor to the archive joined the conversation by telling us how Catholic pupils at the non-denominational school he went to attended Latin Mass every week, despite not understanding any of it, 'but they knew it all, and could repeat it, parrot-fashion!' he said with a sense of scorn. Andrew agreed, stating that Catholics were actually trained by their priests never to open the Bible, a claim I had frequently heard from other Orangemen who explained to me that this policy was motivated by a fear that, if they *did* read the Bible, ordinary Catholics might discover how the 'teachings of Rome' were 'contrary to Scripture'.

Andrew's comments prompted Derek to tell a story of his own about a fellow Orangeman whom he had worked alongside in the coal mines. This particular miner was well known for spending his entire lunch break reading by the light of his mining lamp while the other men relaxed and bantered with each other as they ate. One day, a Roman Catholic workmate who found his reading annoying shouted over to him: 'What are you reading? A lot of fucking rubbish likely!' To everyone's surprise, the Orangeman looked up and replied 'You're right, it is!' as he threw him the book. The book, Derek explained, was a copy of the Catholic Bible with Apocrypha; 'he [the Catholic man] didn't say much after that!' Derek laughed. Somewhat confused by the story, I asked Derek why an Orangeman would spend his time reading the Apocrypha. Derek's answer was that Orangemen needed to be educated, and to know what 'the other side' believed. Andrew firmly agreed, stating how, as a young Orangeman, he had furtively attended Catholic membership classes in order to learn what the Church taught. After weeks of sitting at the back of the class, the information he gleaned, Andrew told us, had been disseminated to Orangemen through a series of lectures he delivered to different lodges on the topic of 'Romanism'.

Derek took the conversation in a different direction by claiming that Tony Blair had converted to Roman Catholicism in an attempt to become President of the European Union. This specific assertion, which I heard repeated by several other Orangemen during my fieldwork, formed part of a wider claim that the European Union was 'a puppet of Rome' (see Webster 2013: 200), and that, likewise, the Roman Catholic Church was a 'pseudo-political organisation'. The other men in the room certainly agreed with Derek. After all, one of them reasoned, many of the world's dictators had been Roman Catholic, including Hitler and Mussolini, a claim also profiled in Bryce's *Irredeemable Papacy* under a section titled 'War Criminals', which appears beside a section on the Vatican Bank which outlines papal 'involvement in Mafia arms and drug trafficking' (2018: 21). Derek, nodding, brought the conversation closer to home by explaining how what was true of the EU was equally true of Scotland; the Labour Party was controlled by Roman Catholics, Derek explained, especially in Glasgow. The only solution, Derek stated, was a revival of Orangeism, the like of which had only been seen after the Second World War. On this point, Derek's reading of history was revealing: as these young soldiers emerged from the War, they found within themselves a deeper sense of being not only British but also Protestant, having fought not only *for* 'Queen and Country', but also *against* Nazism and its Catholic-born Führer.

The catholicity of Catholic conspiracy

Yet, in the absence of this Orange revival, Derek and many of my other Orange informants were pessimistic about their ability to effectively resist 'the menace of Rome'. Because local West of Scotland politics was said to be dominated by Catholics within the Labour Party, and national politics was said to be dominated by the

SNP who sought to appease the Catholic Church, many of my informants felt they had no effective political representation. The daily consequences of this lack of representation merely acted to confirm the existence of a Catholic conspiracy. Access to government funding was an often-discussed example, said to lay bare the institutional sectarianism Orangemen felt themselves to be victims of. Flute bands were a case in point. Many such groups had decided to reclassify themselves as 'orchestras', Derek explained, since, they believed, they would never receive funding if the grant-awarding committee knew that their 'flute band' was Protestant and loyalist. Grant applications submitted by flute bands which refused this name change were not only unsuccessful, but often went unacknowledged, since, Jonathan argued, a formal rejection letter would create hard evidence of discrimination which could then be challenged by human rights legislation. When I asked if Catholic-Republican bands had successfully bid for such grants, I was emphatically told that they had. This same sectarian discrimination, I was assured, also applied to grants for church renovations; while Protestant churches routinely had their applications turned down, 'every Roman Catholic chapel gets renovated!' Jonathan protested.

Such (real or imagined) discrepancies powerfully reinforced Orange beliefs about the long arm of 'the menace of Rome', a menace which, in their experience, had constructed a system of anti-Protestant discrimination overseen by bigoted Catholic politicians and bureaucrats. Importantly, this anti-Protestant system was said to exert control over far more than grants to flute bands and churches. Specific complaints about injustices in public expenditure (see Pilkington 2016: 161–163) were narrated, as above, within a politico-historical context going back many years. Both in the archive and in Glencruix, stories were told about the ethno-religious and political machinations exposed through the scandal of 'Monklandsgate' which 'emerged into the glare of media publicity in 1993 when accusations were made against the ruling Labour Monklands District Council in Lanarkshire' (Walker 2016: 34). The central accusation was that 'vast differentials in public spending and the awarding of jobs and contracts' between 'the mainly Protestant town of Airdrie and the largely Catholic town of Coatbridge' were the product of 'a Catholic "mafia" using the Labour Party as a vehicle for dispensing favours on a religious basis' (ibid.). Despite two public enquiries suggesting otherwise (ibid.: 35–36), what Monklandsgate revealed, according to my Orange informants, was the undeniable reality of the Catholic conspiracy they faced – a reality which, I was told, extended far beyond Labour Monklands District Council and their issuing of colour-coded job applications as a mechanism to only hire Catholic workers.

Indeed, twenty-five years on from Monklandsgate, the scandal still loomed large in the political and religious consciousness of the Order across Central Scotland, partly because it was held by many Orangemen to be the tip of a much bigger 'Romish' iceberg. In political terms, this 'menace' (referred to by one of my informants as 'the green element') extended beyond any local concentrations of Catholic representation within the Labour Party to, as already described above, Scotland-wide claims about the SNP's efforts to court the Catholic vote, most especially in the context of the independence referendum. Much of this conspiracy thinking was framed by wider Orange claims that Catholics in Scotland 'vote however they're told', that is, 'however their priest tells them' (see also Chapter 5). Even (or perhaps *especially*) on the international stage, 'the menace of Rome' was said to exert significant influence, with local parish priests imagined to instruct their parishioners how to vote based on orders received from a global Catholic hierarchy, that is, from bishops, archbishops, and cardinals outside of Scotland who were, in turn, said to be acting on the orders of the Pope himself.

Intriguingly, Manley's ethnographic account of SNP activists has found remarkably similar concerns about occluded agency, albeit ones directed towards concerns about the long arm of the British State, as opposed to fears about Catholicism. Indeed, according to Manley, 'conspiracy theories have been impossible to avoid, ranging from common distrust of the mainstream media to more outlandish theories of actors and infiltrators nefariously tasked with the dismantling of the independence movement' (2019: n.p.). In this purview, claims of BBC television debates being dominated by 'actor[s] paid to slander the SNP' are voiced alongside fears about British unionist spies infiltrating the Scottish independence movement, but also denials that the moon landing ever happened (ibid.).

As such, what Manley's SNP interlocutors share with many of my Orange informants is 'the uncanny feeling that there must be something more to uncover' (ibid.). Of course, for those in the Order in Scotland, the target of such conspiracy accusations was not the British State but the Catholic Church and its purported political puppet, the SNP. Yet, as above, the (Scottish) media was said to be implicated in conspiring to achieve a nefarious agenda, variously by erasing reporting of child abuse by Catholic clergy, depicting Catholics as victims rather than perpetrators of sectarian crime, advocating for independence, demonising Orange parades, and ensuring that Protestant viewpoints were never aired. So too within the Scottish education system, which was said to unfairly monopolise public funding by diverting all new resources to Catholic schools, while reproducing Scotland's sectarian divide through discriminatory employment and pupil-allocation policies. As with Catholic domination of the media, my Orange informants perceived a hidden sectarian agenda woven into the Catholic education system in Scotland. One informant, for example, described how a model Catholic school in Glasgow supposedly had no problems with sectarianism, despite the fact that he had personally observed extensive pro-IRA graffiti surrounding the school site. Another Orangeman related a story of pupils from a Catholic school stoning a public bus full of Protestant pupils from the local non-denominational school, 'that's a product of sectarian schools! They separate them at five years old!' he said angrily. According to the men in the Orange archive, the cumulative effects of this were devastating to popular Scots-Protestant consciousness; not only had many 'loyalist' and 'unionist' working-class communities become politically apathetic, but the very notion of 'Protestant' as a legitimate identity marker had been undermined, and this despite the asymmetrical rise of Catholic confidence in their own religious identity.

Such was the catholicity of Catholic conspiracy that, what was said by my Orange informants to be true of contemporary Scotland – in politics, the media, and education – was also deemed to be true of Scotland's past, as well as its memorialisation in the present. Important Scottish Covenanter sites, for example, were being destroyed according to Jonathan, as a result of the approval of planning applications which literally paved over them. 'History is being lost!' Derek agreed. Despite hearing much in the Orange archive about how these staunch Presbyterians in the seventeenth century had heroically resisted persecution at the hands of Catholics and their Episcopal sympathisers, I only really began to understand the place of Covenanting history within Orange cosmology and conspiracism after spending a day touring various Covenanter sites in Hamilton with Jonathan and his friend Roger. It was a bright and clear May morning, yet the fairness of the weather contrasted markedly with the dark tales of torture and execution that Jonathan and Roger regaled me with as we moved from site to site.

At our first stop, Jonathan told the story of 'The Four Heads Monument', where the heads and right hands of four martyred Presbyterians had been put on public display 'to put the fear of death into the Covenanters'. 'But it had the opposite effect!' Jonathan exclaimed with pride, 'It made them grow stronger!' After this, we visited the main Covenanter memorial in Hamilton, which overlooked the battlefield of Bothwell Brig, where 6,000 poorly armed Covenanters were defeated by a smaller force of royalist troops. Asking for Roger's perspective on these killings, his answer was typical of the sentiments I had heard from Orange informants, despite not being an Orangeman himself. 'It makes you more Protestant in your faith. You see, they [the royalists] wanted to do away with Presbyterianism and to reintroduce Episcopalianism, as the back door to Roman Catholicism. That's what it's all about. Sometimes we feel as if we have been there'. 'It's in your blood, yes, it does make you feel something' Jonathan said in quiet agreement. Going down into the field itself, Jonathan spoke of discussions the Memorials Association had had with the local council about plans to develop the site for housing. The compromise Jonathan hoped to strike, he said, involved the council and developers building not only homes, but also a Covenanter visitor centre. Jonathan remained sceptical as to the council's real intentions, however, suggesting that it was possible they might try to renege on their commitments. Yet, if the visitor centre was built, this would represent a 'victory', Jonathan said. 'But the ultimate victory' he concluded, 'was the Covenanters' at the Glorious Revolution, because they got exactly what they wanted!'

One of the final stops on our tour – Mary Rae's Well – proved to be the most interesting, if also the most banal. At first, I did not even see the monument, which commemorated the place where a wounded Covenanter lay dying, nursed in the arms of his fiancée Mary Rae, after the Battle of Bothwell Brig. The monument, which sat on a small patch of undeveloped land on the edge of a housing estate, was little more than a low stone square. This square, I had to be informed, was the outline of the old well, the top and sides of which had been almost completely swallowed up by overgrown grass and weeds (see Figure 2.1). 'It's a disgrace!' Jonathan said, as he paced the monument, taking photos to send to the council to protest about its state of disrepair. 'Nobody is interested. The council just *aren't* interested' Roger said, shaking his head. As Jonathan continued taking photos, he realised that some of the stones of the wall were loose or missing, and that the commemorative

2.1 Mary Rae's Well.

plaque had been removed. 'That's shocking, that's the worst I've seen!' Jonathan said in horror. 'It's a disgrace' Roger repeated, albeit more glumly. 'What surprises me' he continued 'is that the people who live here havenae complained'.

Once Jonathan had pocketed his camera, he and Roger began to try to account for the monument's poor condition. Their discussions focused on a number of Labour Party councillors who were also said to be Catholics. 'You have to be careful how you phrase things' Jonathan said, as he and Roger planned their complaint against the council. Despite Jonathan's cautionary remark, the substance of his accusation was clear, namely that there was a concerted effort by Catholic politicians to expunge all traces of Covenanting history – a history which stood as a reminder of the persecution of Scottish Presbyterians at the hands of Roman Catholics and their Episcopal lackeys. In this framing, the threat which faced the Covenanters over 300 years ago, 'to do away with Presbyterianism and to reintroduce Roman Catholicism', remained, according to Jonathan and Roger, largely the same threat in Scotland today.

In this reading of the *longue durée* of Scots-Protestant history, Orangemen like Jonathan and Orange sympathisers like Roger can (and do) anticipate the possibility of occasional victories such as the construction of a visitor centre or the renovation of an overgrown memorial. Yet, at the same time, my informants repeatedly made it clear to me that they felt themselves to be under no illusions about how significantly the odds were stacked against them. Indeed, it was those well outside the world of Orangeism, especially liberal-minded middle-class Protestants, who were held to be delusional, blind, as they were, to the control that Roman Catholicism exerted over Scottish society, politics, media, education, and even historical remembrance. Understanding this last claim, that the Roman Catholic Church was seeking to expunge Scots-Protestant history from popular remembrance, is important because it allows us to see how Orangemen like Jonathan, as well as my other key informants from the archive, cast themselves as central figures in resisting a national (and in some cases a global) religious conspiracy.[1]

Much of this resistance took the form of various kinds of vigilance – vigilance against media bias, against injustices within Scotland's education system, and against religiously motivated political nepotism and bigotry, all of which were said to be clear manifestations of 'the menace of Rome'. Importantly, as I have described it above, this vigilance centrally involved talk, that is, the sharing of stories, gossip, news, and remembrances about 'what Rome is up to'. But vigilance also took material (and arguably more mundane) forms, such as vigilance against overgrown weeds and grass, which were themselves said to be part of a more deliberate and insidious policy of anti-Protestant neglect. 'Sometimes we feel as if we have been there' Roger said, speaking of his reaction to being in the place where Covenanters had died in battle; 'It's in your blood' Jonathan had replied in affirmation. In the same way that the Covenanters suffered for their Protestant faith, so too did my Orange informants expect to suffer, and while their injuries were not often understood to be caused by bullets or flames (the Troubles in Northern Ireland being the obvious exception), the intended consequences were said to be similar, namely a degradation of the religious and political forces of Protestantism in Scottish society, both past and present. The logic was clear; as the Covenanters had been attacked in life, so too in death, with their faith (and the faith of their Orange advocates) undermined by a Catholic conspiracy to obliterate the Protestant past by de-memorialising (and thereby demoralising) the Protestant present.

While some of my Orange informants found the Covenanters to provide compelling evidence of an anti-Protestant conspiracy, others found such evidence in relatively more recent times, particularly in the history of the First and Second World Wars, and in efforts to memorialise those conflicts in the present. As already described above, several Orangemen (in the archive, in the Glencruix Social Club, and elsewhere) frequently blamed the Catholic Church for causing the Second World War, a claim that was often justified with reference to Hitler's Catholic parentage and upbringing. Yet, such biographical details were not held to be the only evidence of the Second World War being orchestrated by 'Rome' as an attack upon civil and religious liberty, and particularly upon Britain as a Protestant constitutional monarchy. Stories of British blackouts being deliberately thwarted by Irish towns and cities which left lights on as a way to guide Luftwaffe bombers to Belfast and Liverpool were offered as further proof that supposedly neutral Ireland was, in reality, collaborating with the Nazis to maximise the damage of the Blitz. Such actions were motivated, I was told, by religion as well as by politics, a claim which emerges from wider Orange and loyalist beliefs that Ireland was (and is) a vassal state of the Vatican which sought (and still seeks) to undermine the British State as a way to undermine Protestantism.

Importantly, this conspiracy was said to be ongoing, emerging in ways which further persuaded my Orange informants of the powerful links between Irishness, Catholicism, and anti-Britishness. Sectarian attacks on war memorials were said to constitute a clear case of how the memory of fallen soldiers – as with the memory of martyred Covenanters – was under attack in Scotland. For example, in 2016 the cenotaph in Coatbridge (commemorating those killed during the First World War) was scrawled with pro-IRA graffiti, with phrases including IRA, PIRA (Provisional IRA), Provos, and 1916 – a reference to the Easter Rising, the hundredth anniversary of which was being widely commemorated in Ireland and elsewhere at the time. While local councillors lined up to condemn the attack in the press in the days that followed, loyalists in the town arrived on the scene first, during the hours immediately after the attack, to film the damage that had been done, and to film themselves making statements condemning what they regarded as the overly slow response of the authorities to launch a clean-up. That the attack happened in the same town, which, twenty-five years before, had been at the centre of the 'Monklandsgate' scandal simply confirmed deeply held loyalist and Orange suspicions that the town was still run by a 'Catholic mafia' who pandered to the strongly republican, anti-British, and anti-Protestant sympathies of many of their constituents.

Other key symbols of remembering Britain's war dead were also said to be under attack by Catholic republicans, including use of the poppy. During a brief spell of fieldwork within Edinburgh's Lady Haig Poppy Factory, one of the veterans I spoke to (who was himself a Catholic) explained that they routinely sent orders of poppy wreaths to Northern Ireland packed into cardboard boxes which had been deliberately folded inside out. Shipping these orders in (what appeared to be) plain brown boxes was necessary, he explained, to prevent the parcels from being vandalised or dumped by republican delivery drivers. 'We are still doing things like that! It's crazy!' he said with a shake of his head. Setting aside the complexity that many of these poppy wreaths were manufactured by Scottish veterans who were Catholics, when I related this story to my Orange informants, the larger point struck them as entirely unsurprising. If IRA sympathisers, or 'Catholic republicans', as they were often referred to, were willing to desecrate war memorials, then they would certainly also be willing to vandalise boxes of poppy wreaths. Such was 'the menace of Rome' – a menace which stood accused by my informants of inculcating a hatred within its followers of all things British and Protestant, a hatred which was said to span hundreds of years of Scottish history, from the 'Killing Time' of the Covenanters, through both World Wars, to their memorialisation in the present.

The Orange culture of conspiracism, as I encountered it during my fieldwork, is a highly complex constellation of claims about the true nature of 'the menace of Rome' – a constellation, which, when recognised as a real and coherent pattern, brings the moral value of Protestant exceptionalism alive for my informants. Consider the following summary sketch. Roman Catholic schools in Scotland engage in illegal discrimination by only hiring Catholic teachers, and by prioritising the children of Catholic families when allocating school places. These schools fraudulently inflate their rolls by counting those attending evening classes as new pupils, and by bussing in pupils from outside their catchment area. This allows Catholic schools to receive a disproportionately large amount of the education budget, despite EU law requiring that denominationally specific schools should receive no State support at all. These social and economic injustices, furthermore, are protected and maintained by a cabal of republican Catholic Labour politicians, as well as by self-hating Protestants in the Tory party whose liberal and progressive agenda leads them to reject their real ethno-religious heritage in favour of identifying with the bland and all-inclusive label 'Christian'. That the real political agenda of these schools is treasonous is clearly displayed through the extensive pro-IRA graffiti that covers their walls. Ultimately, then, the wider aim of these schools, which they achieve very successfully, is to maintain Scotland's sectarian divide by separating Catholic children from the rest of the population, and teaching them, from the tender age of five, to hate everything associated with Britishness and Protestantism.

Upon completing this education, Scots-Catholics experience divergent outcomes. Significant proportions go on to practise what their schools preached by committing hate crimes against Protestants and the monuments they hold dear, while perversely maintaining that it is they – the perpetrators – who are the real victims of Scotland's sectarian divide. Others seemingly move in the opposite direction, and, rather than joining the Catholic criminal underclass, become power brokers within the upper echelons of society, in politics, media, the law, and finance. In the Scottish political sphere, these individuals pursue a hidden Catholic republican agenda by variously denying Protestants equal access to government jobs, restricting State funding for Protestant causes and Protestant towns, and campaigning for Scottish independence. Importantly, in the same way that these politicians receive their political orders from Rome, so too do local priests relay these orders to their parishioners from the pulpit, thereby instructing them how to vote. Looking beyond Scotland, Scots-Catholic politicians seek to undermine the Protestant foundations of Britain by campaigning for an end to the Act of Settlement, while concomitantly bolstering the influence of Rome's puppet, the EU. In the sphere of Scottish media, Catholic journalists advocate for the policies of Catholic politicians, while covering up the abuses of the Catholic Church and silencing critical Protestant voices that would seek to expose them, or simply offer an alternative view. In the financial and legal spheres, Catholics dominate the positions of greatest influence, as they do in politics and within the media, while simultaneously claiming that Catholics in Scotland are an excluded and downtrodden minority.

Conclusions: Orange conspiracism as theodicy

Such was the narrative flow of Orange conspiracism, as it was told to me by both the Grand Lodge hierarchy, and grass-roots members. But what are we to make of this? For the remainder of this chapter, I want to argue that Orange conspiracism offers members of the Order a theodicy, that is, an account of, and an explanation for, this-worldly experiences of evil. More than this, Orange-conspiracism-as-theodicy offers Orangemen a model for taking action, for resisting this ostensible evil, by first instantiating a double-mode of *revelation* and *observation*, that is, of seeing and watching. By showing how Orange conspiracism births Orange theodicy via these modes of revelation and observation, I aim to show how the spectre of 'the menace of Rome' constitutes Orangeism as a cosmology driven by the desire to expose nefarious hidden powers believed to be secretly directing Scotland's destiny. As such, in contrast to Csordas's recent account of homodicy, which he offers as 'an alternative to theodicy' (Olsen and Csordas 2019: 12) by taking evil to be 'manifested more in experiential modes than in theocratic frameworks' (ibid.: 10), I deploy the notion of Orange theodicy below to suggest how the experiential and the theocratic are, in reality, inseparable. Before explaining Orange conspiracism further, however, I want to pause to critically consider the better-known term 'conspiracy theory'.

Much of the academic writing on conspiracy theories discusses the importance of emic ideas about a 'New World Order' (NWO) (Barkun 2003, Uscinski 2018), making analytical reference to a wide range of groups or powers said to act as secret global puppet-masters. The UN, NATO, the Bilderberg Group, Freemasonry, the Illuminati, extra-terrestrials, and shape-shifting reptiles have all been identified as sitting at the hidden helm of the NWO. Sometimes discussed in isolation, but more often taken together, these entities are said by famous conspiracy theorists such as David Icke (Robertson 2016) to form the 'who' and 'what' of world control, existing as the *real* government behind the globalist government. As Robertson points out, while a 'conspiracy theory' may be defined easily enough as 'an explanation that conflicts with the account advanced by the relevant epistemic authorities' (Levy quoted in Robertson 2016: 37), it needs to be noted that 'the term's ultimate function is *rhetorical*' (Robertson 2016: 37). Here, conspiracy theories (and conspiracy theorists) come to be labelled (and mocked) as 'inherently irrational', even 'pathological' (ibid.: 38). As a result of this pejorative impulse, like Robertson and others before him, I have chosen not to use the term. Instead, I draw inspiration from Barkun's emphasis on 'conspiracy belief' as 'stigmatized knowledge' (2003: 2), that is, 'knowledge claims that run counter to generally accepted beliefs' (ibid.: 8).

Importantly, however, my use of Barkun's *A Culture of Conspiracy* is not meant to signal direct empirical resonances between his analytical focus on New World Order conspiracy beliefs about UFOs and my own focus on Orange conspiracism. For the avoidance of doubt, I never met an Orangeman who discussed UFOs, nor did NWO conspiracy theories form a part of Orange cosmology more generally. This is because my Orange informants did not believe in a New World Order, but instead subscribed to a different constellation of ideas about an *Old Catholic Order*. Yet, much of what I have already described above (and seek to analyse below) still conforms to Barkun's definition of conspiracy belief as 'the belief that powerful, hidden, evil forces control human destinies' (2003: 2). In this sense, Orange conspiracism can be understood not only as stigmatised knowledge, but also as 'suppressed knowledge' (ibid.: 27), as many Scots-Orangemen firmly believe that claims about Catholic domination are publicly dismissed by wider Scottish society as sectarian nonsense, while at the same time being privately acknowledged (and celebrated) as true by Scotland's hidden Catholic rulers.

Such claims are not new. Indeed, far more so than UFOs, beliefs about Catholic machinations can be seen as something of a conspiracy archetype. While certain strands of conspiracy belief track the origin of Catholic evil 'back to an obscene pre-Christian religion allegedly practiced in Babylonia by Nimrod and his descend-ants' (ibid.: 131), the origin of conspiracy beliefs about Catholic evil emerge across Europe during the Reformation period. In Scotland, such beliefs are found within the Westminster Confession of Faith (1646) and its identification of the Pope as 'that Antichrist, that man of sin, and son of perdition' (Chapter 25.6). Proclamations about immoral religion often came to be linked to proclamations about immoral sexuality – 'libertine priests, the confessional as an opportunity for seduction, licentious convents and monasteries, and the like' (Hofstadter 1964: 21), as seen for example in the 1836 bestseller *Awful Disclosures of Maria Monk*.

Importantly, to the extent that 'anti-Catholicism has always been the pornography of the Puritan' (ibid.), similar tendencies can be observed within Orange conspiracy beliefs about homosexual priests in Scotland, as well as ongoing scandals about historic child abuse within the Catholic Church in Ireland and further afield (see also Chapter 4). For Barkun, anti-Catholic conspiracism in nineteenth-century America can be understood as a kind of 'nativism' which targeted Catholics 'not only for their religion but for their non-Anglo-Saxon ethnicities' (2003: 127). As Finn has argued, this kind of religiously inspired ethno-nationalism can also be observed within certain expressions of Scottish Protestantism, which have historically regarded Irish Catholic immigrants 'as a disloyal, racially inferior ethnic group, who were the enemy within' (1991: 374). And, as I argue below, for some, such views remain formative in the present.

Of course, for many of my Orange informants, concerns about this 'enemy within' are not the product of any conspiracy theory but are understood to be a reasonable reaction to an undeniable reality – a modern-day Gunpowder Plot, minus the gunpowder. Yet, according to these same informants, the truth of Scotland's hidden domination by Rome is being suppressed by virtue of that truth being stigmatised, thereby rendering it largely unutterable within the mainstream of progressive civic society. According to Orangemen like Andy, that this silencing of reality is taking place simply confirms the existence of the menace – a menace which comes to resemble a system, or 'systemic conspiracy' (Barkun 2003: 6), involving not just religion, but also education, politics, journalism, banking, and the judiciary, thereby doing away with the need for gunpowder altogether. As a result of the veiled operation of this system, attributions and experiences of agency take on different forms, whereby nothing happens by accident, nothing is as it seems, and everything is connected (ibid.: 3–4). It is no accident that weeds envelop a Covenanter memorial, for council employees are not, despite appearances, neutral bureaucrats, but rather Catholic republican sympathisers engaged in a calculated campaign to neglect and marginalise Scots-Protestant heritage. As such, Barkun (1997) is also right to point out – in a separate but related account of the British Israelite movement – that claims to special insight into what is *really* going on give men like Andy, Jonathan, and Derek a double sense of privilege and peril, that is, of being 'a self-identified spiritual elite' who are simultaneously convinced 'that God's forces are encircled' (Barkun 1997: 250).

It would, however, be all too easy to dismiss such narratives as a form of irrational 'semiotic arousal' (Landes 2006), whereby all observable phenomena come to be assigned spurious meanings via the identification of false patterns. Given this temptation, it seems worth asking how our interpretations might differ if the patterns being identified were not papal, and the meanings being assigned were not Orange. Would semiotic arousal appear rather more justified, for example, if undertaking a critical ethnography of neo-liberal capitalism? Note, here, how late capitalism is commonly held within anthropological scholarship to be directly responsible for a panoply of evils including climate change, drug addiction, gender-based violence, war, and the wholesale exploitations of indigenous groups and their lands, to name only a (very) few. That it would seem utterly obvious to most anthropologists (myself included) that capitalism is indeed responsible for these phenomena is precisely my point, namely that a semiotic connecting of dots only becomes embarrassingly overenthusiastic if and when such connections are deemed by onlookers to be dependent upon logic which appears 'occultish and oddly prancing'. When applied to neo-liberalism, in contrast, such semiotic tracings appear simply true. For Faubion, this double standard is not only hypocritical, but stultifying, and no more so than within the anthropology of religion:

> Too much of the scholarship of religious activism … now seems to me to be infected analytically and textually with the same defensive strategy that I have so often felt impelled to deploy: a strategy of distancing, which would seek to disguise what is in fact familiar, all too familiar, in the costume of the far-flung exotic. Some of its devices are transparent: rationalist mockery, bemused or belittling, which is content to dismiss as foolish or infantile whatever might threaten to reflect back to it the extra-rational grounds of its own complaisance; and a sort of behavioural scientism that rapidly weaves the feathery headdress of a psycho-pathological profile to crown whoever might threaten to reflect back to it the most arbitrary of those social conventions that saturate its schemas of perception and diagnosis. (Faubion 2001: 33)

The longer I spent with the Order, the more I came to realise that, in certain respects, Faubion was correct for, in the early stages of my fieldwork, I had wrongly judged my Orange informants to be part of an exotic tribe, worthy of my curiosity and bemusement, but unable to offer anything which might unsettle my own view of the world and its moral make-up. Such was the stubbornness of my assumption that sectarianism could *only ever* exist as a social evil that it took five years of fieldwork, and the calamitous failure and eventual repeal of a markedly counter-productive piece of Scottish legislation attempting to ban 'offensive behaviour at football', for me to be able to countenance the possibility that the varieties of Orange exceptionalism might contain something good. More than this, if the exceptionalism of Orange conspiracism (and, as we shall see in Chapter 4, of fraternity and hate) can be *good* it must also be *real*, or at least *no less real* than the goodness of liberal tolerance and inclusive pluralism. It is in this respect, then, that I partially diverge from Faubion's analysis above. Indeed, my instinct is not to treat the inclusive pluralism of anthropology as a schema of perception that is somehow just as arbitrary as that of the Branch Davidians of Waco Texas (Faubion

2001), but rather the reverse, namely to treat the moral commitments of Orange conspiracism as just as real and defensible as those we might more typically find among anthropologists, be they militant (Scheper-Hughes 1995) or otherwise.

Anthropology cannot have it both ways; if the Orange Order is driven by a morality of exclusionism, then so too is anthropology. This seems especially true of anthropology in the United States, where American Anthropological Association resolutions have prohibited holding annual meetings in states with anti-sodomy laws, denounced the government of Honduras, and proposed a boycott of Israeli academic institutions (Webster 2018: 334), as well as, most recently, rejecting the politics of Trump 'in the strongest terms'. For many within anthropology, as within the Orange Order, to be a member in good standing is thus to affirm the goodness of certain prohibitions, denouncements, boycotts, and rejections. Further, just as the Orange Order cannot claim a monopoly over affirmations of 'The Good' of exclusionism, neither can it claim a monopoly over a proliferation of semiotic connectedness so extensive that it comes to appear somewhat conspiratorial. Indeed, anthropology, too, engages in a tracing out and joining up of human experience – of kinship, livelihoods, politics, law, religion, ritual, material culture, art and so on – into a grand ethnographic and theoretical whodunnit. For Faubion, the inescapable conclusion is that he is not so very different from the Branch Davidian prophetess Mrs Roden where:

> In her political and semiotic suspicions, in her alienation, in her passion for making sense, in her scholarly devotions, I could not but recognize emphatic expressions of my own … I am not, after all, so radically alienated from what I like sometimes to tout as the manifold absurdities of the temporal order I inhabit. The hiatus between the two of us has always been one of degree, not of kind … I think that I am far from alone, and think instead that a subjectivity similar to my own lurks in a considerable number of others who have decided – if decision there was – to pursue careers in the academy, especially careers in its hermeneutical sectors and subsectors, anthropology prominent among them. (Faubion 2001: 32–33)

Drawing from Faubion's analysis above, what we see here is something of the hermeneutic elective affinity that exists between anthropology and the Orange Order, for both seem to share a sense of the reality of intrinsic connectedness that exists alongside the impossibility of purely accidental occurrences and purely face-value realities, where, for the Order, weeds growing over a monument forms part of a larger constellation of dots which are ready and waiting to be joined. To try and give a sense of *how* this joining takes place within Orangeism, I want to try and extrapolate up from these weeds, to the office of the Pope. Consider, then, the following. From the perspective of my Orange informants, the groundsperson, as an employee of a council which discriminates against Protestants, is likely to be a Catholic, who, having being educated within a Roman Catholic school, will have been taught to hold instinctively anti-Protestant sentiments. While it is possible that the groundsperson knew that the stone well was a monument to Scotland's Radical Reformation, and chose not to maintain it for that reason, it is more likely that a different Catholic employee, a manager of the council's parks and gardens service, made the deliberate (but undocumented and thus legally unchallengeable) decision not to maintain the monument, out of spite towards Scotland's Protestants, but also due to budget cuts.

Budget cuts, moreover, are targeted on the basis of wider anti-Protestant sentiments within Scotland's Catholic-controlled public sector. Just as reductions to grass-cutting services disproportionately impact the upkeep of Protestant monuments, so too do other spending decisions discriminate against wider Orange interests, with Protestant churches and loyalist bands refused funding, while Catholic churches and republican bands regularly receive local government support. These local decisions are also symptomatic of a bigger regional and nationwide system of economic sectarianism, with Monklandsgate being the tip of an anti-Protestant iceberg. Scotland's religiously segregated education system, funded by public resources but spent by Catholic politicians for the sole benefit of Catholic communities, evidences some of what is just below the waterline. The perpetuation of this unjust economic system (which extends beyond Scotland to the UK as a whole) is guaranteed by powerful Catholics within Britain's financial sector, who lead key institutions such as the Bank of England.

That the majority of Scottish citizens are ignorant of these persistent injustices is the product of a Catholic-controlled media who conspire to hide the truth of their social and economic domination by casting themselves as victims. Moreover, while such institutionalised anti-Protestant discrimination is illegal across all levels of local, devolved, national, and EU governance, its inner-workings are protected and maintained by a judicial system which seeks to preserve Catholic power and privilege above all else. Crucially, each of these elements of Catholic domination, from local parks maintenance, to council funding decisions, to control of education, banking, media, and the judiciary, exert their influence in parallel, doing so with the singular aim of absorbing Scotland into a new Roman empire under the authority of the papal triple crown, which, I was assured, symbolised the Catholic Church's blasphemous claim of holding 'power over all monarchs', including the British sovereign.

It is here, given the intricacy of the Orange cosmology outlined above, that I find myself departing somewhat from Barkun's analysis of conspiracism as it might be made to apply to my informants. For Barkun, 'conspiracy theories … are nothing if not parsimonious, for they attribute all of the world's evil to the activities of a single plot, or set of plots' (Barkun 2003: 7). The result, for Barkun, is as inevitable as is it straightforward: 'conspiracy theories … reduce highly complex phenomena to simple causes' (ibid.). Yet, while it *is* true to say that all theories exist as simplified models of the phenomena they seek to describe, Orange conspiracism (whether or not one treats it as a 'theory', conspiratorial or otherwise) does not seem parsimonious, nor could it be described as an oversimplification. Indeed, I want to argue something rather different, namely that Orange conspiracism is a highly baroque enterprise which takes shape in and though the verbosity of Orange debate, rumour, gossip, storytelling, and reminiscence. As such, rather than being a form of reductionism, the result is a kind of constructivism, a heaping up of interpretation upon interpretation, agency upon agency, and motive upon motive, which builds towards the creation (or identification) of a plot that is both highly singular *and* utterly labyrinthine.

Other anthropological commentators on conspiracy have made similar suggestions. West and Sanders, for example, 'belie the notion, widely held, that conspiracy theories … recklessly reduce the world's complexity at the expense of deeper analyses and accurate understandings' (2003: 17). Indeed, these authors claim that conspiracy theories 'do precisely the opposite, rendering the world more complex by calling to attention its hidden and contradictory logics, by proposing alternative ways of understanding and engaging it' (ibid.). Yet, while I echo West and Sanders' emphasis on the complexification of conspiracy, I do not find their term 'occult cosmologies, as systems of belief in a world animated by secret, mysterious, and/or unseen powers' (ibid.: 6), to be particularly fitting in the case of Scots-Orangeism. This is because, while not pejorative, the term does seem to carry within it an emphasis on magic, which, while befitting the authors' work on witchcraft and sorcery in postcolonial Africa (Moore and Sanders 2001, West 2007), sits awkwardly with the Order's emphasis on (albeit Masonic-style) Reformed Protestantism.

Outside of anthropology, much scholarship has built upon Hofstadter's famous essay 'The Paranoid Style in American Politics' (1964), extrapolating from it an overly 'clinical' (Barkun 2003: 8) view of conspiracism, thereby transforming it into a quasi-pathology akin to Festinger's reading of millenarianism as productive of a kind of 'cognitive dissonance' (1956). Others, like Robertson, view conspiracism as a kind of 'fight back', that is, an attempt to regain some semblance of 'control of epistemic capital' (2016: 35). While certainly displaying greater efforts of empathy than those who would pathologise conspiracy believers, I still find this type of deprivation theory problematic insofar as it positions conspiracism as an essentially reactionary force, a grasping at straws by the structurally and ideologically disadvantaged, if not the mentally infirm (see Hickman and Webster In Press).

What then? If conspiracism cannot be adequately explained as a parsimonious oversimplification, a symptom of pathology, or a battle against one's epistemic poverty, how might it be explained? My suggestion, that Orange conspiracism may be understood as a kind of theodicy, takes semiotics as its point of departure. Remember, then, the inscription on the inside cover of the coffee-table book I found in the Orange archive: '…the menace of Rome is still the same! She has not changed! She cannot change! For were she to relent or change one iota, she would cease to be Rome. The price of freedom is eternal vigilance'. Orange conspiracism, then, is an attempt to explicate Orange ideas about evil, as made manifest by 'the menace of Rome'. More than this, Orange conspiracism is a kind of semiotics, a kind of 'vigilance', which seeks to join up different ethno-religious and ethno-national happenings into complex patterns and ornate constellations.

In joining these dots, veteran Orangemen like Andy, Jonathan, and Derek invite their fellow brethren (as well as inquisitive ethnographers) to see the world as they do, by having 'the menace of Rome' revealed to them, just as Johannes Hevelius revealed eleven new constellations to the Early Modern world in his *Firmamentum Sobiescianum* star atlas, published in that most special year of 1690. And as with constellations, once the pattern has been traced out and then seen (that is, recognised as *really* there), it cannot be unseen. Indeed, the person who looks at Rubin's Vase and initially *only* sees a vase cannot go back to this singular point of view once it has been successfully shown to them that the image *also* contains two faces. In this sense, the semiotic revelation of (material and/or imagined) patterns – Rubin's Vase, Orion's Belt, Monklandsgate – has the power to change the way we see because 'the way we see things is affected by what we know or what we believe' (Berger 1972: 8). More than this, the way we see transforms the very thing which we see: a vase becomes two faces; three stars become a belt; self-interested politicians become a Catholic mafia (see Ball 2014, Keane 2018).

Residing within this transformative inability to 'unsee' something is the necessary fuel to feed a desire to keep looking, to keep seeing, and thereby to maintain one's privileged perspective of seeing what others cannot see, or refuse to see. Here, revelation slips into observation, with the first sight or glimpse of the asterism giving birth to a much more concerted effort, not just to see, but also to scrutinise and track the whole constellation. Now that the belt can be seen, the rest of Orion must also be claimed and conquered by the eye, and soon the entire night sky may be (literally) mapped using dozens of similar images – of centaurs, serpents, lions, goats, and crowns – all made possible by the connecting of dots, and thereby the production of an atlas with which to navigate the cosmos. So too with Orange conspiracism, where singular revelations about 'the menace of Rome' expand, and come to be absorbed, through the transformation of Orange sight, into an interconnected host of related revelations which become atlas-like in their navigational potential. As such, once the plot of the Catholic education system has been seen and believed, the rest of the conspiracy must not only be revealed, but also observed and guarded against. Overgrown weeds, republican graffiti, rejected funding applications, media bias, and constitutional referendums all demand the same vigilance, the same effort of observation, for it is only by continually *seeing* this menace that Orangemen like Andy may stare it down, and thus defeat it.

Crucially, it was the very activity of remaining vigilant, of revealing and observing 'the menace of Rome', in all its verbosity and baroque semiotics, that gave my informants such a concrete sense of the evil they were facing. As such, Orange conspiracism is not only a theodicy, an account *of* evil, but also makes possible its very *creation*. Just as astronomy creates constellations by drawing lines between stars, so too does Orange conspiracism-as-theodicy create 'the menace of Rome' by drawing lines between teacher employment policies, lines of school buses, school roll figures, and local and national funding decisions, via, in some cases, overgrown weeds and papal influence over elections. Equally, just as astronomy creates constellations, so too does it create astronomers, that is, professional revelators and observers of the sky, adept at identifying otherwise difficult-to-see patterns. In the same way, Orange conspiracism-as-theodicy creates Orangemen, or at least the need for Orangemen, by first creating (that is, identifying and imagining), the *semiotic reality* (Ball 2014) of 'the menace of Rome'. What is created through this tautological identification of and vigilance against 'the menace of Rome', is, simply put, a kind of Protestant exceptionalism – a select group, or a 'Chosen Few' (in the words of many a lodge and band banner), who are able to see and stand against that which threatens Scotland's very existence as a Protestant country within the family of British nations. Yet, as we shall see in the next chapter on Orange ritual, being an Orangeman involves more than just a change of sight, for being able to see and observe 'the menace of Rome' is only the first step towards entrance into this Loyal Order, where a defining feature of proper revelation is simultaneously bound up with deliberate acts of secrecy, and the cultivation of concealment.

Note

1 The parallels here to protests over Confederate monuments in America are striking, not least because of their ability to produce counter-narratives about the true purpose of the exercise of power in public space (see Saul and Marsh 2018).

3

A society with secrets

'The Orange Order is not a secret society – *it's a society with secrets*'. This statement, offered to me by several Orange informants as a way to explain what the Order was, and was not, was usually offered as a mild rebuke in response to my clumsily comparing Orangeism with Freemasonry. However, the objection, and thus the rebuke, did not typically emerge from a sense that Orangeism and Masonry had nothing in common, indeed, as described below, the opposite was often said to be the case. What my informants objected to, rather, was, in their view, the false assumption that Orangeism was somehow an entirely closed and private institution which sought to maintain anonymity to the point of invisibility. Nothing could be further from the truth, my Orange informants assured me. After all, Orangemen regularly paraded through Scotland's streets alongside marching bands, and made proclamations in public parks amplified by loudspeakers. Such behaviours, my informants scoffed, were hardly those of a *secret* society.

What, then, does it mean to be a 'society with secrets'? What is it about secrecy that makes us *want* to know what these secrets are? And why is *not* knowing so tantalising, even tormenting? More specifically, within the context of contemporary Scots-Orangeism, how can we make sense of the seemingly contradictory combination of deliberately vociferous promulgation and steadfast ritual secrecy? What happens, for example, to the social and semiotic power of Orange emblems, which, while being central to the secret cosmology of ritual initiation, are also painted on banners several feet high and (literally) paraded through the streets of Edinburgh and Glasgow? And what happens to the neophyte upon being (again, literally) 'let in on the secret' through their admission to an Orange lodge and their participation in Orange ritual?

Georg Simmel's sociological essay 'The Secret and the Secret Society' (1950) provides a useful starting point, being possibly the most cited account of secrecy within the social scientific literature. As a theoretical treatise, it has both breadth and depth. Perhaps its best known and most readily understood claim is that secrecy is a form of boundary-marking insofar as secrecy has the ability to divide the world into those who know the secret, and those who do not. Much has been written about this specific feature of Simmel's argument, which he refers to as 'the fascination of secrecy' (ibid.: 332). Mahmud's penetrating ethnography *The Brotherhood of*

Freemason Sisters, for example, develops this point with real sophistication by showing how female Freemasons in Italy rely on an ethic of 'discretion' (2014: 43–44, passim) to negotiate civic, family, and personal lives lived alongside 'profane' individuals who, as 'non-Mason people', remain 'outside the temple' (ibid.: 38) and thereby outside the Brotherhood. Clawson's historical account of Masonic fraternalism in nineteenth- and twentieth-century America draws on this same aspect of Simmel's work, but does so more bluntly:

> Fraternalism is above all about boundaries, in both their institutional and symbolic aspects … Membership in an organized group of any kind creates a boundary between members and non-members … The ritualized possession and dissemination of secret knowledge substantially strengthens such a boundary. It sets in motion a process of differentiation; the exclusion of some people effects the incorporation of others and bestows a common identity upon them. (Clawson 1989: 248)

Most recently, Önnerfors' account of Freemasonry has drawn again on this aspect of Simmel's argument in order to restate the point that secrecy produces and maintains boundaries:

> For members, who are in possession of (real or imagined) secrets that are only to be transmitted inside the lodge, a line is drawn between freemasons and non-masons; between 'us' and 'them'. These secrets, which are never to be revealed to strangers (or significant others), are in effect privileged knowledge, and represent art that 'transcends the common view', distinguishing freemasons from their fellow human beings. (2017: 56)

My point is not to dispute the role of secrecy in producing exclusivist boundaries, for Simmel himself argues persuasively that one element of the fascination of secrecy is a 'strongly emphasised exclusion of all outsiders' (ibid.). Indeed, so enthralling is this ability to draw boundaries, that it can (and frequently does) eclipse the importance of the content of any given secret. Thus, Simmel observes, children may boastfully chirrup to one another 'I know something that you don't know' even where this 'something' 'is made up and actually refers to no secret' (ibid.). My reading of Simmel, then, partially echoes the authors above in affirming the centrality of boundaries and exclusion, as I outline below, but also especially in the next chapter in relation to fraternity.

Where I depart somewhat from these authors, however, is in their more or less explicit insistence that Simmel's sociology of the secret necessarily places concealment and revelation in a relationship of direct opposition. My objection is that this supposed opposition is founded upon a faulty assumption, namely that the revealing of a secret is a de facto destruction of that secret. Thus, for Önnerfors, 'in freemasonry, secrecy is a constitutive organizational feature and a key element of internal knowledge formation; thus, it is opposed to revelation' (2017: 120). Similarly, for Mahmud, 'discretion, *unlike secrecy*, is characterized not by an exclusive preoccupation with concealment, but rather by a careful balance of both concealments and disclosures' (2014: 180. Emphasis added). Here too, secrecy, in contrast to discretion, is defined as intrinsically opposed to revelation.

But what if this were not always the case? What if we took both of Simmel's suggestions, about the fascination of secrecy and the fascination of betrayal, at face value, and sought to follow them simultaneously? In addition to the necessity of concealment, might we then also observe within secrecy the necessity of revelation? What if, for example, the power of the secret, a Janus-faced power of both 'superiority' and 'self-humiliation', were 'fully actualized only at the moment of revelation' (Simmel 1950: 334)? In this sense, are secrets like money, becoming 'concentrated for the dissipator, most completely and sensuously, in the very instant in which he lets this power out of his hands' (ibid.: 333)? My contention is precisely this, namely that Orangeism does not depend upon keeping concealment and revelation in a relationship of strict opposition, or even in some kind of delicate balance. Indeed, my time among Scottish Orangemen suggested that, very frequently, the reverse was true, that vociferous ritual promulgation and steadfast ritual secrecy *jointly created* the conditions necessary for the Order to be a famous (even infamous) aspect of Scottish society, and, at the same time, a little known and largely hidden 'society with secrets'.

Indeed, unlike Mahmud's Masonic informants, my Orange informants were *not* discreet about their membership of the Order, or about their ethno-religious and ethno-national convictions, nor did they seek to be. Yet, certain key aspects of the ritual expression and symbolic meanings of these convictions were kept avowedly secret, despite much of their content being put on display through Orange marches and other means. Furthermore, many of my informants enjoyed describing to me (often in hushed tones, and with furtive looks over their shoulders) certain aspects of Orange ritual and cosmology. One informant even went as far as pressing upon me official copies of both the Order's *Manual of Ritual and Ceremony for Lodges* and its book of *Laws and Constitutions*. In seeking to make sense of this double reality of Orange secrecy and Orange revelation, I draw inspiration from Simmel's famous essay, not only as a route to tracking the often overlooked 'fascination of betrayal' (1950: 333–334), but also to push Simmel's ideas further, as a way to rethink the relationship between revelation and concealment. In essence, I argue that not only does secrecy contain within it the *fascination* of betrayal, but also the *necessity* of betrayal, a requirement to tell, to blurt out, to 'spill the beans'.

Yet, as I also argue below, spilling the beans is not the same thing as giving the game away. This is because, within the world of secret ritual (Orange or otherwise), revealing a secret does not destroy that secret, because revelation is always partial, secrecy is always layered, and therefore the game is always ongoing. As such, there are constantly more secrets to discover, and thus more secrets to tell, and discover, and tell, ad infinitum. In such circumstances, secrecy does not disappear under the light of revelation, under the gaze of full disclosure, because disclosure is never (and can never) be fully complete. The result is that secrecy is shown not only to be incommensurable, but also, in the very act of any single revelation, still capable of retaining the impetus of the secret. This is the case even where revelation is obtained unwillingly, outside the control of the secret-keepers. Hidden camera footage of various Latter-day Saints temple rituals, for example, is widely available on WikiLeaks as are leaked copies of the ritual manuals of many American fraternities and sororities, such as Sigma Phi Epsilon and Alpha Chi Omega. My suggestion, then, is that this type of once-removed exposé, foisted upon those 'on the inside' and broadcast to those 'on the outside', does little to undermine such organisations, such 'societies with secrets'.

This is the case, I argue below, not only because there are additional layers of secrecy *beneath* any given secret, but so too are there layers of secrecy *within* a single secret. Put another way, pulling back the curtain typically reveals another set of curtains. Revelation, in this sense, is its own kind of secrecy, that is, revelation and concealment do not occur in alternation, or in see-saw fashion, but should be seen as social processes which occur through conflation. Here, revelation can be seen as a kind of ongoing secrecy, whereby parading down the street in an enormous display of Orange symbolism and myth reveals the Institution to be a society with secrets, while still keeping those secrets secret. Conversely, by shifting the focus from public roads to Private Lodges, I try to articulate precisely the opposite claim, whereby secret Orange initiation rituals function as a kind of revelation. Here, the ritual act of 'travelling', whereby Orangemen undertaking the Royal Arch Purple degree re-enact the desert wanderings of the Ancient Israelites, comes to be seen as an engagement with secret esoteric knowledge, which, in line with its structural and thematic indebtedness to Freemasonry,[1] produces revelation not in spite of its secrecy, but in it and through it.

To better explain what I mean here, some ethnography seems needful. I want first to consider how revelation may be seen as a form of concealment by examining the ritual of the Orange parade before going on to consider how concealment may be seen as a form of revelation by examining the rituals that occur within Private Orange Lodges.

Sir Knights on parade

It was a damp and grey afternoon in March 2013 and I was travelling to Glencruix with two prominent Orangemen from Edinburgh for a hundred-and-fortieth anniversary parade of a local Royal Black Preceptory (RBP). 'The Black', as most of my informants referred to it, is a fraternal organisation open only to members of the Orange who have already completed both of the Order's degrees, that is, the Orange and the Royal Arch Purple. In comparison with the Scottish Orange Order's two degrees, the Royal Black Institution has eleven. It is ritually much more elaborate as a result and is often seen to be closer to Freemasonry in this respect. Indeed, one 'Sir Knight' (the title given to members of the Black), who was also a Mason, frequently told me that there was 'only a thin curtain between the Masons and the Black'. Importantly, while the Royal Black Institution in Northern Ireland had a reputation for attracting a more middle-class, sober-minded and evangelical membership, this was not generally recognised as being the case within Scotland. Instead, what differentiated the Black from the Orange within Scotland was its ritual elaborateness, its more formal dress code, and its older membership. It was also the case that these differences in form and structure occasionally exposed social cleavages within the Loyal Orders. Indeed, while members of the Royal

Black Preceptory were keen to impress upon me that being a 'Sir Knight' represented an extension of and an advancement within Orangeism, ordinary Orangemen spoke openly to me about their resentment of what they saw as the 'superior attitude' of those in the Black. Yet, while these differences were real, and should be borne in mind when reading the ethnography below, they should not be overstated, most especially because all members of the Black are also, by definition, Orangemen.

Having been dropped off at the Glencruix Orange Hall where the parade was to start, I was excited to learn that the day's proceedings were scheduled to begin with a short meeting of the Preceptory as well as with a religious service. The hall itself was already humming with activity, as men in black collarettes prepared a central table for the ritual proceedings. The table was draped in a long black and red cloth displaying two key RBI emblems – a skull and crossbones[2] and a red cross. On top of the table were arranged an old Bible, a silver tube containing the Preceptory warrant, a commemorative shield, a gavel used to open and close meetings, and two pictures displaying further emblems, including a sword, a hand, a chequered floor, pillars, and the signature RBI cross and crown emblem. Other Masonic symbols were also prominent; every man, for example, wore a Masonic-style blue apron adorned with a square, compasses, and the letter G, while others also wore this same symbol on their collarette, alongside other Orange and Black 'jewels'. The visual impact of these Sir Knights and their ritual paraphernalia was further heightened by the presence of other esoteric symbols painted onto wall panels within the hall itself. These included the sun, the moon and stars, the 'ladies' tripartite cross-anchor-heart, as well as the depiction of two tents beside a smaller tent – a reference to 2½, the mystical number of the Orange Order, and to the Order's self-identification with Reuben, Gad, and the half-tribe of Manasseh, who led the Ancient Israelites into the Promised Land.

As I stood at the edge of the hall, I watched these men greeting each other with the customary 'grip' used between members, with a thumb pressed between the second and third knuckle of the other man's hand, a further invocation of the mystical number 2½. Shortly after being introduced to the Sir Knights in charge, it soon became apparent, however, that I would not be allowed to observe either the Preceptory meeting or the service, because both would contain rituals which, as a non-member, I was not permitted to witness. Somewhat disheartened, I went through to the social club lounge which was quickly filling up with local Rangers fans ahead of their match against Annan Athletic. These mostly young and middle-aged men drank pints and bantered with each other while they waited for a private coach to take them to Ibrox. The embodied aesthetic contrasted strongly with that next door but was just as striking. Instead of suits and Masonic-style aprons, most of the men wore Rangers tops, and many displayed Rangers tattoos. A different set of customary practices to that in the hall was also notable; as well as the usual pre-match drinking, various forms of ritualised gambling were noticeable. One of the men, for example, was passing around a football scratch card to raise money for their supporters club, with participants paying a pound to select a random team from a list of forty. The person who selected the 'winning team' (as revealed by the scratch-off panel) was given £20, with the other £20 going to the supporters club. A few minutes later, a group of men who looked to be in their early thirties entered the bar, sitting down with a larger group of friends to compare betting slips from the William Hill bookmaker around the corner.

The growing crowd was added to further by the arrival of the Glencruix Protestant Boys, a local loyalist flute band, who had been hired to provide the music for the day's Black parade. Several band members began to put on their military-style uniforms – white peaked caps, white jackets with silver trim, shoulder hoods and large metallic buttons, and royal-blue trousers with white side stripes. Those already in their uniforms wasted little time in ordering pints, a fact which marked this band as less strict than those who insisted their members never drink while in uniform. Pints and bottles ordered from the bar were passed down a line of bandsmen to tables towards the back of the lounge. Not to be outdone, a boy of about twelve years old sat down at a nearby table and opened a bag containing fours cans of Monster energy drink, the weapon of choice for those too young to pass for 18. Those around me seemed unaware of or unconcerned by my presence, with no one asking who I was or what I was doing. The woman in charge of the coach trip to Ibrox was collecting money and ticking names off a list. As she did so, she began recounting the drunken escapades of her recent 'divorce party'. Several of those listening joked with her about various men she might 'go with', to replies of 'he's a bit young!' or 'let me be divorced for a bit first!'

Eventually a few men in black collarettes began to drift through into the lounge, having concluded their Preceptory meeting and service. Their appearance seemed to coincide with the arrival of the bus to Ibrox, triggering an exodus of Rangers fans. With the parade soon to start, the band began to tune up in earnest. Pint glasses were drained and jackets pulled back on as the room filled with the crackle of snare drums and the piercing screech of flutes. Congregating outside, the men organised into a two-line marching formation, while I stood on the pavement taking a few photos. As I did so, the RBP chaplain approached me and explained that he had been told I was a researcher, and proceeded to explain that today's event was best understood as an act of Christian witness, a demonstration of the strength and vibrancy of the Protestant faith in the area.

Soon, the parade was fully formed and ready to set off. At the front of the parade was a Sir Knight carrying an open Bible wrapped in transparent plastic, a practical if unglamorous anti-rain measure. The Bible itself rested upon a wooden tray draped in a small black banner displaying a red sideways leaning cross, the whole assemblage being secured with red cords behind the neck of its bearer. Behind the Bible-bearer were two standard-bearers – to the right a Union flag and to the left a Saltire – and between them, a Sir Knight carrying a bannerette displaying the name and number of their Preceptory. Directly behind the bannerette and standard-bearers marched two lines of high-ranking Sir Knights who occupied various positions within the Grand and District RBI hierarchy (Figure 3.1).

Behind these marched the band, followed by the main Preceptory banner carried on poles and depicting two Sir Knights comforting a bedridden man, framed by the biblical text 'I was sick and ye visited me'. Finally, the rank-and-file Sir Knights who made up the majority of the Preceptory membership processed at the back.

3.1 Sir Knights on parade.

In total, I counted eighty-seven marching. Possibly due to its relatively modest size, the parade had only two police officers assigned to it, one at the very front and one at the very back, while the sides of the parade were flanked by RBP marshals, whose job it was to keep order and maintain a good marching formation.

As the procession made its way around the town, I began to notice discrete groups of supporters following the parade. Two teenage girls walked alongside particular boys in the band. A group of a dozen adults also followed the band, shouting encouragement to those they knew. A lone woman in her twenties smiled and cheered as she repeatedly ran up and down the length of parade. Two men in their thirties, both dressed in tracksuits, and both clearly drunk, danced and swaggered alongside the parade, hollering support to the band and punching the air as the loudest beats of the bass drum reverberated between the buildings. These men attracted frowns from several of the Sir Knights, who knew all too well that such supporters – dubbed the 'blue bag brigade' on account of the off-licence purchases they carried – were the source of much criticism levelled against the Loyal Orders. By the time the parade had made its way through the centre of Glencruix, several shopworkers had emerged onto the street to observe the spectacle, while more deliberate supporters, wrapped up against the cold, stood lining the railings at key intersections, waving to friends and family as they marched past.

As the parade reached the end of its route, the band split into two lines, forming a tunnel of bodies and music through which the Sir Knights marched. As they exited, the Sir Knights divided to form their own tunnel, and stood clapping while this time the band processed down the middle, continuing to play as they went. As the band exited, at the shout of their sergeant, the musicians regrouped into three parallel lines, while the Sir Knights simultaneously organised themselves into three sides of a square, all facing inward. Next, the RBI hierarchy, the bannerette-bearer, and the standard-bearers entered the newly formed square, creating a line of their own, with the exception of the Union flag bearer, who stood in front and to the left of the hierarchy. Separately, standing front and centre, the Bible-bearer entered the square formation, with every Sir Knight directly facing him. Finally, the Master of the Preceptory called out for the national anthem, at which point the Saltire was lowered while the Union flag was kept upright. The band then played *God Save the Queen*, while the Sir Knights, arms held straight down at their sides, sung the words. With the anthem completed, the whole parade formation broke up, and everyone returned to the Orange hall for food and drink.

After a brief moment sitting alone, I was approached by the RBP chaplain, a well-presented man in a blue shirt and clerical collar who walked over and asked with a smile what my 'research findings' had been. Aware that, as yet, I had little in the way of real 'findings' to discuss, I answered his question with a question, by asking why the RBP Bible-bearer had paraded without a plastic crown sitting atop the open Bible, as was present at all Orange parades. By way of explanation, the chaplain simply stated that the RBP was different from the Orange Order in that it was 'less political'. While I could tell that he did not want to elaborate further, our conversation, as it happened, was cut short by a series of presentations to mark the hundred-and-fortieth anniversary of the Glencruix Preceptory, with engraved glass plaques being given to the Grand Master, Master, and chaplain, as well as to Colin, the oldest member, and a close informant of mine from the social club. A Sir Knight from an RBP in Belfast was also in attendance to present the Glencruix Preceptory with a large framed commemorative certificate. After a final vote of thanks, the Master banged the gavel on the table to formally close proceedings, and then, with no warning, asked me to stand to introduce myself. Taken rather by surprise, I hastily explained that I was researching Protestant fraternities in Scotland, thanked the leadership for allowing me to attend the day's proceedings, and said I hoped to be able to speak to some of the Sir Knights during the afternoon's celebration. Despite my feeble words, as was customary whenever a stranger introduced themselves in a formal fraternal setting, I took my seat to loud applause. It only struck me afterwards that the timing of my introduction, directly after the bang of the gavel, was very deliberate, since, as a non-member, I would not be permitted to speak while the formal meeting was still in session.

As the buffet opened, I joined the queue and, along with everyone else, began to fill my paper plate with sandwiches, pies, and chicken pieces. The atmosphere was jovial, with the Sir Knights clearly enjoying the post-parade celebrations. The bar was busy, with most of the men ordering rounds of pints and whiskies, laughing and bantering with each other as they did. Raffle tickets were also on sale, with the prizes being litre bottles of whisky, vodka, and rum. As I prepared to move back to my table, I was called over by Graham, another elderly social club regular, to sit with him and a group of his friends. Glad of this chance to talk to 'ordinary' members, I was soon deep in conversation about the Blacks and the Masons. Graham began by restating his belief that 'there is only a thin curtain between the Masons and the Blacks'. One of Graham's friends, James, a small and wiry man in his sixties, eagerly confirmed Graham's assertion. In an effort to prove the point, Graham's friend began to list the various emblems displayed on his apron and collarette – Noah's ark, a dove with an olive branch, a skull and crossbones, a red cross, and a seven-step ladder. The list seemed to represent conclusive proof for the men around the table, with the mention of each emblem provoking sage nods and murmurs of agreement.

What seemed clear to these men, was not, however, at all obvious to me. Wanting to know more about the symbolic world that these Sir Knights seemed to inhabit with such ease, I asked James about the seven-step ladder, it being the only symbol I could readily connect to the Orange Order, which had a three-step ladder as one of its emblems. Why did the Black's ladder have seven rungs while the Order's ladder had only three? Was this, I reasoned, a way to symbolise the more complex ritual structure of the RBI? The mumbled non-answer that followed made it clear that none of the men around the table wanted to commit to giving me a clear explanation. Undeterred, I suggested a different possible explanation; perhaps this particular emblem was only awarded to Sir Knights upon completion of their seventh degree? Because this suggestion was flatly incorrect, James seemed to feel more able to say so, explaining to me that the emblems did not signify which Sir Knight had passed which degrees, indeed any Sir Knight, no matter how junior, could wear any RBI emblem on their collarette, I was told.

In an apparent attempt to sustain the conversation, while at the same time moving it away from topics deemed unsuitable to discuss with non-members, James turned to me and asked if I had ever thought about joining the Masons. The tone of his query made it clear that what was being voiced was less of a question and more of a direct invitation. As all eyes around the table turned to me, waiting expectantly for an answer, I suddenly became acutely aware that I was probably the only person in the room who was neither a Mason, nor a member of a Loyal Order. My answer, that I hadn't considered joining the Masons, received little reaction, positive or negative. Thankfully, the awkwardness of the moment was quickly dispelled as calls went out across the hall that the raffle was about to be drawn, prompting Graham, James, and the others to turn their attention to the colourful numbered tickets that they pulled from their jacket pockets.

As the afternoon drew on and the rounds of whiskies continued apace, the language became more colourful as the men told jokes and swapped stories. The hyper-masculine, ultra-Protestant mood felt familiar, having the same ethno-nationalist feel to a normal session at the Glencruix Orange Social Club, but with a heightened sense of occasion. As I listened to the men banter, I found myself puzzling over how the fraternal boozing and swearing of these Sir Knights connected to the chaplain's insistence that the day's events represented an act of Christian witness, and I was reminded afresh how utterly different this kind of Protestantism was to the strict teetotalism and reserved piety of the Brethren of Aberdeenshire.

As if to further reinforce the stark contrast, the central aisle of the hall began to fill up with bandsmen scheduled to provide the post-buffet entertainment. The music was incredibly loud, made all the more deafening by the low ceiling. With nowhere to escape, the sound of the drums boomed so loudly that I could feel the reverberations across my chest, while the piercing notes of the flutes rang in my ears long afterwards.

Many of the men, perhaps more used to the volume, seemed to enjoy the experience, tapping their feet and nodding their heads to the tunes. One of the men I had travelled with was obviously less enthusiastic, and checked his watch and phone constantly, looking for word that our lift had arrived to take us back home. When it was finally time to leave, I said goodbye to the men at my table, shaking each of their hands in turn. As I shook hands with James, he looked briefly puzzled, released my grasp, and then attempted another handshake. After a second failed attempt, James frowned, noting that I was not returning his 'grip', gruffly commenting to me that I would need to 'sort out' my handshake. 'Can you tell who is who, by their handshake?' I asked him. 'Oh *def-in-itely!*' he said with a serious expression, drawing out the word in typical Scots fashion. Deciding that a third handshake would be excessive, I gave him a nod, said goodbye to the others, and left.

Loyal Order parades: revelation as a form of concealment

How do secrets work? How are they sustained? Can a secret put on public display still be regarded as secret? Perhaps one way to begin is to acknowledge the challenge faced. Indeed, directing these questions at the topic of Loyal Order parades, and the signs and symbols that surround them, quickly exposes the difficulty of studying secrecy, which, if not an outright oxymoron, is surely a somewhat tense and laboured affair. Yet, this recognition, that studying secrecy is difficult and often tense, helpfully instructs us, I will argue, about how the *revealing* of secrets remains inextricably linked to the simultaneous *concealment* of those self-same secrets, and vice versa. Consider, for example, Simmel's foundational statement that the sociality of secrecy emphasises exclusion (1950: 332). This has, I think, been amply demonstrated by the ethnography above. Remember, for instance, my exclusion from the formal pre-parade meeting and Preceptory service, since this was where secret rituals were to be performed. Remember, too, the simple fact that only Sir Knights and band members took part in the parade, while supporters and observers followed on the pavements, kept at an orderly distance by parade marshals. Finally, remember how secret handshakes or 'grips' acted as a constant affirmation of the in-group, as well as a jarring reminder, when in 'mixed' company, that not all were part of the fraternity.

The ethnography above also demonstrates how the sociality of secrecy cannot be fully comprehended through the trope of exclusion alone. Indeed, the same power within secrecy capable of creating a closed unit – those 'in the know' – also seeks to expand that power by widening the circle of secret keepers, a process which, by definition, is only possible by sharing (that is, by *not keeping*) the secret. As such, the exclusion of outsiders, or 'profane' individuals (see Mahmud 2014: 38), simultaneously galvanises efforts to include, to share, to recruit. Thus, as described in more detail below, while I was not permitted to observe Lodge or Preceptory rituals directly, I was given all sorts of information about Orange and Black ritual normally reserved for members only. Equally, the spatial and symbolic exclusiveness of parading through the streets was itself rendered intentionally porous by those same Orangemen and Sir Knights who were responsible for policing its boundaries. In this sense, the chaplain who described the Glencruix RBP parade as an act of 'witness' appeared to be engaged in far more than an attempt to redefine Loyal Order parades from boozy ethno-nationalist triumphalism to upstanding Christian piety. Indeed, it seems reasonable to take the chaplain's words literally, meaning that the visual and musical spectacle of a parade becomes less of an exclusion, and more of a public invitation, an invitation, that is, for the men of Glencruix to become not only committed Protestants, but also Orangemen and Sir Knights.

Other ethnographic encounters confirmed this interpretation. Just three months after the RBP parade in Glencruix, for example, I was standing at the edge of (yet another) Orange parade, this time in Prestonpans, in the East of Scotland. As the parade moved past, I noticed an Orangeman in full regalia turn and point at one particular spectator, roaring at him 'You should be in here!' The man went red in the face and, with a rather sheepish expression, forced a smile and waved as the Orangeman marched on. Whether the spectator was himself a lapsed Orangeman, or merely a 'loyal Protestant friend' and potential new recruit is beside the point. What this ethnographic moment reveals, rather, is how the exclusivity of membership to 'a society with secrets' is simultaneously compelled to undermine that exclusivity through acts of witness and invitation. In the same way, my failure to reciprocate James's Orange grip led him to invite me to 'sort out' my handshake, a task that would, from his perspective, require my joining not only the Loyal Orders, but also the Masons.

One way to better understand how invitation and exclusion co-constitute each other is through the idea of 'conspicuous secrecy', a comparative term used by Lebra (1972: 204) to describe millenarian movements. While Lebra only uses the term in passing, and offers no definition or even much of a context for its use, I still find the idea of 'conspicuous secrecy' insightful, and want to employ it here as a way to encapsulate how Orangemen, Sir Knights, and spectators experience Loyal Order parades as acts of revelation that are also, at the same time, acts of concealment. I want to do so, furthermore, by connecting the notion of conspicuous secrecy to Simmel's idea of secrecy as 'adornment'. For Simmel:

> The secret also operates as an adorning possession. This fact involves the contradiction that what recedes before the consciousness of the others and is hidden from them, is to be emphasised in their consciousness; that one should appear as a particularly noteworthy person precisely through what one conceals. Although apparently the sociological counter-pole of secrecy, adornment has, in fact, a societal significance with a structure analogous to that of secrecy itself. Adornment intensifies or enlarges the impression of the personality by operating a sort of radiation emanating from it. For this reason, its materials have always been shining metals and precious stones. One may speak of human radioactivity in the sense

that every individual is surrounded by a larger or smaller sphere of significance radiating from him; and everybody else, who deals with him, is immersed in this sphere. The radiations of adornment, the sensuous attention it provokes, supply the personality with such an enlargement or intensification of its sphere: the personality, so to speak, *is* more when it is adorned. (Simmel 1950: 337–340)

Understanding Loyal Order parades as a kind of 'conspicuous secrecy' fits very well, it seems, with Simmel's description of secrecy as an adorning possession. Indeed, not only do such parades use striking colours and loud music to be as conspicuous as possible, but they deliver this assault on the senses to as many people as they can, by marching down the middle of some of Scotland's busiest city streets. Furthermore, the parades I observed during my fieldwork were not only conspicuous in their use of colour and sound, but also in their publicly displaying secret knowledge and esoteric symbols. Think here of the Masonic-style aprons worn by Sir Knights on parade, or the Orange and Black collarettes adorned by countless emblems, often referred to by members as 'jewels'. Just like Simmel's imagined adornments, these Loyal Order emblems are made of shining silver or gold-coloured metals, designed to catch the light and radiate out their symbolic meanings in the process. And these meanings, just like the symbols themselves, are numerous: a pillared archway, a Bible topped with a crown, a burning bush, a set of scales, a coffin, a tripartite spade-pick-rake, a heart pierced by a sword, pursed lips inscribed with the word silence, two hands clasped in a grip, a snake coiled around a wooden staff, a five-pointed star, a sun, a three-branched candlestick, a wheatsheaf, a scroll inscribed with the words Holy Writ, a three-step ladder, a seven-step ladder, and of course, William atop his rearing horse.

Yet, as I have described, enquiring too closely into these meanings can be problematic, and herein lies the seeming contradiction or 'sociological counter-pole' (Simmel 1950: 338) between revelation and concealment, between things which are consciously hidden, and, at the same time, consciously emphasised (ibid.: 337). How can this be? How might something be kept secret, while, at the same time, be paraded through the streets as an adorning possession? The answer, simply put, is that revelation can exist as a form of concealment when the secret in question is put on display but remains incomprehensible. This incomprehensibility, moreover, operates on different levels. The coffin, for example, is likely to be acknowledged as a symbol of death by members of the Loyal Orders and members of the public alike, yet, as described in more detail below, this acknowledgement does not inform the non-member as to the precise embodied and symbolic status of the coffin within Orange initiation ritual. As such, parading through the streets of Edinburgh with the 'adorning possession' of a coffin lid collarette jewel does nothing to undermine the integrity of the Order's system of secret esoteric knowledge about the movement from death to resurrection, or darkness to new light. Indeed, the opposite seems to be the case, whereby parading down the street displaying coffin pins, or the square and compasses apron, exists as an act of conspicuous secrecy, announcing to all who are caught within the 'radiations of adornment [and] the sensuous attention' (Simmel 1950: 340) it provokes, that the bearer, like Simmel's imagined boastful child, knows something that you don't know.

The power of this incomprehensibility is elevated when the symbols on display are sufficiently unusual so as to be protected against commonly available (that is, 'profane') interpretations. Here, it is not even the case that the uninitiated have access to some symbolic surface meaning such as coffin = death, while being left unaware of their ignorance as to the deeper meanings at play. Instead, where the adornment of secrecy is both highly conspicuous and profoundly incomprehensible, the 'radiation emanating from it' (Simmel 1950: 339) seems to be of a different quality, provoking both 'wonder' (Scott 2014) and a sense of semiotic 'defeat' (Gell 1998: 69). I experienced this twofold effect of the incomprehensibility of secrecy during my fieldwork, as I photographed Loyal Order marches and as I talked with Orangemen and Sir Knights. Lodge and Preceptory banners, for example, were often adorned with highly complex assemblages of symbols, leaving the viewer in little doubt that one was in the presence of inaccessible secret knowledge (see Buckley 1985: 9). Consider, for example, the RBP banner below (Figure 3.2), the design of which is used by several Preceptories across Scotland, including not only the red cross, open Bible, and hand, but also the Eye of Providence (or the all-seeing eye), the sun, the moon and stars, Noah's ark, a heart pierced by a sword, the spade-pick-rake, the lamb and flag, a sling and stones, the square and compasses with G, the burning bush, Moses with the Ten Command-ments, Aaron in priestly garb, a skull and crossed bones atop a coffin, and the Latin phrase *In hoc signo vinces* (In this sign you will conquer).

As I photographed this banner for the first time, I remember feeling simultane-ously enthused and discouraged – enthused, that is, by the richness and complexity of Loyal Order symbolism and visual culture, and yet discouraged by the fact

3.2 Royal Black Preceptory banner.

that, to a non-member like me, much of this symbolic content would remain conspicuously secret, and therefore inaccessible. I now recognise, however, that both of these reactions, my sense of wonder and my sense of defeat, were precisely those which this type of revelation-as-a-form-of-concealment sought to elicit. Indeed, as I became encompassed by the radiation of adornment, I felt in that moment as if I knew more than I ever had done about the ritual and symbolic secrets of the Loyal Orders, as their forms and subjects were literally paraded before my eyes. Yet, at the same time, I found myself confronted by how little I knew, both of the actual use of these symbols within the live ritual practice of 'travelling', and of the wider social and ethno-theological assumptions that underpinned their esoteric meanings.

Beyond simply observing Loyal Order marches, this latter recognition was also frequently reinforced to me during discussions with Orangemen on parade days. One such conversation took place while spectating at an Apprentice Boys of Derry parade in Perth, about forty miles north of Edinburgh. Before the parade had formally begun, I had the chance to browse the various loyalist fancy-goods stalls dotted around the edge of the park. As well as the normal collection of memorabilia – Orange collarette pins, Rangers fridge magnets, loyalist flute band CDs and the like – there was a stall selling a large collection of flags, including one which combined the Israeli flag and the Ulster flag into a single design (see Figure 3.3). Intrigued by the combination, not least because I had also seen spectators at Orange parades displaying standard Israeli flags (see Figure 3.4), I asked the vendor what the flag represented, specifically mentioning the blue star in the centre. To my surprise, he suddenly looked embarrassed, and, without mentioning anything about Israel, glanced at the other customers at the stall before hastily explaining that the star was a Masonic symbol. Unsure what to make of his answer, and wanting to know more, I bought the flag, planning to show it to some of my Orange informants in the hope of getting further information.

As it happened, I didn't need to wait long, for shortly after leaving with my vexillologically dubious purchase, I bumped into Wilson Wood, an Orangeman from Glasgow. As well as a member of the Orange Order, Wilson was also an ardent Rangers fan, an amateur historian with a passion for studying the Battle of the Somme, and an ex-paramilitary prisoner, having served time during the Troubles for his involvement in the UDA. After showing me his purchases – two baby bibs, one inscribed with the words 'Orange feet all over Ulster' and the other 'Proud to be a Baby Prod' – Wilson introduced me to several friends visiting from Northern Ireland, explaining to them that I was doing research on Orangeism in Scotland, and was also, more importantly, 'a real gentleman'. With Wilson having vouched for me, the stern expressions of his friends seemed to relax somewhat, and the conversation began to flow. Seemingly in response to Wilson's description of my research, one of the men, called Sam, began detailing to me how the plight of Rangers Football Club was due to the bigotry and jealousy of its enemies. Having admitted that I had thought Rangers had been relegated to the third division due to financial irregularities which had forced the club into liquidation, Sam patiently explained that this was simply being used by Celtic as an excuse: 'You see, Rangers

3.3 Loyalist fancy-goods stall showing Ulster/Israeli flag.

3.4 Spectators at Orange march holding Israeli flag.

is an institution, like the Church of Scotland, and they want to get rid of us' he said with real resentment.

As if to further illustrate his point, Sam went on to describe how the marble staircase at Ibrox was based on the design of a Masonic temple, a claim, I learned later, which had been popularised by the circulation of an art print called 'Entrance to the Temple', depicting Masonic tools on the black and white tiled floor of the main entrance hall to the stadium. Puzzled by the links Sam was forging between Rangers, Freemasonry, and the Church of Scotland, but sensing an opportunity to learn more about the flag I had just purchased, I asked Wilson and Sam about it. Was I right that the design combined the Ulster and Israeli flags, and if so, what did this combination mean? Sam was quick to answer, but, as with my conversation with the flag seller, no direct mention was made of the modern state of Israel. Instead, Sam answered my question in a way that to me felt rather cryptic, but to him, I am convinced, seemed straightforward. The Red Hand of Ulster, he stated with complete confidence, could be found in the Bible, as could the other British nations of England, Scotland, and Wales. 'Why do you think the Ulster flag has the Star of David on it?' he asked me with a knowing look, as if the answer were obvious.

Far from being an outlier, my conversation with Sam resonated with other discussions I had with Orangemen, both on parade days, and more generally. Travelling back to Edinburgh after the Perth Apprentice Boys of Derry parade, for example, I found myself in conversation with Bill Paterson, a high-ranking Orangeman, Sir Knight and Freemason, and Trevor, a new recruit whose Orange initiation was scheduled for the following week. As Elizabeth, Bill's wife, and a prominent Orangewoman in her own right, drove us down the motorway, Trevor announced that he was a fan of Barry Rumsey Smith, a Protestant preacher from New Zealand who had published several books on 'end times' prophecy. Trevor explained that, having read Smith's books on the New World Order and the Illuminati, he found his teaching persuasive. Soon, he and Bill were deep in conversation about what connection, if any, there was between the Freemasons and the Illuminati, with it becoming clear that Bill was less persuaded by Smith's views than Trevor was. As Trevor spoke, he passed me his phone, which displayed a web page listing various topics of Smith's teachings, one of which stated that Freemasonry was satanic. Knowing Bill to be a Mason, I quietly suggested to Trevor that Bill probably wouldn't like that particular aspect of Smith's work, to which Trevor agreed.

Changing tack slightly, Trevor asked Bill what he knew about the Knights Templar, who were they, and what did they do? Bill, who had obviously done some reading of his own on the topic, confidently explained that the Knights Templar were a group of medieval warrior monks who protected various Christian shrines around Jerusalem. When the Templars grew in power, Bill continued, they attracted the attention of various Popes, who began to persecute them. This hostility, Bill said, culminated in the Templars being rounded up and tortured into making false admissions that they were secret Satan worshippers. Some believed, Bill added, that the remnant of the Knights Templar existed as the present-day Freemasons, although there was no evidence to suggest that this was true, he stressed. 'Still' said Elizabeth, breaking a silence that she had kept from the start of the conversation, 'Roslyn Chapel is a fascinating place to visit!'

Taken together, these two conversations represent something of the richness and diversity of the kinds of esoteric knowledge that frame Loyal Order parades as occasions for the display of conspicuous secrecy. As is the case when parading behind a banner which contains close to twenty secret emblems, discussing the anti-British conspiracy against Rangers FC, or the Masonic architecture of Ibrox, or the Old Testament origins of the Red Hand of Ulster, or the descent of British peoples from Ancient Israel, allows the speaker to use words, just as the marcher deploys symbols, to adorn themselves in secrecy. By its very nature, this adornment of secrecy seeks to be conspicuous, that is, it seeks to display something of the *actual content* of the secret to a watching and listening public, a public, importantly, who are not themselves 'in the know'. In this same way, Bill, Trevor, and Elizabeth were able to talk of the New World Order, the Illuminati, the Knights Templar, papal persecution, contemporary Freemasonry, and Roslyn Chapel in ways which adorned them in the garb of secret knowledge, thereby revealing to a non-member such as me something of this knowledge while simultaneously keeping that knowledge secret.

The result is that revelation-as-a-form-of-concealment maintains the integrity of secrecy by ensuring that what is spoken of remains largely unintelligible to the uninitiated, allowing some commentators to blithely dismiss such semiotic displays as 'mumbo jumbo' (Gray 1972: 172). Here, talk of the biblical origins of the Red Hand of Ulster reveals nothing to the hearer without their first being steeped in British Israelite theology, a set of teachings popular among some Protestants in the nineteenth century, and many Orangemen today, which claimed that British peoples made up part of the Ten Lost Tribes of Israel, and were thus literally, *biologically*, part of God's chosen race. More specifically still, Sam's claim about the Red Hand remains unintelligible until one combines the broad claims of British Israelite theology with a specific reading of Genesis 38, a passage which details how Judah's son Zerah had a scarlet thread tied around his hand during his birth, only to lose this birthright upon the 'breach' of his twin brother Perez. 'Why do you think the Ulster flag has the Star of David on it?' Sam asked me with a knowing look, a look which affirmed our mutual recognition of his knowledge and my ignorance.

In such moments, as I was immersed in the sphere of secret knowledge radiating outwards from the 'enlarged' and 'intensified' personalities (Simmel 1950: 340) belonging to Sam, Bill, and my other informants, my ignorance concerned not only the hidden meanings of flags, but also of Rangers FC, Masonry, the Knights Templar, and Roslyn Chapel, among many other things. And I wondered at my informants' knowledge of such matters, of their being able to see that which was veiled, a wonder made all the more intense by my own lack of knowledge. This sense of wonder was thus a double sense of knowing that I *did not know*, while, at the same time, knowing that others *did know*. I had come to realise that the Orange Order was indeed a 'society with secrets', for this society had been revealed to me through parades and other means, and yet had remained secret, hidden, concealed. Occasionally, moreover, this wonder of being confronted by conspicuous secrecy gave way to a more pessimistic sense of defeat, whereby my knowledge that I did not know collapsed into a sense that I *could not know*, and *never would know*, not, that is, until I entered into the Orange Order as an initiated member. Only then could the defeat of conspicuous secrecy – of revelation-as-a-form-of-concealment – be itself defeated. It is to this that I now wish to turn, that is, to the secrecy of Orange initiation rituals and to concealment-as-a-form-of-revelation.

From Orangemen to Royal Arch Purplemen

When Orangemen in Scotland describe the Order as a 'society with secrets', what they primarily have in mind are the secrets which surround Orange degrees, and particularly the ritual of the Royal Arch Purple. Crucially, unlike in Northern Ireland, in Scotland, the Royal Arch Purple does not form a parallel Order as is the case with the Royal Black Institution. Instead, in contemporary Scottish Orangeism, the Royal Arch Purple forms a second degree *within* the Orange Order proper and has done so since 1902 (Malcomson 1999: 20). As such, while many Orangemen in Northern Ireland choose not to join the Royal Arch Purple Order, all Orangemen in Scotland undertake the ritual of the Royal Arch Purple simply by virtue of being Orangemen, normally (but no less than) three months after their first degree initiation as an Orangeman. By giving an account of the ritual of the Royal Arch Purple, then, what I am detailing is foundational to the experiences of *Scottish* Orangemen, even if not all of their Northern Irish brethren recognise it as foundational to their Orange experience.

This difference in structural organisation needs bearing in mind for two reasons. First, the difference highlights a theological and ideological disagreement between some Orangemen in Northern Ireland and in Scotland over what kinds of ritual activity are appropriate for Protestants to engage in. In Northern Ireland, where 'born again' evangelical Protestantism is still comparatively influential, both within the Orange Order (McAuley et al. 2011: 158), and within society at large (Ganiel 2008, Bruce 2009), there are some Orangemen who feel that the elaborate Masonic-inspired rituals and oaths of the Royal Arch Purple Order are unbiblical, even sinful, both in form, and in their bearing on the free expression of Christian conscience. As such, because the Orange and the Royal Arch Purple Orders are separate in Northern Ireland, some evangelicals may choose to join the former but not the latter, while others, influenced by more uncompromising evangelical exposés of the Loyal Orders, such as those published by W. P. Malcomson (1999, 2009), choose to stay away entirely. In Scotland, however, the situation is different, not only because the Orange and the Royal Arch Purple are contained within the same Order, as two successive degrees, but also because the influence of evangelical-ism is much less marked. As a result, not only would it be practically impossible for Orangemen in Scotland to function within the Order without eventually taking the second (Royal Arch Purple) degree, but, more importantly, such a course of action would be unlikely to occur to most rank-and-file Scots-Orangemen, since the kinds of objections raised by Malcomson (ibid.) struggle to get a hearing in the absence of a strongly evangelical subculture.

The second reason for bearing in mind these structural and theological differences is that, in addition to my ethnographic data and my use of the Loyal Orange Institution of Scotland *Manual of Ritual and Ceremony for Lodges* (1983), it has also been necessary to make use of Malcomson's *Behind Closed Doors* (1999). This is because Malcomson's book offers the only detailed published description of Royal Arch Purple ritual. Gray's account, for example, only states that 'the initiation ceremonies of ... the Purple [in the nineteenth century], were ... much more challenging and frightening than the present rituals' (1972: 210). And while Buckley's account does confirm that Orange Order 'symbolic and ritual activity' (1987: 31) draws on images from 'the Israelites' sojourn in the desert' (ibid.: 32), he only manages to state that 'the Royal Arch Purple ritual is something of an ordeal for the candidate' (ibid.). Such lack of scholarly sources has forced me to draw on other published accounts of the ritual.

However, my using Malcomson as a source is somewhat problematic, not only because he refers to the Royal Arch Purple Order in Ireland, but also because the rhetorical language he offers is so fiercely critical of the Order that it encumbers his otherwise accurate description of the ritual. Indeed, Malcomson decries the Royal Arch Purple ritual as 'heathenish' (16), 'injurious' (19), 'abhorrent' (20), 'deceptive' (25), 'distorted' (31), 'offensive' (32), 'occult' (35), 'humiliating' (36), 'obscene' (37), 'vulgar' (37), 'pagan' (38), 'superstitious' (38), 'repulsive' (39), 'blasphemous' (41), 'pathetic' (42), 'pitiful' (42), 'dismal' (42), 'undignified' (43), 'intimidating' (50), 'Satanic' (50), 'sinister' (54), 'apostate' (56), 'godless' (56), 'irreverent' (56), 'indecent' (57), 'unseemly' (58), 'polluted' (60), 'idolatrous' (61), 'corrupt' (62), 'devilish' (77), 'barbaric' (78), 'repugnant' (78), 'wicked' (78), 'monstrous' (79), 'abominable' (79), 'debased' (80), 'bloodthirsty' (80), 'degrading' (82), and 'ungodly' (86), in addition to over forty other negative descriptors.

Clearly, as a 'born again' evangelical who considers the Royal Arch Purple (RAP) 'an anathema to holy living' (80), Malcomson is no friend of the Orange Order, either in Ireland or in Scotland. Nonetheless, once stripped of its adjectival flourishes, the bare description Malcomson offers of the Royal Arch Purple ritual appears accurate. This seems to be the case not only because, as an ex-member, Malcomson himself undertook the degree and would have witnessed others doing so, but also because several Scots-Orange informants of mine, having read Malcomson's book, objected not to his factual account of the ritual, but to his religious reinterpretations. Indeed, with the exception of differing levels of violence associated with various aspects of the ritual (which may be accounted for both historically and regionally), those Scots-Orange informants of mine familiar with Malcomson's work begrudgingly admitted to me that the details of the degree had been *described* correctly, even if they had been *interpreted* wrongly as a result of, in the words of one informant, Malcomson's 'Pentecostal over-excitement about devils'.

By drawing on Malcomson's description in *Behind Closed Doors*, in addition to the GOLS *Manual of Ritual*, as well as the *History of the Royal Arch Purple Order* (Murdie et al. 1993), a book written by and for RAP members in Ireland, what I present below is as full and accurate an account of the Scottish Orange Order's second degree as I am able to give, without having myself been initiated into or present at a live performance of the ritual itself. Such is the nature of doing research on the lived experience of secrecy (see Gray 1972: 209, Mahmud 2014), that one has to rely on critical exposés and leaked documents, as well as developing the kind of rapport which offers partial revelations, half-answered questions, and furtive non-denials. To be clear then, my description below is given neither as a member nor an ex-member, but as a non-member, that is, as someone who has never joined the Orange Order at any level, and thus remains 'outside the camp'. As such, while all of the information contained in my description has already been published elsewhere (and does not, as a result, represent any real breach of secrecy), what is new is its being collected together into one source, and written up as a neutral account.

According to the *Manual of Ritual,* the degree takes place within the Orange hall, with only those who have already received the RAP degree (and are wearing 'the Regalia laid down') permitted to be present, a process managed by the 'Tylers', or door guards. Because the initiation often follows a normal lodge meeting, brethren present who have not received the RAP degree are dismissed by the Worthy Master of the Lodge with the words 'please come before the Bible, make the sign of salvation, take off your collarettes, and retire' (Loyal Orange Institution of Scotland (LOIS) 1983: 31). The Lodge Secretary then reads the names of the candidates, and the Worthy Master asks if the candidates have been Orangemen for at least three months, and if they have 'proved themselves worthy of advancement in our Order' (ibid.). Next, all those present 'give the RAP Degree Annual to the Deputy Master', that is, the annual secret password, to confirm that they 'are RAP men and as such are entitled to remain in the Lodge Room'. With all brethren upstanding, the Worthy Master then 'raises the Lodge' with the words:

> I Bro. .... by virtue of the authority vested in me hereby declare this Lodge No. .... raised from the First or Orange Degree, taking this for our sign and G .... for our password and raised to that of Second or R.A.P. Degree taking this for our sign and G .... our password. I hereby declare the Lodge legally raised. (ibid.: 32)

The Worthy Master, Deputy Master, and Substitute Master then use gavels to give a series of knocks, followed by this prayer offered by the Worthy Chaplain:

> Gracious and Almighty God, Thou who didst raise a wall of water round Thy servants the children of Israel and who didst save them from the power of Pharaoh and the perils of the Red Sea; by whose Divine permission in after times our liberties have been secured and our most holy religion preserved; continue unto us Thy Almighty favour; may Thy heavenly love be the arch of our protection, and the increase of Thy Spirit amongst us the special mark of our seal and covenant with Thee. These, with all other needful blessings, we humbly beg through the mediation of Jesus Christ our Lord and Savious (*sic*). Amen. (ibid.)

The Worthy Master then says: 'I now declare this R.A.P. Lodge open in due form – GOD SAVE THE QUEEN' (ibid.), followed by a knock, whereupon the brethren resume their seats. The Worthy Master continues with the words: 'Worthy Deputy Master will you come forward to the Dias and act as supporting pillar to the keystone,

Worthy Substitute Master you will act as Guard to the inward camp' (ibid.: 33). Just as cryptically, the next lines of the *Manual of Ritual* simply state that 'the mysteries and solemnities will then be explained which will be followed by the explanation of the working sign of the Degree' (ibid.). The Worthy Master then reminds the brethren present of the solemnities of the degree, and requests that 'order and decorum be observed' (ibid.). Next, the Worthy Master asks that the Lodge Room be prepared for 'the travel'; a square path of leaves and twigs are strewn on the floor, running along the inside walls of the hall, an arch is erected, and other items described below are set in place. While these arrangements are made, the sponsors enter the anteroom to prepare the candidate by asking him to take an 'obligation', or oath to:

> Solemnly declare that I will faithfully keep all matters and things confided to me as a Royal Arch Purpleman from an Orangeman, as well as from one who is not a member … Nor will I admit … any member into any other Degree purporting to be part of the Orange system, than the Orange and Royal Arch Purple, which are the only Degrees recognised by the Orange Institution of Scotland. I will be true and faithful to every Royal Arch Purpleman in all just actions, and will not wrong or know him to be wronged or injured, if in my power to prevent it. And I will not be present and see this Degree given, unless the Candidate pay such sum as the Grand Lodge shall authorise to be charged, which sum I have paid. All this I declare with a firm resolution to abide by and keep me steadfast in this my Royal Arch Purple obligation. (GOLS 1983: 35)

The candidate then has his socks and shoes removed, his left shoe replaced on his bare foot, his trouser legs rolled up above the knee, his left breast exposed, a blindfold put on, and a purple ribbon attached to the front of his shirt (ibid.: 35). Once the hall has been prepared, the sponsors then knock for admission and the candidate is led into the centre of the hall as the assembled brethren stand singing '*I to the Hills Will Lift Mine Eyes*' (LOIS 1983: 33). The candidate is then instructed to kneel on their right knee and repeat with the chaplain and the brethren the Lord's Prayer. The *Manual of Ritual* then simply states: 'The Travel of the Degree will here be gone through' (ibid.). Because this ritual 'travel' is not detailed at all in the *Manual*, what follows below is taken mostly from Malcomson's account, stripped of its critical language. Importantly, what Malcomson describes coincides with the little that my informants shared with me about the ritual, namely that the ritual involves the candidate re-enacting the Old Testament Exodus of the Ancient Israelites (see Cairns and Smyth 2002: 150) as they 'travel' from Egypt into the Promised Land by perambulating the hall along a path of twigs and leaves.

The ritual continues with the candidate having their naked left breast pricked three times with a sword or other sharp implement, symbolising a sting to the conscience as a reminder not to divulge the secrets they are about to receive (Malcomson 1999: 49–50). Following this, the candidate then hears a 'loud and unexpected bang' (ibid.: 51) symbolising God's wrath towards the children of Israel for their disobedience. This bang, according to one of my informants, was achieved by dropping the lodge's banner poles on the floor. The candidate is then made to kneel and pray for deliverance, after which they are led around the hall three times, walking partially barefoot along the path of foliage as a symbolic re-enactment of the desert wandering of the Ancient Israelites during the Exodus. During these three circuits of the hall, the brethren whip the candidate's legs with brambles, while imitating goat bleats (ibid.: 55). Malcomson continues:

> The three journeys of the candidate round 'the wilderness' are accompanied by three great falls symbolising the candidate's victory over death and the grave. As the candidate is led round the room the first time he sustains a fall, and is raised up, on the words '*O death, where is thy sting?*' He is then led round again and receives the second fall, and is raised up, on the words 'O grave, where is thy victory?' [...] On the third and final lap round the Chapter room, the initiate sustains his third and final fall, which results in him being ... raised to a figurative new birth by the five points of fellowship. This practice involves the candidate being raised from the floor [and]... the brother raising the candidate then embraces him and acts out each individual point of fellowship. (ibid.: 58–59)

These five points of fellowship, which differ slightly from Masonry, are explained as follows: (i) foot to foot – to serve fellow Orangemen; (ii) knee to knee – to pray for fellow Orangemen; (iii) hand in hand – to go hand in hand with fellow Orangemen in all just and lawful actions; (iv) breast to breast – to keep the secrets of fellow Orangemen, murder and treason excepted; (v) left hand behind back – to be true and faithful to fellow Orangemen (ibid.: 59–60). After the five points of fellowship have been explained, the candidate is then led to within five feet of a ladder (or set of steps) symbolising Jacob's ladder. Next the candidate advances two and a half steps towards the ladder, representing the mystical number of the Orange Order, and the tribes of Reuben, Gad, and the half-tribe of Manasseh who led Israel into the Promised Land (ibid.: 65–66). The candidate, still blindfolded, is assisted in climbing each step of the ladder (representing faith, hope, and charity, as well as youth, manhood, and age), while the chaplain reads 1 Corinthians 13: 13 (ibid.: 68, 70).

At the top of the steps, the candidate kneels on a representation of a coffin while the assembled brethren gather behind the steps and unfold a large blanket. The candidate, with his back to the blanket, crosses his arms and is asked 'In whom do you put your trust?' After answering 'God', the candidate is pushed backwards, caught in the blanket, and is then roughly kicked and tossed in a part of the ritual called 'riding the goat' (ibid.: 73, see Gray 1972: 210). This aspect of the ritual may explain the prominence of goat symbolism within the Order more generally. Not only is the image of a goat used as a collarette emblem, but also provides the inverted initials of a central password of the Royal Arch Purple ('The-Ark-of-God') representing g-o-a-t spelt backwards, a detail told to me by an Orange informant prior to my reading Malcomson's account of the same (1999: 66).

After 'riding the goat' the candidate is wrapped up in the blanket and taken to the north-west corner of the hall where he is warned of 'the three great and solemn penalties' (ibid.: 77) for divulging the secrets of the Order or its members. These include, first, having one's throat cut, one's tongue torn out, and one's body buried in the sands of the sea, second, having one's left breast torn open, and one's heart and vitals fed to vultures or wild beasts, and third, having one's body severed in two, the parts separated and burned, and the ashes scattered to the four winds (ibid.: 77–78). Having heard these penalties, the candidate has something cold and something hot pushed into their chest. After this, the candidate is asked 'what do you stand most in need of' to which he is prompted to answer 'light' (ibid.: 83–84). The candidate's blindfold is then removed, an act which symbolises their having received spiritual enlightenment. In a further symbolic warning to keep the secrets of the Order, the candidate, having his blindfold removed, is immediately faced with three of the brethren pointing weapons at him – a spear, a sword, and a gun (ibid.: 88). Following this, the candidate is shown a three-branched candlestick, ('spiritually') representing 'the three great lights' of the Father, Son, and Holy Ghost and ('carnally') the Sun, Moon and Stars, and the Worshipful Master (ibid.: 89).

At this, the conclusion of the 'travel', the *Manual of Ritual* states that the candidate is told 'Brother, you have been deemed worthy of advancement in our Institution and have been promoted, according to your desire, to the Royal Arch Purple Degree' (GOLS 1983: 33–34). The candidate is then given a collarette with the words:

> I now invest you with the badge of that Degree sincerely trusting that your greater power of serving this religious and loyal Brotherhood will by you be well and duly employed, and that as your opportunities will now be advanced with your station amongst us, so also you will increase in diligence, in season and out of season, to promote the interests of true Protestantism in your native land, and to the ends of the earth and may God enable you to do so. (ibid.: 34)

The *Manual of Ritual* continues: 'two Instructors will then repeat the Lecture and Candidates will be instructed on the signs, grips and passwords, including the working sign. Emblems will then be explained' (ibid.). As was the case with 'the travel', however, the actual content of this lecture is not included within the *Manual* itself. Malcomson's account gives some indication, stating that 'after alluding to the Bible and other symbols' the candidate hears 'a solemn address on the subject of death' (100), including these words:

> Whilst reflecting upon the solemn thought of death, this degree teaches us that all must die; we follow our brethren to the brink of the grave, and, standing on the shores of a vast ocean, we gaze with exquisite anxiety until the last struggle is o'er. We see them sink into its fathomless abyss, and feel our own feet sliding from the precarious brink on which we stand. A few more suns, and we too shall be whelmed neath death's awful wave to rest in the stilly shades, where darkness and silence shall for ever reign, around our melancholy abode. But this is not the end of man, nor the glorious aspirations of the brethren of our Order, who, true to their principles, look for the manifestations of the three great lights in the east, representing Death, Resurrection, and Ascension. And bid us turn our eyes with faith and confidence beyond the silent grave towards the dawn of a glorious eternity. Finally my brethren, by the careful regulation of our lives, pondering well our words, and the cultivation of brotherly love and loyalty, we may obtain our Great Grand Master's approbation. Then, when the embers of mortality are faintly glimmering in the sockets of existence, and death does come, and we are ushered into the Grand Lodge above, there shall be revealed to us the real secrets of the Ark of God; and we shall realise, for all eternity that the Great Jehovah has been our Guide. (ibid.: 100–101)

The *Manual of Ritual* concludes by stating that the brethren then stand to '*Abide with Me*', after which the Master, taking the candidate by the right hand, says: 'In the name of the Brethren, I bid thee heartily welcome, believing that you will continue with unabated earnestness and zeal to love the Brotherhood, Fear God, and Honour the Queen' (GOLS 1983: 34). The candidate is then welcomed into the lodge, after which the chaplain concludes with the Aaronic blessing. Finally, the Master lowers the lodge from the second to the first degree, giving the required knock with his gavel (ibid.).

Orange initiation rituals: concealment as a form of revelation

If, in acts of conspicuous secrecy, Orangemen parade the emblems of their Order through Scotland's city streets without betraying the secrets they contain, then what kind of secrecy can be said to be at work within Orange initiation rituals? Put another way, if the work of Orange banners is to hide and conceal, what is the work of the blindfold? My suggestion is that the blindfold, and the Royal Arch Purple ritual generally, exists as an inversion of the Orange banner, showing concealment to be a form of revelation, just as parading shows revelation to be a form of concealment. This is, I argue, because the secret ritual of the second degree is experienced by Orangemen not as an adorning possession to be flaunted, or an act of witness to be proclaimed, but rather as a series of mysteries to be traversed and pondered. Crucially, where the adornment and witness of parading is undertaken in a spirit of outward-facing engagement for the benefit of a (largely uninitiated) watching and listening public, the 'mysteries and solemnities' (GOLS 1983: 33) of the second degree are strictly reserved, by sword-carrying Tylers no less, for Royal Arch Purplemen only. As such, the ritual described above faces inward, concealing from all outsiders, including the liminal neophyte, both the true meaning of 'The Travel' and the (suddenly transformed) identity of those who undertake it.

Consider, first, the candidate, whose experience is veiled, both literally and symbolically. Entering an anteroom separate from the main hall where the ritual occurs, the candidate must swear an oath of loyalty to a segment of the brotherhood they have not yet joined, just as they had to swear an oath of loyalty to 'every Brother Orangeman' (GOLS 1983: 25) before they completed their first degree, and thereby entered the Order. While evangelical critics like Malcomson view this as an inappropriate act of concealment – 'here the Order unfairly demands adherence to an oath the contents of which the initiate knows nothing about' (1999: 26) – emic perspectives on Orange ritual and fraternalism lead to a different conclusion by strongly emphasising trust in both God and the brotherhood. From this standpoint, being confronted with the requirement to state one's willingness to undergo an unknown ritual, or vowing to keep secret a body of esoteric knowledge one has not yet been taught, exists as an honourable act of concealment, which, by virtue of remaining veiled, reveals to the candidate their need to trust, and thereby also makes plain their status as one who, being uninitiated, remains symbolically 'in the dark'.

This concealment-as-an-act-of-revelation concerns not only the theological and fraternal ideal of trust, but also addresses the embodied experiences of lostness and helplessness. Here, by donning a blindfold, the candidate's symbolic experience of being left in the dark also becomes physical. Being led into the centre of the hall, being pricked on the chest by a sword, hearing a loud and unexpected bang, walking barefoot on twigs, being whipped by brambles, pushed backwards off a platform, and tossed and kicked in a blanket, all while blindfolded, reveals to the candidate that they are indeed helpless, and must trust those around them to lead them through the ritual. Perhaps more importantly, by being blindfolded, by having all that is around concealed, the candidate has the fact of their spiritual blindness revealed to them in physical form. Here, the blindfold becomes an embodied metaphor, inverting the work of the Orange banner. Indeed, rather than using public display as a way to *hide* the mystery of secret emblems, the blindfold takes away sight as a way to *impart* secret esoteric knowledge. Thus, by asking 'what do you stand most in need of?' and then prompting the candidate to answer 'light', the candidate is helped first to identify and then to alleviate the lostness and helplessness that is dramatically enacted through the physical stumbling of their perambulation. In short, the blindfold becomes an aid to sight, that is, to being shown the Order's mysteries and let in on its secrets.

Importantly, this concealment-giving-way-to-revelation only ever takes effect, as in Masonry, with the benefit of hindsight. Indeed, once the candidate's blindfold is removed, they can expect to understand little of what they see immediately afterwards, be it candles burning on a three-branched candelabrum, or three brethren facing them with raised weapons. Even after the ritual is completed, and the explanatory catechism and lecture delivered, the revelation such words offer does not stand alone or complete, but is continually added to as the Orangeman moves from being a 'candidate' who has just undergone their own initiation, to a full RAP man who has, over time, witnessed the blindfolded initiations of many others.

Of course, noting the interplay between concealment and revelation (in this case, concealment *as* revelation) is not to suggest that such revelation is offered to all equally, in the same manner, or on the same terms. Consider, here, the fact that the very first action of the second degree is to expel all Orangemen who have not yet become Royal Arch Purplemen. So important is this separation of Orange from Purple, that, after the Worthy Master's initial order for all first degree Orangemen to retire, the Deputy Master is then subsequently instructed to 'uplift the R.A.P. Degree Annual' (GOLS 1983: 32) to make doubly sure that 'all Brethren present are R.A.P. men and entitled to remain' (ibid.). Here too we see concealment functioning as a kind of revelation, with first degree Orangemen, who have had the RAP ritual concealed from them as a result of their expulsion from the room, gaining a simultaneous revelation of their non-RAP status. Just as the blindfold physically demonstrates to the candidate their pre-Purple blindness, so too does the experience of finding oneself shut out of the hall as the ritual proceeds. Divested even of one's collarette, the most outwardly visible adorning symbol of one's membership, the first degree Orangeman has it revealed to them that they are, as yet, not ready to wear a blindfold or to experience the mystical vision that it affords.

Outside of the ritual of the second degree, there are other equally stark acts of separation which divide not Orange and Purple, but Orangemen and Orangewomen, and, indeed, Orangemen and non-Orangemen. One brief ethnographic example will suffice to highlight both. I was in a large hall in the basement of Glasgow Evangelical Church, nicknamed the 'Orange Kirk' due to its connections to the Order, awaiting the commencement of a special 'banner unfurling' service. I was with Bill and Elizabeth, a prominent Orange couple, who were talking with several Orangemen about the upcoming Scottish independence referendum. As more Orangemen streamed into the hall, several men began setting out the room for a lodge meeting, with two long tables standing opposite each other, flanked at right angles by two rows of chairs. A smaller table draped in a Union flag stood in the middle of this square, and atop it rested a Bible, into which an old collarette had been inserted, functioning as a kind of bookmark. As another man began to set out a gavel, a *Ritual Manual*, and a warrant tube atop a table which had been draped in a cloth displaying a lodge number, it became clear that a formal Orange meeting was about to begin.

Several of the men started to banter with Elizabeth, a high-ranking Orangewoman, that it was time for her to leave. 'It's a men's meeting!' one man said, only half-jokingly. 'No women allowed!' another man chuckled. Possibly because I was a stranger, no one commented on my presence. 'Am I not allowed to stay? Am I being banished?' Elizabeth said in mock hurt. Then, turning her attention to me, she said 'Come on Joe, we're being banished! I'm a woman, and you're not a member, so we can't stay'. As we made our way upstairs to the main sanctuary, we met several Orangemen going in the opposite direction, late for their meeting in the downstairs hall. 'We've been banished! We've got to go upstairs and freeze in the church!' Elizabeth declared to them as they hurried past. Despite her good humour, it was clear that Elizabeth felt acutely the experience of being ejected from the hall before the Orangemen's meeting had begun. In addition to the inescapable fact of the institutionalised gender inequality of the situation, whereby Orangemen may attend Orangewomen's meetings, but not vice versa (see MacPherson 2016), it was clear that Elizabeth also shared my more general sense of frustration at being reminded afresh of our limited access to the ritual world of the Orangemen downstairs.

Like the first degree Orangemen shut out of the wilderness 'travel' of the second degree, having these rituals concealed from us revealed much about the inferiority of the vantage points we were forced to adopt. That my own vantage point on the Order's rituals was limited was a fact of which fieldwork among Orangemen frequently reminded me. These reminders came in different forms. My attempts to pry into the secret rituals of the Order often elicited awkward non-answers, seen, for example, in my attempt to learn more about the emblem of the seven-step ladder from a group of Sir Knights in Glencruix. Others were more frank in their answers, stating clearly that they could not share certain information with me because doing so would break the oaths they had taken when they were initiated. Requesting a list of Bible references used in the RAP ritual elicited several such refusals. However, when an Orange informant of mine finally agreed to provide me with such a list, its value proved limited. The reality was that I had simply been given a list of books, chapters, and verses, which, stripped of all mystical knowledge and internal explana-tion, stood like an incomprehensible banner on parade, revealing to me only my ignorance of the 'live performance' (Önnerfors 2017) of Orange ritual.

A different realisation of the inferiority of my vantage point on the secret world of Orange emblems and ritual came when spending an afternoon with Orangemen who were distributing 'independent unionist' leaflets during the Scottish referendum campaign. Walking back down the path of one particular house, Russel, the Orange-man I was with, closed the front gate to leave, and, as he did so, pointed out its design, which clearly and prominently featured a square and compasses with G, the kind of which was used not only by Masons all over the world, but also by every Sir Knight on parade. Having confessed that I hadn't seen the symbol when first walking up the path, Russel laughed and said 'You have to be born free to see the signs'. Here, the fact that such symbols remained concealed from me by hiding in plain sight revealed to Russel (and reminded myself) that I was not an Orangeman, or a Sir Knight, or a Mason. More than this, my failure to spot the presence of such an emblem revealed something deeper about the status of my 'birth' and the state of my 'sight', since, as a non-member, I was metaphorically (and in some cases, literally) blind to signs which stood, wrought in iron, in front of my very eyes (see Mahmud 2014: 42). What Russel's comment demonstrates, then, is that, for initiated Orangemen, the eyes are indeed a window onto the soul, yet what one *cannot* see, what remains *concealed*, is just as revealing as what one can see.

In sum, taking part in secret Orange rituals was imagined by those who did so (and often by those who did not or could not) to change one as a person. This is because, in the social functioning of concealment-as-a-form-of-revelation, what initiated members see (and what uninitiated members cannot see) is shaped by a confluence of secrecy, ignorance, and mystery. In contrast to Mitchell, then, I do not regard these as 'relatively specific, defined, and bounded intellectual deprivations of three sorts' (1993: 7), but as a trinity of partially overlapping intellectual and perceptual experiences. Thus, as my encounter with the garden gate taught me, secrecy can share with ignorance an experience of 'the absence of knowledge accessible via at-hand epistemologies' (ibid.) Similarly, as my experience of receiving the unenlightening list of RAP Bible references made clear, secrecy can share with mystery a recognition that certain facts and forms of knowledge 'may be accepted as irreducible to conventional discourse' and must therefore be 'encountered on their own terms' (ibid.: 8). Secrecy, then, is a kind of ignorance (*my* ignorance) just as secrecy is also a kind of mystery – a mystery which may be entirely hidden from the uninitiated, while remaining partially veiled, but, at the same time, progres-sively revealed, with the benefit of hindsight, to initiates.

Conclusions: secrecy, enlargement, and confirmation

The result of all of this, of the double interplay between revelation-as-a-type-of-concealment and concealment-as-a-type-of-revelation, not only concerns the *sight* (or blindness) of the individual, but also the *size* of the world they inhabit. This is because, to return to Simmel, what we find within the sociality of secrecy, and what we observe within Scots-Orangeism understood as 'a society with secrets', is a process of enlargement. Indeed, for Simmel:

> The secret produces *an immense enlargement of life*: numerous contents of life cannot even emerge in the presence of full publicity. The secret offers, so to speak, the possibility of a second world alongside the manifest world; and the latter is decisively influenced by the former. (1950: 330. Emphasis added)

For Orangemen, a key part of this enlargement was experienced fraternally, opening up a new (or 'second') world of engagement within a brotherhood, which, as explored in the next chapter, offered much social and familial engagement to those who were members. Yet, as described above, another key aspect of the enlargement of secrecy was experienced ritually, symbolically, even cosmologically. The ritual of the parade, for example, allows every Orangeman to enter a second world of banners, collarettes, emblems, band tunes, flags, parade formations, and platform declarations. This world, displayed materially and symbolically to spectators as an adorning possession, remains, as a direct result of the 'full publicity' (Simmel 1950: 330) of this revelation, simultaneously concealed. Furthermore, by shifting our focus from the adornment of emblems on parade to the 'mysteries and solemnities' (GOLS 1983: 33) of re-enacting the Exodus wanderings of Ancient Israel, we see the workings of revelation and concealment in reverse. Here, the 'travel' of the Order's second degree creates for Orangemen 'a secret and sacred space' (Önnerfors 2017: 64) which uses concealment as a form of revelation. As such, the ritual of the second degree allows Royal Arch Purplemen to enter again this 'second world' of Orange esotericism – a world of swords, ladders, coffins, and candles, as well as oaths, passwords, grips, and catechisms.

Importantly, whether this second world, this 'society with secrets', is only partially entered into via the kind of concealment afforded by Orange banners, or is entered into more fully via the revelation afforded by a blindfold, the fact remains that the world is reframed, as are those who find themselves enveloped (to a greater or lesser extent) within its radiation and influence. For my Orange informants, this 'reframing' was experienced not as a transformation but rather as a confirmation. This is because the double work of Orange secrecy (the work of establishing the knowledgeable membership of the initiated and exposing the ignorant non-belonging of the uninitiated) does not, in direct contrast to Freemasonry, seek to remake the world in its own universalist image, but rather seeks to preserve and protect it as it already is, in all its ethno-religious and constitutional distinctiveness and divisiveness. This is crucial, for in contrast to Masonry, Orangeism does not seek to foster 'a morality that can be experienced by everybody' by forging 'universal solidarity' via the creation of 'a common spiritual/mythical past … for the benefit of humankind as a whole' (Önnerfors 2017: 61). Instead, Orange ritual secrecy – through parading, and through lodge initiations – seeks to advance a Protestant morality for a Protestant people. As described in the next chapter, this morality produces not 'universal solidarity' but ethno-religious fraternalism based on hatred as well as love. Equally, the Orange rituals described above do not celebrate a common spiritual past shared by all of humankind, but instead celebrate a very particular past, that is, of the

Reformation, the Battle of the Boyne, the Battle of the Diamond, and, more mythically, the history of the Exodus and the entry into the Promised Land.

How, then, is this morality, fraternity, and history experienced, in and through ritual secrecy, not as a kind of transformation, but as a kind of confirmation? The answer is that the Orange rituals described above, functioning through both revelation-as-concealment and concealment-as-revelation, take the Protestant religion upon which they are constructed to be a kind of essence, or an immutable substance, which may be recognised, identified, reframed, and even awoken, but not brought into existence *ex nihilo*. Indeed, as Russel explained to me, 'you have to be *born free* to see the signs'. Within Orange ritual, this birth involves new entry into the brotherhood, but this in no way equates to new entry into Protestantism. Indeed, before a candidate may undertake even the first degree of Orangeism, the Master of the Lodge must be satisfied that the man to be initiated is *already* 'a true and faithful Protestant, and a loyal subject' (GOLS 1983: 25). Here, ritual confirms one's Protestantism, and perhaps even consolidates it, but it does not create it.

So too within the second degree, where, in line with the British Israelite theology at its centre, the candidate is mystically identified with 'Brother Joshua' and with Reuben, Gad, and the half-tribe of Manasseh, an identification that is ritualised through their barefoot perambulation, as explained in the catechism that follows:

> Q. How were you dealt with?
> A. *I was led three times around the wilderness, once across the Red Sea, and the river Jordan, to testify that I was duly prepared to receive the degree of a Royal Arch Purpleman.*
> Q. What befell you on the way?
> A. *I was beaten and torn by brier and bramble, bitten and stung by fiery serpents, I received three great and mighty falls with my back to the earth, and my face towards the heavens.*
> Q. What did these three great and mighty falls represent?
> A. *Three times the children of Israel fell in the wilderness for their disobedience unto the Lord.*

Here, the candidate finds their ethno-religious identity confirmed, but not transformed. As British Protestants they are conjoined to Ancient Israel as divinely elect, and, in the minds of my informants most committed to British Israelite theology, are shown to be literally, biologically, God's chosen people. 'Why do you think the Ulster flag has the Star of David on it?' Sam asked rhetorically. So too while parading, where a different kind of ritual perambulation – this type being done always behind that Orange symbol of Protestantism, the open Bible – again confirms the Orangeman as one who will always 'support the Protestant religion' and 'give no countenance … to the unscriptural, superstitious and idolatrous worship of the Church of Rome' (GOLS 1983: 26). Walking within the ranks of parading Orangemen allows these men to affirm their fraternity with each other, while at the same time proclaiming to all those 'loyal Protestant friends' spectating that this too is their proper place. 'You should be in here!' the Orangeman shouted to his (undoubtedly Protestant) friend who stood, at that moment, outside the brotherhood. The sentiment was clear; you *should* be in here because, like me, you are a British

Protestant man who is loyal to the Queen; you *already* meet the qualifications of an Orangeman and stand in need of nothing more than to have your pre-existent Protestant religion and ethnicity *confirmed*; come, join our brotherhood and enter into our society of secrets.

Yet, it stands to reason that such confirmation necessarily goes hand in hand with disconfirmation and disqualification, for every potential Orangeman accosted while spectating at the edge of a parade with the words 'you should be in here!' is likely to be matched (outnumbered even) by those with neither the ethno-religious background, nor the personal desire required to be let in on the secret. As already described in Chapter 2, these un-Orange and anti-Orange persons (Catholics, Scottish nationalists, republicans, Celtic fans, and others) are imagined to have secrets of their own, secrets said to conceal a nefarious plot against British Protestantism. Yet, more than this, as described in the next chapter, it is the identification and exclusion of such nefarious anti-Orange individuals, which, in part, constitutes the very essence of this 'society with secrets' as a society, that is, as a religious and political fraternity driven not only by love, but also by hate.

Notes

1 Yet, as non-Orange Freemasons are generally quick to point out, the kind of Orange revelation gained here remains radically different (in tone, in scope, and in purpose) from the Masonic quest for enlightenment. While still a form of revelation only truly accessible *after the fact*, that is, through reflection and hindsight, Orange secrecy-giving-way-to-revelation seeks to produce not a Masonic-style universalist humanistic fraternity under the generic and spiritually all-inclusive Grand Architect of the Universe, but instead seeks to produce a highly particularistic form of Protestant fraternity open only to men with a certain ethno-national pedigree.
2 Which Gray reports as being a symbol of Sir Knights' mourning of Joseph, 'who was sold into slavery in Egypt … [and] was given up for dead' (1972: 217).

4

Fraternity and hate

It was a cold, dry afternoon in late December 2012, and I was in Glencruix, North Lanarkshire, an ex-mining town in Central Scotland. As I walked up the road to the Orange hall and social club, I was acutely aware of the possibility of being seen. The distinctiveness of the hall's architecture was difficult to miss: a huge Masonic-style blue-painted metal arch stood beside the hall itself, which was bedecked in Scottish, Ulster and Union flags, as well as a mural of King Billy, Prince of Orange. The fact that the vast majority of Scots would immediately identify such a building, along with all those who entered it, as belonging to the Orange Order, and to its political and ethno-religious ideology, made me nervous. Glancing at passers-by as I turned under the arch, I wondered if I had been noticed and silently judged. It was certainly not beyond the bounds of possibility given the Order's less-than-positive public reputation, a fact already documented in earlier chapters. Although my concern was surely heightened by the fact that this afternoon was one of my first trips to the Glencruix Orange Hall, it is also true that, while over time the club and its members had become familiar to me, I was never entirely free of that mild anxiety-cum-guilt whenever I walked under the large blue arch, as if entering a place that was both hazardous and unsavoury.

Importantly, this unflattering prejudice of mine – honesty demands that I call it such – was both confirmed and challenged by my time spent in Glencruix. My prejudice was confirmed, then, by the words and actions of many of the men who came to the club to drink and socialise. As described below, these informants spent much of their time joking, gossiping, debating, and storytelling in ways that almost invariably placed Catholics and Roman Catholicism centre stage when the strongest abuse was being meted out. Indeed, some of the men I came to know during my time in Glencruix openly admitted to me that they were – in their own words – 'bigots' who 'hated Roman Catholics'. One aim of this chapter, then, is to make sense of how such words and lives can be made to fit within certain understandings of what a good Protestant life looks like.

Of course, there was much more going on within Glencruix than self-proclaimed hatred and bigotry, and it was here, within the very same Orange social club, that my prejudices about the hazardous and unsavoury nature of Scots-Orangeism came to be challenged. Frequently, the challenge came as a result of hearing different, more tolerant, attitudes spoken by various regulars to the club, sometimes by those same individuals who had previously articulated such strongly sectarian vitriol. These seemingly contradictory speech acts were justified in diverse ways, drawing on everything from differing familial experiences of 'mixed marriages', to conflicting footballing loyalties, to contrasting personal interpretations of British history, Protestant theology, and Orange initiation vows. My prejudice also came to be challenged indirectly, by observing over a period of five years the embodied fraternalism which existed between my informants, binding them together as fellow Protestants and fellow Orangemen. From this perspective, the full complexity of the social lives lived within the Glencruix Club was not, and *is* not, comprehensible through a narrow focus on anti-Catholicism, no matter how enthusiastically this theme was embraced by many of my informants there. This is because fraternal love is the other side of sectarian hate; both matter, and deeply. In presenting the ethnography below, I have sought to balance these expressions of love and hate in an explicit attempt to avoid emphasising one to the analytical neglect of the other. This seems important, not only in light of Faubion's (2001: 32–33) warning against pathologising religious activism (in this case, by viewing Orangeism as singularly and pathologically hateful), but also because, by neglecting fraternalism, one would be unable to understand what it is that hate actually *does* for many of my Orange informants. To better explain this generative power of Orange hate, I want first to present two ethnographic encounters.

Difference, hate, and the morality of detachment

First, consider this early trip to the Glencruix Orange Social Club in December 2012. Despite having only been there a few times, most of the faces were familiar, it being the same group of a dozen or so retired working-class men who came every Thursday to drink and chat. The men ordered single measures of whisky topped up with water. One face I didn't recognise was Don's, a hard-bitten man in his seventies. Dennis, who managed the club, called Don over to talk to me as soon as he came in the door. Don and I shook hands and we sat down at one of the corner tables. As was often the case during such first encounters, Don asked me a few questions about who I was and where I was from, designed, in part, to ascertain if I had a Catholic or a Protestant background. I explained that I was raised in Canada but had lived in Scotland all my adult life. I was also careful to mention that I was a Presbyterian, as was my wife, and that she had been raised in Northern Ireland, where religiously mixed marriages were still unusual and sometimes risky. By this point I had known Don for less than two minutes, a fact which I still find astonishing, given what he said next. Levelling his gaze at me, Don described how, when his children first started socialising with the opposite sex, he sat them down and explained two basic rules, which, in his own words, were as follows: 'no blacks and no Roman Catholics'. He continued, 'I said to them, "if you bring a black or a Roman Catholic into this house, or if you marry a black or a Roman Catholic, you can find somewhere else to live"'. And with that, he stood up, and walked to the bar.

While I was certainly taken aback by such an open admission of racism and sectarianism made to a complete stranger, what I found most striking was the way in which Don's comments chimed with the other men's wider conversations that afternoon. At one point Dennis announced that he considered himself to be a bigot. He explained how some Orangemen claimed that they didn't hate Roman Catholics as *people*, but merely hated their *religion*. Dennis couldn't agree with that perspective, he explained, because he *did* hate Roman Catholics as people. 'I do! I do! I hate Roman Catholics! And I'll tell you why – it's because Roman Catholics hate Protestants and hate the Orange Order as much as it is possible to hate anything!' His diatribe was lengthy and wide-ranging, detailing, among other things, how Hitler was a Catholic and how the Catholic Church agitated to create both World Wars. As Dennis spoke, he grew red in the face, swore frequently, and occasionally pounded his fist on the table, causing the men's drinks to bounce and tremble. Composing himself, Dennis repeated his explanation that he was simply taking his cue from Catholics' hatred of him. His logic was clear; such hatred was mutual, and, by extension, was expected and acceptable, perhaps even honourable.

Second, consider this trip to the Glencruix Social Club more than two years later, in February 2015. I had spent the day in Glasgow, having managed to get a ticket to the most infamous derby in Scottish football. Known as the 'Old Firm', this meeting of rival teams was also, crucially, a meeting of rival fans, supposedly that of 'Catholic' Celtic supporters and 'Protestant' Rangers supporters. After ninety minutes of energetic flag-waving, passionate hate-filled chanting, and rather lacklustre football, as predicted, Celtic beat Rangers 2–0. As the crowds, kept entirely separate by the overwhelming police presence, slowly dispersed into the surrounding streets and pubs, I made my way by train to the Glencruix Club to say some goodbyes before taking my flight back to Belfast.

When I arrived, the club was packed with drunk, but philosophical, Rangers fans. While I recognised some of the older faces, there were many younger people I didn't recognise. Everyone had watched the game on the club's flat-screen TV, and, by the time I arrived, seemed fully immersed in boozing and singing the night away. The jukebox was blaring popular loyalist tunes full of anti-IRA and anti-Catholic lyrics. The noise was so loud that it made conversation nearly impossible. Quickly realising that I was unlikely to get much contact with the club regulars, I offered my commiserations to a few, and then headed for the door. Just as I moved in that direction, however, Dennis, possibly remembering that I was leaving possibly for good, grabbed me by the arm, pulled me close and roared in my ear: 'Joe, Joe, we don't dislike them, we fucking hate them! We fucking hate them!'

That the 'them' Dennis was referring to was Catholics, should, I hope, be clear. But what are we to make of all this? In what sense do Orangemen like Dennis and Don think of themselves as Protestants in relation to the Roman Catholic 'other'? While knowing their words to be offensive, in moments of more sober reflection, Dennis and others repeatedly urged me to give what they called a 'warts and all' account of life in the Order. On one level, then, it seems that what Dennis was asking me to do was 'take seriously' his world of hate. But can anthropology really take such a world 'seriously', *in its own terms*? Can such sectarian vitriol, for example, be properly described as forming a kind of 'ethical life'? If it *can* be described thus, how might anthropology not only learn *about* it, but learn *from* it? (Laidlaw 2014: 46). It is questions such as these which this chapter will explore.

Running in parallel to Laidlaw's description of 'the ethnographic stance' as 'gaining an imaginative understanding from the inside of a set of ethical concepts and of a form of life, and to learn to use and think with those concepts' (ibid.: 45), the beginnings of a possible answer have already been discussed in the Introduction of this book, as found in Webb Keane's suggestion that 'we shouldn't decide in advance what ethics looks like' (2014: 444). If Keane is right (and I will argue below that he *is*), then the task confronting both the anthropology of Christianity and the anthropology of morality is challenging. It seems that what the anthropology of morality must do is grasp the nettle by developing ethnographically informed theories of ethics capable of encompassing social exclusion and religious bigotry within anthropological accounts of 'The Good'. The alternative, of course, would be to reject Keane's proposal by insisting that inclusivity, tolerance and respect be regarded as essential elements of 'The Good'. This position, however, would seem to force anthropology into theorising Orange morality as 'evil' (Csordas 2013, Olsen and Csordas 2019), which, by definition, would require an abandonment of 'the ethnographic stance', and a foreclosure of the possibility of learning anything about the ethics of Orangeism 'from the inside' (Laidlaw 2014: 45).

Another step towards developing an ethnographic theory of the goodness of religious bigotry is taken, I suggest, by Candea et al. in a recent volume on the subject of 'detachment' (Candea et al. 2015). Not only do these authors affirm that detachment is 'a real phenomenon' worthy of being 'taken seriously' (ibid.: 16), but they do so by, among other things, compiling a list of sixty possible usages of the word (ibid.: 17–18). I have written elsewhere, as part of an analysis of Exclusive Brethren theology and sociality (Webster 2018), how this typology might helpfully be focused on a much smaller number of concepts that share a closer evaluative family resemblance – one that emphasises Brethren preoccupations with detachment from worldliness via acts of 'closing off', 'turning away', 'distancing', 'removal from public view', 'separation', and 'renunciation' (ibid.). The same initial point can be made regarding the Orange Order, where a shorter list of evaluative modes can be seen at work in the ethnography presented above (some of which also find resonance among the Exclusive Brethren). Here, we might understand Orange detachment from Catholicism as emphasising 'untouchability', 'exclusion', 'expulsion', 'disgust', and 'repugnance' (ibid.).

Yet, such lists do not seem to take us very far (ethnographically or theoretically), providing, as they do, little more than a catalogue of possible 'symptoms', with all the analytical problems that a normative epidemiology of this kind draws us into. While Candea and his co-editors seem to agree on this point, my second step beyond typological definitions is rather different to theirs. Indeed, where their broader aim is 'to highlight the ways in which, as conceptual abstractions, the foundational status of the terms sociality, relationality and engagement naturalises a relational view of the world that then acts to render detachment as a specific and secondary quality' (ibid.: 18), my aim (couched in their terms) is to give an account of what Scots-Orange detachment does socially and morally.

In pursuing this objective, I argue below, how, in empirical terms, Orange fraternity and sectarian hatred co-constitute each other, that is, fraternity and hate make each other possible, socially and morally. My argument here orbits around two simple ideas; first, that people like people like themselves and, second, that people dislike those they regard as somehow fundamentally different from and opposed to themselves. Following Barth's classic thesis in *Ethnic Groups and Boundaries* (1969), attributions of human difference – made by recourse to highly specific cultural details as attached, for example, to ethnicity, religion, gender, sexual preference, political allegiance, nationalism, localism, class, or age – engage in a kind of double work, producing groups of people who are 'us' (similarity) and groups of people who are 'not us' (difference). Put another way, the Orange Order know who they are only and insofar as they also know who they are not. This (somewhat reactionary) process of identification-in-the-negative seems particularly acute among Protestant cultures whereby the legacy of the Reformation defines the 'us' of similarity as, in the first instance, a product of the 'not us' of Catholicism. Thus, according to the origin myth of the Reformation, Luther knew which door to nail his *Ninety-five Theses* to well before they were fully written, for it was this Catholic door which materially and symbolically pre-existed his own nascent Protestant disputations. Importantly, while much of the content of the Wittenberg myth is fanciful, the ideational impetus of the Reformation did indeed emerge from a logical negation, that is, Protestantism was defined by what it was not and what it did not do; it *was not* Catholic, because it did not grant indulgences. (Very similar binary processes of identification-in-the-negative are also central to footballing rivalries, and these are discussed below).

Yet – and this is important for the wider relevance of the argument of this book about exceptionalism and apophasis – while Orangeism seems to be a particularly clear and forthright example of identity formation by logical negation, such processes are not at all restricted to Orange, or indeed Protestant, culture. Just as my Orange informants defined themselves as Protestant unionist loyalists via (very) frequent negative references to Catholic nationalist republicans, similar apophatic processes are observable across much of the ethnographic record. Ayala Fader, for example, documents how Hasidic Jewish women in Brooklyn define themselves and their families in oppositional (and openly racist) terms to their 'goyim' or Gentile neighbours (2009: 160). In the same way, Maryon McDonald (1989) examines negative identity through language politics among Bretons in her aptly titled monograph *We are not French!* So too among travestis in Brazil, who, Kulick (1997) describes, experience gender differently to the more common male–female dichotomy, insisting instead that all human bodies can be classified as either men or not-men. What all of these cases show, then, is the continued relevance of Barth's boundaries thesis, and thus the near-universal occurrence of the sociality of exclusionism, even among those whose morality has come to be defined by the principle of inclusivity.

Barth was certainly not the first to indicate the social importance of what I have been referring to as apophasis. Indeed, such logical negation, I argue below, returns us to the very origins of the anthropology and sociology of religion – to Hertz's

1909 account of right-handedness and religious polarity, and, by 1912, to Durkheim's account of the 'negative cult' in *The Elementary Forms of the Religious Life*. As such 'the sacred thing is *par excellence* that which the profane should not touch' (Durkheim 1915: 40. Emphasis added). My point here is not to rehearse old debates about the validity of the sacred/profane distinction, but instead to suggest that their being defined in the negative (X is that which is *not* Y) is suggestive of a more fundamental role given over to negation (in general) than many in anthropology recognise.

In the analysis that follows below, I take inspiration from Kenneth Burke's writing on 'the negative', and specifically his claim that all human language and symbolism, by creating a strong distinction between sign and referent (that is, the sign is *not* the referent), concomitantly produces a state of affairs whereby 'every experience will be imbued with negativity' (1966: 469). However, where Burke's focus rests on theorising the negative origins of language per se, my focus is upon the negative content of social identification, of knowing which group one belongs to by first knowing which group(s) one does *not* belong to. My claim is that collective identities, Orange or otherwise, are unavoidably marked by apophasis, whereby positive statements about who one *is* are impossible to make, they literally 'cannot be said' (see Franke 2007), in the absence of what I suggest are sociologically parallel statements made in the negative. Just as the sign is not the referent, Group A is not Group B, thus being 'not B' is an essential part of 'being A'. Examples of this kind abound. A Jewish person is Jewish because they are not a Gentile; a Muslim is Muslim because they are not a kafir; a Christian is Christian because they are not a heathen; an atheist is atheist because they are not religious; a virgin is a virgin because they have never had sex; a vegan is a vegan because they do not consume animal products; a teetotaller is teetotal because they do not drink alcohol; organic food is organic because its production does not use artificial fertilisers, pesticides, growth regulators, or feed additives.

Of course, these examples do not suggest that positive statements about group belonging are somehow permanently unsayable. The kind of apophasis I have in mind, then, unlike certain discourses on divine transcendence found within apophatic theology (see Franke 2007 vol. 1), does not refer to being silenced by the sublime, but refers instead to a process whereby positive group belonging is always experienced *alongside* negation and non-belonging. My claim is that neither the negative nor the positive are socially dominant but are instead mutually dependent on one another. As such, while I address a similar empirical phenomenon to that investigated by Stasch (2003) my argument runs somewhat counter to his. Indeed, I argue that Orange fraternity (that is, Orange engagement) is constructed through intense reciprocal *dis*engagement from the Catholic 'other'. In this sense, while Stasch is primarily concerned with the 'engaged separation' (2003: 325) between sons-in-law and mothers-in-law, I am interested in engaged connectedness between Orangemen and their fellow brethren as they *simultaneously* engage in collective acts of detachment. Similarly, while Orange sociality may be described as engaged in 'cutting the network' (Strathern 1996) via its exclusion of Catholics, it is equally true that Orangeism is engaged in highly selective acts of *sticking*, of joining up previously separated Protestant individuals, through the fraternal establishment of an Orange brotherhood.

What, from this standpoint, does a good Protestant life look like? What I argue below is that for many of my Orange informants in Glencruix and elsewhere, a good Protestant life is constituted by a 'loving hatred' – a love of ethnic Protestantism that is itself socially and emotionally inseparable from a hatred of ethnic Catholicism. Conversely, we can also speak of a 'hateful love', whereby, in this context, hating Catholics becomes a key way to express and experience love for fellow Protestants. Such statements are anthropologically possible, however, only where hate is conceptualised not so much as 'good' (although this certainly seems to be the case for Dennis) but as part of 'The Good' (capital T, capital G), that is, as a real and compelling element of human ethical life. To make this case, some more ethnography seems needful, starting with an account of hateful enmity, then moving to consider loving fraternity, before ending with some final remarks on how these two forms of sociality may be seen as co-constitutive.

I had spent the morning at Olympia House, the Order's headquarters in the East End of Glasgow, interviewing the only Orangeman widely known to be a vocal and committed member of the Scottish National Party (discussed in Chapter 5). As had become routine, my plan for the afternoon was to travel to Glencruix, to spend some time at the Orange social club. Derek Reid, a heavily built ex-coal miner in his seventies who volunteered in the archive during my time at Olympia House offered me a lift, as he lived in a village just outside the town. As we drove into Chapelgeddie – the 'Catholic' town adjacent to 'Protestant' Glencruix – Derek pointed out a pub called the Tall Elm. 'That's a right papist pub' he said with disgust, describing how drinkers would congregate outside during Orange parades simply 'to defy you'. 'They would try to break your ranks', Derek recounted, an act which involved Tall Elm patrons deliberately walking through the lines of loyalist flute bands as they marched in formation. This provocation, Derek explained, frequently ended in fights on the street.

Recounting this story led Derek to tell another, this time about a Royal Black Preceptory parade in Bridgeton, which was forcibly halted by two groups of Catholic men simultaneously emerging from two different Catholic pubs, one at the top of the parade and one at the bottom, trapping the marchers in the process. Things turned violent, Derek said, when one of the men tried to wrestle the Union flag from the hands of the standard-bearer, triggering a brawl between loyalist bandsmen and the pub-goers. Because of his leadership within the Bands Association at the time of the incident, Derek was asked to conduct an investigation. This ended with the band being entirely exonerated. Derek's final conclusion was as simple as it was unequivocal: 'they had to defend their flag'.

When I arrived at the club, the men were discussing an Orange parade that had occurred the previous weekend in Glasgow, which had had concerns hanging over it as a result of it being scheduled for the same afternoon that Celtic was to be awarded the Scottish Premier League trophy. While the parade passed without incident, the men noted with incredulity the large police presence outside a particularly infamous Celtic bar along the parade route which had had its licence revoked; 'it's closed now – it's been closed for ages!' commented one of the younger drinkers. 'They could do with closing some of those other ones, with the fenian flags outside!' another added. These comments drew Dennis's attention, who began speaking again about how much he hated the fact that there were Roman Catholics attending the pensioners club in the main hall adjacent to the bar where we sat. 'It does my head in!' he bawled, 'if it were up to me I would fling them oot!'

The discussion continued along similar lines for most of the afternoon. At one point Dennis began to fill me in on the entertainment put on for social club members the previous Saturday night. They had booked a singer who worked in the loyalist music scene, touring clubs and bars across Central Scotland. Comparing him to similar acts they had booked in the past, Dennis was enthusiastic: 'I really think he's up there. He's maybe no as good at the bigotry, but I think he's fantastic!' The fact that bigotry was mentioned by Dennis as an important skill seemed odd to nobody, nor was it seen as a humorous quip. On the contrary, Dennis was being matter-of-fact, for alongside instrumental and vocal ability, bigotry was seen as a key measure of talent for any loyalist session musician. Later, the conversation drifted to stories about previous trips to Ulster for parades; where to find accommodation, where the good pubs were, which towns were Protestant and which were Catholic, all featured in the men's discussion. 'You're better going to Ballymoney – Ballymena is full of fenians!' one man declared. Another man agreed, stating that Ballymena had changed: 'it used to be a Protestant town, but now there are more Tims than Protestants!' One of the younger men nodded, drawing a local comparison: 'it's the same in Glencruix – you never used to see any Celtic scarves; now there's loads of them!' The conflation of Celtic Football Club and Catholicism was, from the perspective of these Orangemen, absolute and unchallengeable. Indeed, to suggest otherwise, that Protestants might legitimately choose to support Celtic, was tantamount to a kind of ethno-religious blasphemy.

As more of the social club regulars arrived, several rounds of whiskies and lagers were bought, and the tone of the conversation became more strongly anti-Catholic. The highly publicised case of Cardinal Keith O'Brien, Scotland's most senior Catholic, took centre stage, provoking revulsion and intrigue in equal measure. Just weeks before, it had been reported in the Scottish media that, having first denied accusations of sexual misconduct with four men, O'Brien had since issued a press release stating 'I … admit that there have been times that my sexual conduct has fallen below the standards expected of me as a priest, archbishop and cardinal … I will now spend the rest of my life in retirement. I will play no further part in the public life of the Catholic Church in Scotland'. A late development in the story, that O'Brien had been ordered back to the Vatican having initially planned to retire in Scotland, provoked particular offence. All the men agreed that it was outrageous that O'Brien had been permitted to leave the country and had been spared being defrocked or charged with any offences by the Vatican. The collective view was unanimous – the Roman Catholic hierarchy was engaged in a concerted effort to avoid scandal and prosecution by keeping O'Brien safe within the religious and legal confines of the Vatican. 'That shows what they think of it! He should be thrown out!' one man concluded, with a shake of the head.

The discussion continued by confirming the popular Orange view that Scottish politics and Scottish Catholicism were cut from the same nefarious cloth: 'it's the same with the government! It's full of poofs!' one man offered. In reply, another man proclaimed 'I still think there is something to come up about that fucker [Pope Benedict] who resigned', arguing that his resignation, and his decision to remain living within the Vatican, was motivated, as had been suggested regarding O'Brien, by a desire to avoid prosecution. Possibly noting my surprise at this suggestion, he continued by asserting that Pope Benedict knew much more about the child abuse scandal within the Catholic Church than he ever admitted, and criminally chose not to act, a claim mirrored by Bryce's *Irredeemable Papacy* which accuses his successor, Pope Francis, of 'protecting thousands of evil Priests who have raped and molested boys and girls' (2018: 23). Referring back to O'Brien, a third man directly accused the Church of a cover up: 'they're just trying to get him out the road, but it's not going to work! It's gonna come back to bite them!' With murmurs of agreement, another man offered: 'that's why Benedict isn't going to leave the Vatican, because the polis and the FBI canna touch him!' In response, one of the men offered a different interpretation, suggesting that the history of fascism, not the history of sexual abuse, is the cause: 'That Benedict was in the Nazi youth, the Hitler Youth! There's something still to come out about him!' Despite these interpretative differences, the collective opinion of the assembled drinkers was clear, regardless of the specific reasons for keeping Cardinal O'Brien and Pope Benedict within the Vatican, the underlying motive of the Catholic hierarchy was deeply corrupt.

In the middle of this discussion, one of the younger men, a son of one of the regulars who was also present that day, told a story about how, while working on a building contract at a Catholic school, he was amazed to see a full-size mannequin of the Queen surrounded by a large display of royalist memorabilia set up in the main reception area. 'I said to one of the teachers "what's that about?" and she said "she's my Queen too." I had to take my hat off to her' he said with real amazement. 'Not all Catholics are republicans' another man said with a serious expression. 'I ken that' he replied, 'I had to take my hat off to her. "You ought to get that in Chapelgeddie!" I said to her'. Despite (or possibly, in order to spite) this brief moment of relative tolerance, Dennis announced to the assembled drinkers that he had recently obtained an organ donation card, on the reverse side of which he had written 'No Catholics allowed'. When a few of the men laughed, Dennis angrily insisted that he wasn't joking, emphatically restating that he did not want any of his organs to go to Catholic recipients.

While shocking at the time, as the months passed, I came to realise that the tone and content of that afternoon's debate and storytelling was typical of the men's interactions in the Glencruix Orange Social Club. Indeed, over the course of the most intensive window of my fieldwork in Glencruix, for twenty-six months between December 2012 and January 2015, I observed many similar performances of hatred and enmity, which, taken together, show Renton and Sick Boy's impromptu rendition of 'No More Catholics', in the recent sequel to *Trainspotting*, to be a relatively tame portrayal of an Orange social club. Outside the world of cinema, common derogatory names for Catholics included not only 'fenian' and 'Tim', but also 'bead-rattling bastard' – referring to the Catholic rosary – and 'IRA bastard', used if the person was deemed to have not only Catholic but also republican sympathies. While some of this language of hate was undeniably angry, much of it sought to combine hate with humour, a process that Katherine Smith also observes within a working-class social club in Manchester (2012: 131). The day after the election of Pope Francis, for example, I visited the Glencruix Social Club, bringing with me a copy of the Scotsman newspaper I had been reading on the train. The front-page headline 'Habemus Papam' (We have a Pope), accompanied by a large photo of a smiling Pope Francis, attracted the attention of the sole female drinker in the club that afternoon – 'Ha! Frank the Pope!' she said, pointing at the paper, causing the men to laugh at her pun on the common sectarian phrase 'fuck the Pope'. Later, a more serious tone returned when Dennis came over and, seeing my paper still unopened, said gruffly: 'Joe, no harm to you, but either read that, or put it in the bin!', picking it up and turning it over, so the Pope's picture was now face down on the table.

Performances of sectarian difference concerned not just national and international affairs, but also local events, and these too mixed humour and hate. On discovering that a republican flute band from Chapelgeddie had obtained approval from the council to parade through Glencruix for the first time in thirty years, the men at the club were outraged, and immediately began to make plans to resist the event by all means possible. Adding insult to injury, the parade was scheduled for 13 July, a day after the Order's annual flagship Boyne parades in Northern Ireland and the highlight of the loyalist calendar. 'They'll need to withdraw! There'll be riots!' exclaimed one man. 'How did they get permission for that?' demanded another. 'They want to get barred so they can say "we got barred, so the Orange Order should get barred"' reasoned a third. Within minutes, mobile phones were ringing and a protest was being organised. Eric, one of the most cool-headed of the group, explained the difficulty of the situation. As an organisation, the Orange Order believes in civil and religious liberty, 'but I don't want a republican parade in Glencruix!' he exclaimed, to which Dennis indignantly replied that, in these circumstances, he *didn't* believe in civil and religious liberty.

A collective decision was reached that complaining to the council was a 'non-starter' as this would cause Orange parades to be banned in response. 'We won't object to the council, we will just physically assault them!' one man declared, further explaining to me how he would speak to 'certain people' to 'organise the troops' as a way to ensure that 'unsavoury elements of the loyalist community will do their thing'. This threat of violence was as explicit as it was pragmatic, with one Orangeman offering to contact councillors 'unofficially' to inform them of the likelihood of 'major trouble' if the event was allowed to proceed. 'Hopefully it will reach a crescendo and the parade will be banned' was Eric's matter-of-fact conclusion. Such forthright enmity contrasted somewhat with a story about the republican parade in Glencruix thirty years earlier. The route of the parade went straight past the Orange hall, which, at the time, was opposite a building site. As local republicans congregated to watch the parade, some lifted bricks from the unfinished building and began to hurl them at the Orange hall, one of which accidentally (and hilariously, in the view of the storyteller) struck one of their own supporters. The final irony simply added to the humour; the man, having been injured badly, was taken into the closest building for first aid, receiving treatment within the very same Orange hall that he and his fellow republicans had just attacked.

Other accounts of attacks on the Glencruix Hall underline how humour and enmity (and humour *about* enmity) exist as important social elements of Orange storytelling. Eric, for example, took great delight in recounting how, one year, on the evening before St Patrick's Day, he had received a phone call from Dennis who was so upset he was almost in tears. Being barely able to speak, Dennis simply demanded that Eric come to the hall as quickly as possible. Dennis sounded so urgent, Eric explained, that he wondered if one of Dennis's children had been killed. On arriving at the hall, Eric was relieved (and greatly amused) to see that what had upset Dennis so much was the fact that a prankster had removed the Union flag flying over the hall, and had replaced it with an Irish tricolour. 'I thought it was funny!' Eric told me with a smile, 'No harm had been done!' Eric laughed as he recounted Dennis's fury: 'He was in a complete rage, threatening to burn down the local chapel!' Two weeks later, Eric said, a parcel was posted to the hall containing the stolen flag neatly folded up inside.

As was often the case, one story followed another, with Eric proceeding to describe how, just two days before a major Orange parade in Glencruix, the hall had been daubed in anti-Protestant graffiti. Having worked hard to scrub it off before the parade, Eric organised a group of local Orangemen to stay overnight in the hall to keep watch in case the vandals returned; the group would take them by surprise and 'give them a good doing'. The vandals, as it turned out, did not return. Indeed, all that their night in the hall had involved, Eric admitted, was staying up until 5 a.m. getting extremely drunk. 'And then' Eric said, bursting into laughter, 'we had to wake up the next morning to parade!'

Other ethnographic encounters reveal how enmity, humour, and hate occurred simultaneously. Many of these moments emerged unexpectedly during my fieldwork, occurring within the 'ordinary' ethical acts of everyday life. For example, Steve, a regular at the Glencruix club, having borrowed a pen from Dennis, joked: 'I was going to steal that pen, but it's got fucking *green* on it!', as, much to everyone's amusement, he dropped it, recoiling in mock disgust. Other examples abound. Regularly choosing to place bets at William Hill rather than Paddy Power because of the latter's Irish branding and colour scheme; grumbling about placing a bet on a horse called 'Green Door' 'against my better judgement'; mockingly classifying Indian immigrants to Scotland as either 'Catholic Hindus' or 'Protestant Hindus'; joking that historically teetotal Orange 'temperance' lodges were, much like the Catholic Church, full of 'perverts and deviants'. As already described, the Old Firm derby between Celtic and Rangers was a key outlet for the expression of sectarian hate within the social club. On one such occasion, many of the spectators, including, most vocally, the middle-aged woman sitting beside me, repeatedly shouted vociferous abuse at the Celtic players on the TV, typically 'fenian bastard', but also 'dirty fucking fenian bastard', 'rodent', and 'scum, scum, scum'. While such language was often accompanied by embodied rage, throwing fists and thrusting shoulders towards the screen, these words also produced amusement, as those chanting often sought to outdo one another in the strength and creativity of their insults (see Millar 2016).

A loving hatred and a hateful love

What are we to make of this? Having outlined in some detail what ethnographically constitutes hateful enmity, where might we find examples of loving fraternity, of love for the Orange brotherhood? Returning to Kenneth Burke's work on the negative is useful here, because of the way it draws attention to the expansive work that negativity undertakes, both linguistically, and, in my reading, socially. Consider, first, Burke's suggestion that:

> Implied in the use of the negative, there is both the ability to generalize and the ability to specify. That is, you cannot use the negative properly without by the same token exemplifying the two basic dialectical resources of merger and division. For you can use *no* properly only insofar as you can classify under one head many situations that are, in their positive details, quite distinct from one another. In effect, you group them under the head of 'Situations all of which are classed in terms of the negative.' And in the very act of so classifying, you distinguish them from another class of situations that are 'not No-Situations'. (1966: 425)

Burke's initial point, stated simply, is that negativity, as an act of classification, is reliant on the creation of both similarity and difference – similarity here being achieved by 'merger', and difference by 'division' (ibid.). Yet Burke also notes that negativity is not monolithic, it classifies in different ways, bringing about different effects as a result. Burke distinguishes here 'between "the idea of nothing" and "the idea of no"' (ibid.: 430), with the former being understood as a thing, or a material absence, whereas the latter is understood strictly as an idea, or a conceptual negation. While I find this a helpful starting point in challenging overly uniform theorisations of negativity, this dual conceptualisation of 'nothing' and 'no' still appears to be insufficiently variegated to produce a good account of Orange expressions of enmity and fraternity.

My suggestion is that what is needed is a third category, namely 'the idea of not', which, I suggest, resides at the very heart of the kind of Orangeism that my informants cultivated for themselves and each other within the Glencruix club. This is because 'the idea of not', as I frame it, is neither a material absence, nor a conceptual negation, but rather a relational rejection. In contrast to Rupert Stasch's account of mother-in-law avoidance, then, I argue that, within the context of Scots-Orangeism, separation and avoidance do not 'make "difference" a positive basis of social connection' (2003: 317) with the differentiated other, but rather make difference a negative basis of social disconnection. Crucially, however, this does not mean that Scots-Orangeism is devoid of positive sociality. Indeed, my contention here is that by embracing 'the idea of not', what my Orange informants produced *alongside* negativity were *positive* identifications of fraternalism. The key difference here is that this positivity emerged not from difference, but from similarity.

Before advancing this argument, however, I want first to affirm Burke's suggestion that 'there are positives in which the negative is necessarily implied, even though we would deny or overlook its presence' (1966: 461). An Orange grip, for example, is offered as a positive act of greeting one's fellow brethren, but, by its very nature as a 'secret handshake', it is also a gesture that carries within it a negative statement, as those who fail to reciprocate the grip, thereby exposing their non-membership, quickly realise. Other examples are equally obvious, if often denied or overlooked. Orangemen who refer to each other as 'Brother' do so as a positive enactment of fraternalism, yet do so knowing that not every man in Glencruix can be called or treated as such. Likewise, the greeting 'loyal Protestant friends', issued from Orange platforms during parade-day speeches, not only positively affirms the presence of Orange sympathisers, but also negatively implies the existence of disloyal Catholic enemies. What Burke rightly draws our attention to, then, is the necessity of the presence of negativity within the realm of the positivity.

Yet, as stated above, the opposite is also true, that is, positivity is necessarily (and often powerfully) present within the realm of negativity. Where, then, is loving fraternity, of love for the Orange brotherhood? My argument here is that much of the above ethnographic description of hating one's enemies has, in effect, already described such love. This is because, within 'the idea of not', what we find is a relational rejection which is simultaneously a form of relational embrace. In order for my argument to get a better hearing, I want first to present two examples from Burke's philosophical account – about modern dance and bananas – before making the morally more challenging case as related to hatred. On modern dance, Burke makes the simple but insightful observation that 'the best teachers of the best modern dance taught the new art by noting always what rules of the old art their modern method was negating' (Burke 1966: 449). In this view, what modern dance *is* comes to be defined primarily in apophatic terms, in terms of what it *is not*. What is modern dance? It is not traditional dance. Here, 'the idea of not' comes to function positively, transforming, as a result, into 'the idea of is'. The similarity here with common (and historical) understandings of the Protestant Reformation is striking, for Protestantism may also be defined (in the first instance) in apophatic terms, as a religion that is not Roman Catholic because it does not grant indulgences.

Burke's second example, framed as a story about a hungry boy, is just as insightful:

> A child, visiting, had been admonished by his mother not to ask for things, but to wait until they were offered to him. He was standing before a bowl of bananas, looking at them hungrily. The hostess asked him what he was doing. He answered: 'I am *not* eating a banana'. (ibid.: 470)

One way of interpreting this story would be via Grice's (1975) theory of conversational implicature, which looks for the suggested or implied meaning in any utterance, as framed by a general cooperative principle that speakers should (and generally do) make truthful, informative, relevant, and clear contributions to the conversations they take part in. Yet, of particular relevance to the story above, Grice also developed his theory to understand implied meanings that emerge via utterances which deliberately violate specific elements of the cooperative principle (ibid.), for example, by deliberately providing incomplete information. So when the hostess asks the child what he is doing, and the child replies 'I am *not* eating a banana', the implied meaning would be something like 'I am hungry and want you to offer me a banana to eat'.

While I find these two examples from Burke instructive, I am less convinced as to the helpfulness of Grice's theory of conversational implicature, despite the seemingly obvious and common-sense logic it is founded upon. This is because, assumed within Grice's theory are hidden (or implied) meanings located 'behind' utterances which deliberately violate normal conversational conventions. Moreover, Grice assumes that these implied meanings (or inner states of being) pre-exist the original transgressive answer, just as the child's hunger pre-existed his negative statement about non-eating. In the context of Scottish Orangeism, these assumptions are problematic, I suggest, because they reduce the role of negativity to something secondary and derivative, making negativity into a sign or indicator of an ostensibly more important (but still implied) meaning, rather than treating negativity as a primary and socially constitutive phenomenon alongside that of positivity.

Treating negativity as such – as a primary and socially constitutive phenomenon that creates its own meanings directly, rather than implying or hinting at the meanings of other (more positive) utterances and experiences – changes the way we interpret Burke's examples. What is modern dance? It is 'not-traditional' dance. Imagining this as a positive answer may seem less far-fetched if we pose the exchange as a real conversation, so, in response to the question 'What type of dancer are you?' someone might reasonably respond 'Non-traditional', just as a social scientist might positively identify as an anti-relativist or an anti-positivist. But can the same be said of religion? Can we imagine an Orangeman ever responding to the question 'What religion are you?' with the answer 'I'm a not-Catholic'? As strange as it seems, I want to suggest that this *is* a core part of how my Orange informants in Glencruix engaged with Protestantism, as occurring not through the semantics of implied meaning, but through the semiotics of explicit narratives and behaviours. With this positive reframing of negativity in mind, imagine again a child looking hungrily at a bowl of bananas. What is he doing? He is positively engaged in the activity of *not* eating a banana, or, expressed more positively still, he is fasting. Now imagine a person writing 'No Catholics allowed' on the back of his organ donor card, or dropping a green pen in mock disgust, or hurling sectarian abuse at Celtic players on the television. What are these people doing? They are engaged in the activity of *not* being Catholic, or, expressed more positively still, in the context of Glencruix Orangeism, they are being Protestant.

Conclusions: alternation and rejection

This inseparability of the positive and the negative, can, I think, be detected throughout the Orangeism I witnessed in Glencruix. Consider, for example, Derek's descriptions of public opposition to Loyal Order parades; of Catholic men emerging from a 'papist pub' to 'defy' Orange marchers by walking through their ranks. Similarly, although more violently, a second case describes two groups of Catholic men trapping a Royal Black Preceptory parade in an attempt to wrestle away their Union flag, an act which triggers a full-scale sectarian street brawl. As such, what Derek offers is a sectarian description of sectarianism, a negative account of his animosity towards 'papists' as justified by their animosity towards Orangeism. But this is only, at most, half of the story. Indeed, of equal importance within Derek's narrative is the story it tells about fraternity, of marching together through hostile territory, of fighting together to defend one's flag. Seen from this perspective, Derek is making a positive statement about what it means to be an Orangeman alongside one's fellow Orange brethren. Put simply, Derek is talking not just about hate, but also about love, a love of British Protestantism that is inseparable from a hatred of Irish Catholicism.

Much of the ethnography above can be interpreted thus. In wanting to eject Catholics attending the pensioners club in the Orange Hall, or in writing 'No Catholics allowed' on the back of an organ donor card, Dennis is positively enacting fraternal love, a love that embraces Protestants as rightfully present and deserving, while rejecting Catholics as wrongfully present and undeserving. So too among the other club members, where dropping a green pen in mock disgust, calling for the removal of 'fenian flags', criticising the visibility of Celtic fans, or planning to disrupt a republican band parade, as well as negatively expressing hatred and enmity, also positively express love and fraternity – a love for the colour Orange and its symbolic meanings; a love for the Union flag, a love for Rangers, and a love for loyalist parades and music.

Equally, casually referring to a Catholic as a 'bead-rattling bastard' or an 'IRA bastard' allows the speaker to remind those who hear him that, in positive terms, he (and, in the context of the Orange social club, they too) are Protestant and loyalist, and proudly so. As such, gathering in the Orange social club to hurl anti-Catholic abuse at Celtic players on television, safe in the knowledge that neither the players nor any rival fans will hear you, is not primarily a negative communicative act designed to hate and hurt the sectarian 'other', but is instead focused upon positively demonstrating to fellow Rangers fans the strength of one's Protestant and loyalist convictions. In this context, even the sectarian refrain 'We hate Catholics, Everybody hates Roman Catholics' (sung to the tune of Tiffany's 1987 cover of the aptly titled pop classic *I Think We're Alone Now*) can be seen as a positive act of love. This is the case because, when sung by Rangers fans, the lyrical emphasis is on 'we' and 'everybody', being typically sung in the absence of rival fans by groups of men who bounce on the spot in unison with arms around each other's shoulders. Expressions of antipathy and hate, then, can and do produce powerful positive experiences of fraternal togetherness. Again, to be clear, the Order have no monopoly over such experiences, nor do 'non-liberal' (Fader 2009) groups in general. That Hillary Clinton's (now infamous) jibe describing half of Trump supporters as a 'basket of deplorables' was initially met with applause, cheering, and laughter (and was only later recognised as an ironically mean-spirited critique of those she regarded as mean-spirited), is a powerful example of this same process, but directed by 'liberals' against 'non-liberals'.

As such, the extent of this co-dependence between love and hatred is, I suggest, often underestimated. Theodoropoulou's (2007) analysis of anti-fans within football culture in Greece, for example, makes hatred out to be derivative of, or perhaps parasitic upon, what he regards as the more primary power of positivity. As such, Theodoropoulou insists not only that 'fandom is a precondition of antifandom' (ibid.: 316) but that 'the dislike of object A results from liking object B' (ibid.: 318). My suggestion is that, within the context of Glencruix Orangeism, the opposite assertions are equally true. Hating Celtic, then, is an essential part of loving Rangers because antifandom is a precondition of fandom. So too a love of Rangers might result from a hate of Celtic because like results from dislike just as often as dislike results from like. Here, the causal logic is almost Shakespearean – 'My only love sprung from my only hate' – not because Orangemen 'must love a loathèd enemy', but because it is loathing that (in part) facilitates their love, just as love facilitates loathing. As such, Steve Bruce is equally wrong to understand the sectarianism surrounding Old Firm matches in purely negative terms, when he says:

> The Old Firm have only each other to hate. The vast majority of fans of Rangers and of Celtic do not actually care about religion, about ethnic origins, about the Troubles in Northern Ireland, or about the constitutional future of the British Isles. They only pretend to care in order to maintain an identity that offends the other side and in order to have an excuse to offend the other side. What are at stake are not actual shared social identities built on real differences but pantomime costumes. The fans of both teams wear false noses. Each lot pretends to find the noses of the other ugly and grotesque while claiming to be deeply hurt by the cruel remarks that those scumbags have made about our noses. That a very small number of Old Firm fans are also violent drunken hooligans is deplorable but it does not make them a symptom of a deeply divided society. Most Scots are not football fans. Most football fans do not support the Old Firm. And most Old Firm fans are law-abiding men whose 'sectarianism' is confined to the ritual abuse of opposing fans. (Bruce 2012: 72)

Several points of contention can be raised in relation to Bruce's analysis here. First, and most obviously, Glencruix Orangemen *do* care deeply about religion, their ethnic origins, the Troubles in Northern Ireland, and (as we shall see in the next chapter) the constitutional future of the British Isles. Whether this makes them the exception to some wider sociological or demographic rule is not at issue here, for this is an ethnography of Scottish Orangeism, not an ethnography of 'most Scots', 'most football fans', or even 'most Old Firm fans' (ibid.). Second, it seems to me that what is at stake within the interactions at the Glencruix club are indeed 'actual shared social identities' (ibid.). The question then becomes, are these social identities purely negative? Are Orange expressions of enmity and hate only about the giving and receiving of offence via attributions of ugliness, or could the noses in question (false or otherwise) be just as apt at allowing the identification of beauty and love? By suggesting the latter, I have sought to provide the basis upon which I might finally turn to directly address the questions with which I opened this chapter, namely: how do Orangemen understand their Protestantism in relation to Catholicism; how can anthropology make sense of the sociality of hate in its own terms and; can hatred be described as forming a kind of ethical life?

Orangemen understand their Protestantism positively and negatively; to be an Orange Protestant is to embrace both 'the idea of is' and 'the idea of not'. This is because what someone *is* is inextricable from what they are *not*. The 'is' and the 'is not' are bound tightly together, just as love and hate or fraternity and enmity are bound together. Seen from this point of view, within the context of Glencruix Orangeism, hating Catholics is a kind of love. It is a way to embrace a specific imagination of national history and ethno-religious identity, as well as a way to embrace those who share this same imagination. Among my Orange informants, the reverse was also true. Loving Protestants involved its own kind of separation from and hatred of the Roman Catholic Church and, in some cases, Catholic individuals. One way to make sense of the interplay between what I have called a 'loving hatred' and a 'hateful love' is via Rodney Needham's (1983) essay on alternation in *Against the Tranquility of Axioms*. By reflecting on the process of alternation within a numerical set of one to twelve, Needham makes the observation 'that 1, 3, 5, 7, 9, 11 make up one set, and 2, 4, 6, 8, 10, 12 make up another set' (ibid.: 125), visualising the phenomenon as in Figure 4.1 below:

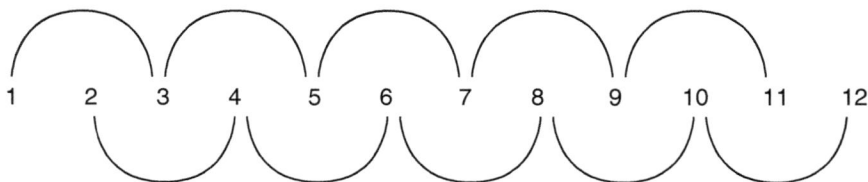

4.1 Needham's visualisation of alternation.

What the ethnography above suggests, it seems to me, is that the production of such sets (be they mathematical, ethno-religious, or otherwise) is not only an act of selection, but also an act of rejection. For Babcock, 'this means that group membership is determined not only by what members share, but by what the members recognize that "significant others" do *not* share' (1978: 27–28). Thus, 1 goes into a set with 3, 5, 7, 9 and 11, and, simultaneously, *does not go* into a set with 2, 4, 6, 8, 10, and 12, as visualised in Figure 4.2 below:

4.2 Alternation as rejection.

I am convinced that this idea seems banal to my Orange informants in Glencruix, who, in their initiation to the Order must vow not only to 'bear true allegiance to Her Majesty the Queen' and 'support the Protestant religion' but also 'avoid and discountenance all societies and associations composed of persons who seek to subvert the just prerogatives of the Crown' as well as 'give no countenance … to

the unscriptural, superstitious and idolatrous worship of the Church of Rome'
(GOLS 1983: 25–26). So seriously is the co-constitutive power of selection and
rejection, that an Orangeman who makes an inappropriate selection (for example,
by marrying a Catholic) or fails in their duty of rejection (for example, by attending
the funeral Mass of a deceased colleague) will be expelled from the Order. As such,
hate comes to be understood as a primary and non-derivative social phenomenon,
not as a by-product of love, but as a core constituent of love, and even as a type of
love, just as love may be seen as a core constituent and type of hate.

From an anthropological perspective at least, what seems less banal is the
suggestion that hate is good – or at least that it is part of 'The Good' – and can
thus be described as forming part of human ethical life. For the Orangemen of
Glencruix, the irreducible goodness of hate hinges on the goodness of Britishness
and Protestantism, as well as on the concomitant badness of Irish Catholicism and
republicanism as directed by the 'Church of Rome'. For some Orangemen, a love
for Protestantism means that being 'sectarian' is simply a natural and inevitable
consequence of having the courage of your religious convictions. 'What is sectarianism?' a leading Orangeman once asked me, before going on to offer his own answer.
'I'm tired of being called a bigot when I'm not. It's just a political thing, it's the
'ism' – what does it mean? All people are sectarian. It comes from 'sect' – it's just
deciding to follow a certain way of life'. Here, 'The Good' of moral decisiveness is
conflated with 'The Good' of being sectarian, albeit as partially distinguished from
sectarian*ism* and bigotry. For others, like Dennis and Don, 'The Good' of hate
requires no such distinction, for bigotry too, is a constitutive part of what a good
Protestant life looks like. 'I do! I do! I hate Roman Catholics!' Dennis proclaimed,
having just labelled himself a bigot, 'And I'll tell you why – it's because Roman
Catholics hate Protestants and hate the Orange Order as much as it is possible to
hate anything!'

But the irreducible (and thus unavoidable) good of Dennis's hate is not fully
encapsulated by these words alone, for, as I have also argued, Dennis's hatred of
Roman Catholics remains inextricably linked to his love for Protestantism and for
the Order, which he identified as his 'church', and its membership as his 'brethren',
a strikingly similar claim to that made by one of Pilkington's EDL informants,
who, when asked if he is religious responds 'English, that's my religion' (2016:
144). In Dennis's imaginary, then, he hates Catholics because they hate what he
loves – the Orange Order – just as EDL supporters hate Islamists because they are
said to hate Englishness. And yet the ethnographic tautology described above is
that hating those who hate you is co-determinative of how and why one loves.
Love and hate, fraternity and enmity, connection and separation, fandom and
antifandom make each other possible. Neither is secondary because both are logically
primary. For Needham, such oppositions are not only socially primary (insofar as
they instantiate certain forms of sociality) but they also exist as 'innate predisposi-
tions' (1987: 7). Indeed:

> The seeming universality of the concept of opposition … may respond to an
> intellectual necessity in coming to terms with representations. In other words, if
> men are able to take reliable account of their positions physically in relation to one

another, or if they are to be able to describe the disposition of material objects in relation
to one another, they may stand in absolute need of the idea of opposition. (ibid.)

Whether or not such oppositions are truly innate or universal is beyond the
scope of my argument here. What I *have* argued above, however, is that such
oppositions, within the context of the Glencruix Orange Social Club, are as
morally desirable as they are socially inescapable. They are, in short, what constitutes
a good Protestant life.

Crucially, when viewed from the vantage point gained by adopting what Laidlaw
terms 'the ethnographic stance', one may genuinely come to see how the good of
hate may become an irreducible good. No longer 'the feathery headdress of a
psychopathological profile' (Faubion 2001: 33), nor something that may be par-
ticularised to the point of 'reifying alterity into an Otherness that belongs nowhere
better than among exhibits in a believe-it-or-not museum' or in an 'asylum' or
'prison' (ibid.), the good of Orange hate may become simply 'the good of hate'.
Here, the good of hate becomes an unsettling and near-universal social fact, being
something most people share to some degree, even if (just occasionally) to indulge
in the not-so-guilty pleasure of hating haters. And, as we shall see in the chapter
that follows, for Orangemen, this moral desirability and the pleasure it affords is
wedded not only to the sociality of Protestant fraternity, and the religiosity of
Protestant ethnicity, but also to the politics of Protestant unionism.

5

'British Together'?

My dear Brothers and Sisters, the 13th of September 2014 – this very day – will be remembered as the day the Orange Order showed again that in any national crisis, our faith is in Almighty God. We stand as God's people – one faith, one heart, one mind, and one voice that declares 'No' to the breakup of our beloved United Kingdom! Dear friends, we thank God today that our brothers and sisters from Northern Ireland, from England and Wales, have travelled many, many miles to support us in our campaign against the nationalist attempt to divide our United Kingdom. We have come out of a sense of duty to God [and] to our country – one united, close-knit, Protestant family. Scotland must remain within the United Kingdom!

Let me remind you in this, the 100th anniversary of the supposed 'War to end all wars', that side by side, as one nation, as one people, we fought, we suffered, we bled and died, as the red poppy of Flanders fields so poignantly reminds us. Have these poor nationalists – who are obsessed only with separation – learned nothing from the massacre of one million British soldiers, nothing about love for one another, or standing side by side, heart to heart, against tyranny and evil? How can they ignore a lesson written in the blood of heroes? They died for our nation! Your vote can save our nation!

This great deception [of independence] has slowly but surely been brainwashing the Scottish people by its misguided patriotism – the manipulation and mind-games of devious politicians who will never have the spiritual wisdom or insight to know what is right or wrong for Scotland because they do not know Scotland's saviour. We know that nationalism is a part of the secular, humanist, liberal agenda to rid Scotland of its Protestant heritage and way of life. We are looking for a modern day Reformation!

God is never ever silent on any issue. Speaking of this crisis, God had this to say in Second Chronicles: '"The battle is not yours but Mine" sayeth the Lord. "Just take up your position and see the victory I will give you"'. And in obedience to God's Word today, we are taking up our position! So we as proud Scots, who are passionately British, come today out of our devotion for our nation, that we rightly call Great Britain – a land of hope and God's glory!

How did these British people have such a successful way of life, and a united country? The secret is this: believing in Almighty God, believing in His Son, The Lord Jesus Christ, and His way of reconciling Man to God through Calvary's cross. It's called salvation: the blessing of brotherly love. It is based on civil and religious freedom which we cherish and will always fight to protect. That way of life is called Protestantism!

When an enemy came against the city of Londonderry, God's people famously said 'There will be no surrender to this evil enemy!' It's a cry we made in 1914, a cry we made in 1939 – a cry British people make every time we face an enemy who seeks to destroy who and what we are. A divisive and evil enemy has arisen against Scotland in a nationalist referendum against our beloved United Kingdom! Our reply, as God's people, is 'No Separation!' We believe that God, who has been our help in ages past, will be our hope and our victory! Our prayer today is 'No Separation!'

So said the Rev. Bro. Alex Forsyth, Grand Chaplain of the Grand Orange Lodge of Scotland, as he stood to address crowds of Orangemen prior to a 15,000-strong march of the Order's members through the streets of Edinburgh, just five days prior to Scotland's independence referendum. By the conclusion of the ballot on 18 September 2014, with a turnout of nearly 85 per cent, the Grand Chaplain's prayer had been answered. Faced with the question 'Should Scotland be an independent country?' 55 per cent of voters had answered 'No', with only four regions in the country deciding for 'Yes'. Given this result, what are we to make of Forsyth's proclamations? What, from an Orange perspective, does voting on the future of Scotland's constitutional arrangement have to do with one's 'duty to God'? Why might this be a uniquely *Protestant* duty – a duty to protect one's 'close-knit Protestant family' by facing down an 'agenda to rid Scotland of its Protestant heritage and way of life'? Who is understood to be the 'divisive and evil enemy' behind such an agenda, and why do they stand accused of wilfully ignoring 'a lesson written in the blood of heroes'? Beyond rhetorical flourish, what does the Ulster politics of 'No Surrender!' have in common with a Scots-unionism of 'no separation'? What, in this context, does it mean to call for 'a modern-day Reformation'? How does the Orange Order's staunchly Protestant 'British Together' campaign relate to the thoroughly secular civic-unionism of the mainstream 'Better Together' campaign, from which it pointedly took its name? It is questions such as these that this chapter will consider.

My argument is that the Rev. Forsyth's words, and the way they speak to wider Orange ideas about Britishness and Scottish independence, can be best understood as offering a counter-politics to both the mainstream 'Yes' and 'Better Together' campaigns. Importantly, by referring to 'counter-politics' I do not mean to suggest that Orange perspectives on the referendum developed in reaction to these 'mainstream' positions, since the former predated the latter by a long number of years. By 'counter-politics', then, I mean to refer to *where* Orangeism locates what is at stake within the referendum. As I argue below, for 'Better Together', debate about the Scottish independence referendum was primarily rooted in the civic sphere, focusing on the rights and responsibilities that different types of citizenship afforded, such as how to sustainably fund the NHS, or how to ensure that Scotland, as part of the UK, has a voice on the 'international stage'. Conversely, for Forsyth and many other members of the Order, their Orangeism placed religious and ethnic identity centre stage, transforming the referendum from a constitutional question, into an existential one.

As such, debates about economics and international relations were sidelined by declarations about Protestant family, the blood of heroes, evil enemies, and divine victory. Drawing on the logic of Orange conspiracism, described in Chapter 2, many of my informants went further and actively inverted the case for independence, contending that, far from liberating Scotland from the yoke of oppression, a 'Yes' vote would instead plunge Scotland into a deeper (and more formal) bondage to 'Rome'. The result, I suggest, was that Orangemen in Scotland came to regard the independence referendum as a referendum on the Protestant Reformation, as well as a referendum on Protestant ethno-nationalism. Shunning the secular insistence on separating religion and politics, as well as the liberal insistence on separating ethnicity from politics, the Scottish independence referendum thereby became a unique moment within which to enact and reclaim a different kind of (ultra-British) nationalism, namely the triumphalist Protestant exceptionalism which resides at the very heart of Orangeism. In order to more fully explain the whys and wherefores of this 'counter-politics', I want first to briefly consider the 'Better Together' campaign, and its views on the Orange Order.

Better Together, 'unsavoury' Orangeism, and the mark of Cain

Attending the Edinburgh launch event of 'Better Together', the largest cross-party campaign for a 'No' vote in the Scottish independence referendum, in the Surgeons' Hall in Newington was a very un-Orange affair. I was greeted by two clean-cut-looking young men in smart-casual office attire. 'Are you here for Better Together? Great – just through there', one of them said, pointing the way with a broad smile. The meeting room was large and already very busy, despite my early arrival. The coffee had run out, so I opted for Earl Grey tea, which I sipped while watching the crowd of well-dressed, middle-aged, middle-class Scots in front of me. Indeed, while understated, the wealth in the room was hard to miss, contrasting strongly with the less affluent aesthetic of working-class Scots-Orangeism. Taking a seat beside a woman in her late fifties, we were soon chatting about her efforts to distribute 'Better Together' leaflets across the city. When I asked how people had reacted to being offered campaign literature, she explained that the reception was generally positive, and that any negative reaction was confined to poorer areas of the city. Despite her awkward and apologetic admission that such observations made her sound 'awfully snobby', she continued by detailing how one woman had angrily thrust a leaflet back into her hands as she was exiting down the stairwell of a block of flats, and that a group of young men from a similar social background had been physically repulsed by the literature – 'they weren't white-collar workers, put it that way' she concluded with an uncomfortable smile.

After a few minutes, the lights dimmed and a video appeared on-screen behind the stage, featuring a carefully curated selection of individuals – a businessperson, a soldier, a young mother, a group of industrial workers. Both the production and video content were slick, capturing the overall theme of the campaign: 'I'm a proud Scot, and I'm British – I'm a member of the United Kingdom, and I stress *united*'. As the video played, a young woman took photos of the audience with a large SLR camera. Next, the lights went up and Alistair Darling MP, the chairman and public face of the campaign, strode onto the stage. 'There's our hero!' my conversation partner cooed above the rapturous applause. Eventually having to raise a hand for quiet, Darling's speech was delivered with the kind of relaxed authority and practised earnestness that was so reminiscent of the Blair administration:

> Remember this: from the nationalist point of view, they only have to win once, by one vote. We are on the road to a deeply uncertain future. We need to engage the hearts and minds of the public. I *don't* argue that Scotland couldn't go it alone. What I *do* say though is that being part of the United Kingdom is better. We have massive economic problems at the moment – and why is separation the answer? It isn't!

The substance of Darling's speech went on to outline three broad arguments for staying within the UK: first, for economic reasons, second, for reasons to do with international profile and political influence (what he called 'clout') and third, for 'emotional' reasons to do with pride in one's national identity. On this third point, Darling's words received vocal (if still measured and mannerly) approval from the audience:

> I'm Scottish, and I'm British, and I'm proud of it! And my guess is that most of you are too! We cannot win this unless 'Better Together' becomes a popular movement. This is something we need to win, and we need to win well!

It was notable, moreover, that the cheering and clapping that Darling's sentiments provoked contrasted markedly with a related (if differently formulated and more forthright) comment from a man in the audience, who stood during the Q&A to address his own 'emotional' reason for supporting 'Better Together':

> I just want to say how angry I am! The Union Jack is *mine*! And the Saltire is *mine*! When I go to see famous English landmarks, they are *mine*! When I go up into the Scottish hills, they are *mine*! I am angry! What is being proposed [by the 'Yes' campaign] is to steal what is mine!

The embarrassed sideways glances around the room during the man's emotional plea made it clear that his sentiments jarred with the more understated and concilia-tory arguments generally deployed by 'Better Together' campaigners. The muted applause he received confirmed my suspicion that expressing raw anger – the like of which was commonly heard among Orangemen – was not felt, by this audience at least, to be a particularly prudent way of galvanising potential 'No' voters. Equally, that the man's accent, clothing, heavy-set frame, and shaved head made him sound and look more like a typical Orangeman than one of the 'white-collar workers' invoked above suggests that the aesthetics of class prejudice were again at play (see also Chapter 1). Darling's joking response to the man – that someone from 'Better Together' needed to 'sign him up' on account of his passion – did little to break the tension in the room, prompting a ripple of nervous laughter that merely confirmed how 'off message' his anger had been. That the last word, as well as the biggest applause given to an audience member during the Q&A, went to a well-spoken English woman who made a comparatively muted plea for 'more inclusive language' further reinforced the sense that 'Better Together' was to be a campaign with decidedly moderate messages and messengers.

Given the above, it is perhaps unsurprising that when the Grand Orange Lodge of Scotland began to plan how it too might campaign for a 'No' vote, such efforts were generally not well received outside its own ranks. Yet, while the 'awfully snobby' attitude admitted to above goes some way in explaining this negative reception, given the Institution's solidly working-class membership, class prejudice alone cannot fully account for the Order's ostracism from the otherwise big-tent unionism of 'Better Together'. As such, we also need to consider the incommensurability of Orange and non-Orange ideologies. From this perspective, the writing was on the wall at a very early stage. In October 2012, for example, Past Grand Master George Martin described to me how Grand Lodge had set up a monthly 'strategy group' tasked with organising opposition to Scottish independence. As part of the group's work, efforts had been made to forge links with 'Better Together', although George was already clear that any such links were likely to be 'informal' since 'Better Together', he predicted, would fear being 'tarnished with the sectarian brush' if they publicly associated with the Order. As it turned out, George had underestimated just how fearful 'Better Together' would be.

George's hope, and the hope of many of my Orange informants, from those in the hierarchy, to rank-and-file members, was that the Order would have an important role to play within the 'Better Together' campaign alongside other interested parties. The hope was relatively simple, and, arguably, not unreasonable, namely that the Orange Order would be allowed to mobilise its large membership to provide a significant source of leafleting 'manpower'. As an Orangeman in Glencruix mused to me, the Tories could raise the money, Labour could supply the political power, and the Orange Order could provide 'boots on the ground'. The reality, however, was that 'Better Together' refused all help from the Order, including any formal assistance with the distribution of leaflets, much to the frustration of the Grand Lodge strategy group and many grass-roots Orangemen. In conversation with several Edinburgh Orangemen, leading Orangewoman and key member of the Grand Lodge strategy group, Elizabeth Paterson, complained that 'Better Together' 'seem to have an agenda against the Orange Order', explaining that one 'Better Together' staffer had compared the Institution to the far-right British National Party. 'Our members vote Labour, Tory, and Lib Dem!' she retorted, 'It's so unfair, because Orange members are *so* willing and *so* able!' One of the Orangemen from Edinburgh echoed Elizabeth's sense of injustice, but shifted the blame onto the liberal political climate in Scotland, which made associating with the Orange Order risky. '"Better Together" don't want anything to do with the Orange Order; whether we like it or not, people hate us, so any link to us would be used against them', he explained. 'We don't want *official* recognition from "Better Together"', Elizabeth interjected. 'All we want is to be *used*' the man agreed, 'Just *use* us! We can do the donkey work – leafleting!' he said with a despondent shake of the head.

The conversation above echoed many similar discussions I heard between Orangemen during my fieldwork, with members of the Institution painfully aware that 'Better Together' and the Scottish general public tended to view the Order as a sectarian anathema to be shunned on that basis. 'There is some young pup running the "Better Together" campaign, going around saying there are some organisations they can't work with, and that the Orange Order is one of them! But we don't have the "Mark of Cain" on our foreheads!' one Orangeman protested to me. 'They just want bland people, bland unionism' agreed his Orange companion. Others took a slightly different view. While one informant, for example, openly admitted to me that '"Better Together" wouldn't touch the Orange Order with a bargepole for fear of being labelled sectarian by the SNP', he also predicted that the two organisations would establish a 'subterranean' working relationship, with groups of Orangemen distributing 'Better Together' leaflets under the guise of being private citizens. For the most part, however, Orangemen remained pessimistic about the role they would be permitted to play (as Orangemen) within the 'No' campaign. Many shared with me their anger at how excluded and ignored they felt, explaining that all they wanted was for 'Better Together' to recognise that they had a right not only to exist, but also to campaign openly.

The fact that no such recognition was ever given merely confirmed to my Orange informants their suspicions that 'Better Together', and 'mainstream' Scottish politics generally, was exclusivist, paranoid, and, above all, bigotedly anti-Orange. In addition, some in the Orange hierarchy feared that if Scotland's wider loyalist community, especially those in the band scene, learned of how negatively they were perceived by 'Better Together', then this might undermine their willingness to turn out on polling day, thereby unintentionally undercutting the strength of a 'No' vote. This worst-case scenario looked increasingly possible, when, just two months before the referendum, a twelve-year-old girl was struck in the face by a bottle thrown during an altercation at the fringe of an Orange march. In the ensuing media furore – complete with graphic bloody images of the injured girl – Jim Murphy MP publicly condemned the Order by announcing that he and 'Better Together' wanted 'nothing to do with them', further stating that 'elements which attach themselves onto the edge of an Orange Order demonstration' were 'pretty unsavoury'. While some of my Orange informants were angered by these comments given that the 'elements' in question were not members of the Order, others were wearily resigned to what they saw as the inevitability of this kind of guilty-by-association media verdict. Others went further, pointing out that Jim Murphy was simply courting the Catholic unionist vote the best way he knew how, by publicly denigrating the Orange Order. Still others regarded such efforts as a fool's errand, believing that Scotland's Catholic community held deep-seated anti-British views and would vote 'Yes' regardless of how fiercely Murphy and others in 'Better Together' slated the Order.

That my own attempts at setting up participant observation among 'Better Together' were stymied by my university staff web page because it listed 'Orangeism' as a research interest is also worthy of note. During a frosty lunch meeting with Ross, a campaign staffer at 'Better Together', his opening gambit was to question me about my work among Orangemen, since this, in Ross's own words, 'would make my boss twitchy', especially if my research attempted to link the two organisations in any way. When I asked if there *were* any links, Ross's denial was strenuous, going as far as to state that 'Better Together' would refuse all donations from the Order. When I asked why this would be necessary, Ross levelled his gaze at me and said 'We see the Orange Order for what they are'. Asking for clarification on what this might mean, he simply repeated the same phrase a second and then a third time, becoming marginally more aggressive with each repetition. Later, when I asked what ethnographic opportunities there might be among 'Better Together' – could I shadow a local campaign group, for example? – Ross was clear that I would be welcome to volunteer with 'Better Together' as a private citizen, but that since all volunteers were required to sign a confidentiality agreement, I would not be permitted to write about any of my observations or experiences. I left the meeting frustrated that a potentially revealing field site seemed closed to me, not least because my research focus on Orangeism rendered me an object of suspicion among Scotland's union-supporting 'social democrats' (the term Ross applied to himself upon objecting to my apparently clumsy use of the term 'unionist').

The irony here was that research access to the Orange Order was both more generous and more easily obtained, despite the Institution being commonly labelled a 'secret society'. Why might this be the case? Why would a liberal, progressive grouping like 'Better Together' be so 'twitchy' about granting access to a researcher who had *also* studied Orangeism? What makes Orangemen and Orange sympathisers so 'unsavoury' that their offers of leafleting labour and financial donations must be turned down? Why go so far as to reject the label 'unionist' during a campaign to remain within the United Kingdom? The answer, I argue below, is that contrary to my Orange informants' views, Scottish Orangemen *are* seen as carrying a metaphorical 'Mark of Cain'. Importantly, this 'Mark' takes many forms. As already outlined in the previous chapter, one form has to do with the relationship between fraternalism and hate. Here, the Mark of Cain often translates into simple accusations of sectarianism, whereby the Order is shunned as an anti-Catholic aberration. A different form of this Mark, discussed in the Introduction and Chapter 1, has to do with a class prejudice which regards Scots-Orangemen as a 'rough' band of drunks whose noisy, garish marches disturb the public peace and offend good taste. Yet, in the context of the Scottish independence referendum, this 'Mark of Cain' is given two additional iterations. The first has to do with the Order's insistence that the referendum was a religious event, while the second has to do with the Order's insistence that the referendum was inextricably bound up with ethnic identity.

Taken together, these two Orange visions of (and for) the independence referendum positioned the Institution against the secular and civic commitments of the 'mainstream' political parties in Scotland, who strove to exclude religious and ethnic particularisms from the debate, not only as a divisive vote loser, but more fundamentally as a kind of category mistake. While the former move may seem unremarkable (Forsyth's ultra-British Protestant/Orange religiosity and ethnicity having a limited appeal among many Scots-Protestants, let alone among non-Protestants), the latter move needs more explanation. Why regard Forsyth's words with which

I opened this chapter not only as exclusionary, but also as a category mistake, a kind of ontological error? My suggestion here is that, from the perspective of 'Better Together', the religious and ethnic claims of Scots-Orangeism are simply *not* properly political, having a status akin to inadmissible evidence. Claims that 'Home Rule is Rome Rule', or that retaining a *British* monarchy is the only way to preserve a Protestant State, came to be regarded not only as wrong, but also as nonsensical, even pathological. In my conversation with Ross about the absolute non-interaction between 'Better Together' and the Orange Order, he also said the same applied to 'Scottish Defence League nutters' and the British National Party. For Ross, then, the Orange Order – just like the far-right SDL and BNP – was not engaged in politics proper, but in the propagation of a religious and ethnic delusion. Crucially, from Ross's perspective, this delusion, which misunderstood the referendum as being about British-Protestant destiny as opposed to Scottish civil and economic policy, threatened to contaminate wider efforts to achieve a 'No' vote unless publicly repudiated. Such was the toxic power of the Order's 'Mark of Cain' that Orangemen carried with them (most knowingly, but some unknowingly) whenever they found themselves denigrated as 'unsavoury', condemned as 'sectarian', or mocked as 'nutters'.

Scots-Orange party politics: divided opinions and split loyalties

Perhaps unsurprisingly, the ethnographic reality of my Orange informants' party-political loyalties was more diverse than the stereotyped view of the Order as a monolith of anti-Catholic sectarianism might suggest. Yet it was certainly true that many of my informants were on the political right. Some, for example, were committed lifelong Tories, most of whom remembered Thatcher's uncompromising public statements against the IRA, and the hunger strikers in particular, with real admiration. Jonathan Henderson, who was one such individual, explained to me that he had continued to vote Conservative even after the betrayal he felt had been shown to Ulster Protestants and their supporters when Thatcher signed the Anglo–Irish Agreement in 1985, thereby granting the Irish government an advisory role in Northern Irish affairs. While Jonathan and others continued to speak of this pact with real bitterness – as an unacceptable compromise to Irish republicanism which, like the Scottish independence referendum, threatened the integrity of the United Kingdom – they and other Orangemen I spoke to still felt that the Conservative Party best represented their unionist convictions.

Where many Scots-Orangemen continued to be ardent Tories up until 1997, for some, this began to change with the advent of devolution in September of that year, with the Scottish Conservatives suffering a series of catastrophic electoral defeats in the wake of their failed campaign against the introduction of a new parliament in Edinburgh (see Smith 2011). In this context, several Orangemen admitted to me that they began to view support for the Scottish Conservatives as a 'wasted vote'. Opinion on this remained divided, which made the issue a popular topic for debate within the Glencruix Social Club, where Conservative and Labour voters drank and bantered together on a regular basis. With the Tories no longer seen as having a monopolistic claim to being effective defenders of the union, some of my key informants in Glencruix candidly told me that they now voted Labour. Their rationale was that Labour was the only party who could effectively challenge the SNP, a matter which became all the more pressing for many Orangemen during my early fieldwork in 2012, in the wake of the SNP's resounding 2011 Scottish Parliament election victory. Compared with the SNP's sixty-nine seats, the Conservative's fifteen seats looked very weak indeed. Orangemen faced with the SNP holding a historic parliamentary majority (despite the electoral system being a version of proportional representation) understandably began to wonder with real foreboding what a future independence referendum might hold, with switching their support to Labour seen as the least bad choice.

This tactical switch had not been easy for some Orangemen. Eric, a key informant from Glencruix, for example, described to me his decision to run as a Labour councillor, and the reaction this provoked. Walking into the Orange social club with a red Labour rosette pinned to his jacket had attracted the horror of fellow drinkers who, he explained, still instinctively associated the Labour Party in Scotland with Catholicism and republicanism. Regardless, both Dennis and Eric had pressed local Orangemen to vote Labour in response to the rise of the SNP. As my fieldwork progressed, I was able to witness the fruits of these efforts during a meeting between Glencruix Orangemen and local councillors held in the Orange hall in March 2013. It was notable that while there seemed to be good rapport between Orangemen and the Labour councillors, relations with the SNP councillor seemed markedly less warm. The meeting itself was taken up by a lengthy discussion about the inefficiencies of the council's handling of parade applications, as well as a number of non-Orange issues including local parking problems, the rise of vacant shops on the high street, and concerns about planning approval for a new supermarket.

While offering an interesting view on issues of local concern, what I found more insightful was how, at the end of the meeting, two of the councillors present that night jointly introduced themselves to me as being 'of the other persuasion'. Not understanding what they meant but guessing they might be referring to a shared political affiliation, I replied 'Oh, so you're from the same party?' 'No, well ...' came the awkward response. Realising I had made a mistake, but not knowing what it was, I guessed again – 'Oh, so you're Independents?' 'No, we are both Labour' he replied patiently. Possibly noting my growing puzzlement, one of the Orangemen interjected with good-humoured frankness: 'Joe, what he's trying to tell you is that they are both *Romans*'. 'Oh!' I said, rather more loudly than intended. 'Just so you know ...' explained the councillor, almost apologetically. Yet it was not until later that evening that I came to fully realise the relevance of the 'other persuasion' comment, when it was explained to me that the SNP councillor, who had been pointedly ignored for most of the meeting, was both a Protestant and a Rangers season ticket holder. The reality, then, was that Glencruix Orangemen were choosing to support two Catholic Labour candidates over an SNP candidate with whom they (ostensibly) shared far more in ethno-religious terms. Importantly, this was not a quirk of the Glencruix context, with Glasgow Orangemen sharing precisely this same conviction that *constitutional* commitments to remaining within the UK trumped any *religious* taboo about not voting for Catholics.

While some Orangemen were willing to become 'tactical' Labour voters to try and stem the tide of Scottish nationalism, others remained unconvinced and sought out alternative political mechanisms for safeguarding Scotland's place within the UK. Prominent Glasgow Orangeman Andy Cooper, for example, was involved in the founding of the Scottish Unionist Party in 1986, set up in the wake of the Anglo–Irish Agreement. In this context, Cooper and others in the SUP hoped to receive significant support from disaffected Tory voters within the Orange community across Scotland's Central Belt, choosing to campaign under the slogan 'Proudly Scottish, Proudly British'. By 2005 and 2007, the SUP's policies had outlined their opposition not only to Scottish devolution ('Get rid of Follywood') and the EU ('Say no to a Federal States of Europe') but also to Scotland's Catholic education system ('End religious apartheid in our schools!'). In addition, Cooper's own election communication for the 2005 general election attacked the SNP by warning of 'other parties [who] wish to break up the United Kingdom and turn Scotland into a cut-price Cuba – without the sun and samba'. Many of the SUP's other policies – zero tolerance on crime, cuts to business rates, protection for armed forces budgets, a freeze on immigration – placed it squarely on the political right, which, in addition to accusing 'leading members of the SNP of echoing the bigoted rantings of terrorist apologists in Northern Ireland with fanatical outbursts of hatred against the [Union] flag', sought to bolster the party's Orange appeal.

Yet despite these best efforts by Cooper and others, the party struggled in local council, Scottish, and general elections, often failing to retain their deposit due to lack of votes. While Cooper complained that the SUP was held back primarily by the indifference of working-class Protestants in Scotland – 'The problem is apathy; a lot of these so-called unionists don't vote' – others in the Orange Order suggested that the SUP was too small and too closely associated with Cooper as an individual personality to offer a real challenge to any of the mainstream parties. In addition, several Orangemen I spoke with during my fieldwork went as far as to be openly critical of the SUP's efforts, suggesting that all the party did was further fragment the already divided unionist vote by undermining the Scottish Conservatives at a time when they needed Orange support the most. Whatever the case, the failure of the SUP did not signal the beginning of a new era of unionist unity. Indeed, Orangemen who remained sceptical of the Labour Party as a true defender of unionist/Orange interests found themselves drawn to the United Kingdom Independence Party. 'I'm voting UKIP!' bellowed Steve, a fellow Orangeman, in response to Eric's story about his efforts to become a Labour councillor. Over time, I came to realise that Steve's comment was more than banter, with a significant minority of my Orange informants talking with me about their support for UKIP, not only because of their concerns about EU immigration, but also because UKIP candidates were seen as pro-union and pro-monarchy in the same way that the SUP was, but with the additional credibility of having a UK-wide political platform.

Importantly, while it was generally acceptable for an Orangeman to vote for a Labour politician who was a Catholic simply out of a desire to see a unionist remain in power, the opposite did not hold true. Indeed, voting for an SNP candidate was seen by the vast majority of my informants as a betrayal of Orangeism, regardless of the ethno-religious background of the nationalist politician. As my experience of meeting with councillors in the Glencruix Orange Hall taught me, not even being a Protestant Rangers season ticket holder was enough to redeem a nationalist in the eyes of my informants. That this was more than a hypothetical taboo was repeatedly highlighted to me during my fieldwork, since it was well known that prominent Orangeman and Grand Lodge archivist Andrew Watson was both a member of the SNP and a supporter of Scottish independence. Watson himself explained his views to me in an interview, which, he admitted, were 'not popular' in Orange circles:

> I have been now for fifty years a member of the Scottish National Party, which, at the time of the great independence debate – which I believe in – I'm very much out of step with the majority [Orange] opinion in Scotland. My political affiliation is not popular in the eyes of many [Orangemen], certainly not in the leadership. I see my membership of the Orange Institution basically as my Protestant tradition, and the defence of Protestantism, which I believe the Orange Order is in the vanguard of. And I see my long-active part in the Scottish National Party as being part of a political party. I have no dilemma in living with both of these, and I go back to King William III, Prince of Orange – he was the monarch, the King of Scotland, because we were independent. There is nothing in either of these institutions that decries your right to be part of either.

> I would be wrong in trying to infer that the Grand Orange Lodge of Scotland doesn't look for its members to support the union, but there is licence for such as me, and I think it's based on the fact that they know that my commitment to Orangeism is not under question. I am not British. I see myself as Scottish. I know the history of my land. I know my culture as a Scot – I know my culture as a Scottish *Protestant*, and the struggles from the Reformation on. I've always felt Scottish; I love Burns, I love Scottish music. I have a strong sense of Scottish identity, and I don't have any sense of a British identity.

As it turned out, I didn't need to wait long to learn just how 'out of step' Watson's views were from his fellow Orange brethren, since, directly after the interview, I was due to travel to Glencruix. Arriving at the Orange social club, I was greeted by the regular faces and, before long, Dennis came over to talk, quizzing me about what Watson had said. Much to my relief, I didn't need to sidestep any awkward questions which would break confidentiality, because before I had a chance to speak, Dennis had launched into an angry tirade about how, if Watson was a full member of the SNP as he suspected, then a formal complaint should be made and he should be thrown out of the Order. There were rules, Dennis said, which prohibited Orangemen being members of any organisation with aims that contradicted those of the Order. Arguing precisely the opposite of what Watson had suggested in his interview just hours previously, for Dennis and for the great majority of Orangemen I met, because the Order was not only a Protestant, but also a *British* and therefore *unionist* organisation, the SNP, in campaigning for Scotland to leave the UK, directly contravened the very essence of Orangeism, as did Watson's political views.

Similar to my argument in the previous chapter, we can see here that Dennis's fury at Watson's SNP membership is not just a negative statement against Scottish nationalism, but also a positive statement in support of the Union, and the Orange Institution's commitment to uphold the current constitutional arrangement of the United Kingdom. Dennis was angry, then, not only because he hated the SNP, but because he deemed Watson, a fellow Orangeman, to have shown insufficient love for Britishness and the Union. Other Orangemen shared Dennis's anger, but expressed it differently, focusing instead on what they saw as the SNP's 'hijacking' of Scottish identity, in which Watson, as a supporter, was held to be complicit. During a formal Grand Lodge awards dinner, for example, an Orangeman at our table attracted several comments for wearing Scotland's flag in the form of Saltire tartan kilt. Turning to a notably unresponsive Watson who was sitting opposite, the wearer leaned forward with an angry glower and shouted 'Yes! *I'm wearing the flag*, and Alec Salmond's *no* getting it from me!' The nervous laughter this provoked around the table suggested, yet again, that such statements were intended to be more barbed than humorous. Others didn't feel the need to use humour, with one Orangeman describing support for Scottish independence (albeit not in Watson's presence) as a kind of violent treachery: 'Some things are unforgivable, and *stabbing your country in the back* is unforgivable', he said with seething resentment. Such was the Orange loathing for the SNP, and for Watson's support for them.

As was often the case, it was Dennis who offered the most concise summary of Orange reasons for supporting Labour as the only bulwark against Scottish independence, which he did by repeating with relish the phrase 'the enemy of my enemy is my friend' whenever he was pushed to justify voting tactically. Dennis's logic was clear, namely that, since the SNP were the enemy, and were strongly opposed by Scottish Labour, then Orangemen were right to ally themselves to Labour despite subscribing to the commonly held belief that the party was dominated by Catholics. Bill Paterson, a leading Orangeman from Edinburgh, echoed this same logic, explaining that while tactical Orange support for Labour could be seen as a temporary move, any decision to break away from the UK would have permanent consequences – 'the SNP only need to get their way once, and that would be the decision made' he said with a grim expression. Dennis's use of the ancient Sanskrit proverb also helps clarify why Watson's support for the SNP positioned him as a kind of enemy, despite being (at least by official membership) Dennis's Orange brother. Indeed, if 'the enemy of my enemy is my friend', then it would also seem reasonable to suggest that 'the friend of my enemy is my enemy'. For Dennis, the reality of Watson's friendship with the SNP produced, at best, a strained fraternity, and, at worst, a partial enmity, and this despite Watson's insistence to me during interview that, contrary to my own observations above, he had never been shown any animosity from Orangemen as a result of his nationalist political convictions.

Watson's membership of the SNP is an instructive case, and not only because Watson stands as an Orange nationalist who very much proves the Order's unionist rule. Indeed, the real insight Watson's words offer is how they stand in contrast to dominant Scots-Orange sentiments on Britishness, as typified by the men at Glencruix, but also by Forsyth's words with which I opened this chapter. Thus, where Watson clearly states he believes in Scottish independence, Forsyth calls independence a 'great deception' and its political supporters a 'divisive and evil enemy'. Where Watson states that Orangeism only concerns Protestantism and is separate from his political support for the SNP, Forsyth explicitly conjoins religion and politics by stating that defending the UK is part of one's duty to God and to one's country, both of which he defines as inalienably Protestant. Similarly, where Watson states that his SNP membership does not call into question his commitment to Orangeism, Forsyth states that Scottish nationalism is part of a 'secular, humanist, liberal agenda to rid Scotland of its Protestant heritage' – a heritage which all Orangemen must vow to uphold. Dennis goes even further here, by publicly stating that Watson's SNP membership is grounds for him being expelled from the Order. Finally, where Watson explicitly states that he is not British and has no sense of British identity, Forsyth rejects such claims as 'misguided patriotism', stating that Orangemen are 'passionately British' and, as such, are members of 'one united, close-knit, Protestant family'.

Given the above, in what remains of this chapter, I want to explore in more detail how (and in what ways) the religion and politics of Protestantism came to be conjoined within Scots-Orange efforts to resist independence. I want to begin by examining Scots-Orange unionism as a kind of divine battle which frames loyalist Protestants as defenders not only of a British constitution, but of a God-ordained British 'way of life'. Following this, I want to examine Scots-Orange unionism as a kind of blood-bought and blood-bound birthright which frames loyalist Protestants as carriers of a divine essence or ethnic substance which is understood to be both politically and materially essential for the survival of Britain as 'a land of hope and God's glory'.

'A Second Reformation': Scots-Orange unionism as ultra-Protestant religiosity

I want to return to the question with which I opened this chapter, namely, what might voting on the future of Scotland's constitutional arrangement have to do with one's 'duty to God'? More specifically, why, from an Orange perspective, was achieving a 'No' vote considered to be imperative for the survival of Prot-estantism in Scotland? I have already described above how the 'mainstream' 'Better Together' campaign regarded such claims as a kind of category error, as pathological, even, within the context of their own assumptions about the secularity of constitutional politics. How, then, had Scotland's Orangemen fallen so very far from the tree? What was it that allowed them to persist in their assertion that the independence referendum was a decidedly religious affair? The answer, I will argue, has to do with themes already discussed in Chapters 1 and 2 – on Orange historicism and Orange conspiracism – but combines these themes, producing new accounts of enmity, persecution, and hope as a result. As a starting point, consider the following speech given by Grand Master Todd Walters in

May of 2013, as part of a Grand Lodge 'education night' designed to teach new members of the Order about Orange heritage:

> It is a great privilege to be members of the finest institution in the world. Why? Because we have the greatest core foundation: the inspired Word of God. It is on that book that Orangeism is founded, and by it, the principles of Orangeism must always be maintained. So where have we come from in this Protestant religion, and Orangeism in particular? We've come from the great Reformers of the sixteenth century such as Martin Luther, John Calvin, George Wishart, John Knox, and the Glorious Revolution of 1688, cemented at the Boyne in 1690, by King William III, the Prince of Orange. And also we have to thank God for the great Covenanters of the seventeenth and eighteenth centuries, and that great message 'For Christ, Crown, and Covenant'. Salvation is not corporate. You don't pay to get into heaven, although 500 years ago that was in the peoples' minds. Yes, the Protestant religion we will maintain. We are charged with that responsibility, of the promotion of our principles.

> And here we are, Sisters and Brethren, in 2013, and we are still being seriously challenged for promoting our heritage and culture. We continue to face the serious challenges from councils on our parading rights. We will not be discriminated against, or treated as second-class citizens! This is our Orange heritage and culture, and we are here to stay! Sisters and Brethren, we must stay focused and active to the serious situation that we as a unionist organisation face next year, on 18 September 2014. We must be aware of the threat of nationalism and the separatist referendum. Yes, a *separatist* referendum, to separate Scotland from the rest of the United Kingdom of Great Britain and Northern Ireland! As a Loyal Orange Institution, we are loyal to God and our Queen. The union is under threat by the nationalists. We cannot let this happen – we cannot sleepwalk our way to national-ism. We cannot have any apathy. We must stand together to make sure that all Protestants vote 'No'. And always remember: united we stand, divided we fall.

That Walters' speech is a tour de force of Orange themes – the Reformation, the Glorious Revolution, the Covenanters, Catholic indulgences, parading rights, loyalty to God and Queen, unionist rejections of nationalism – is hard to deny. More interesting, then, is the logic by which these themes are woven together, a logic which equates campaigning against Scottish independence with Luther's struggle to establish the Protestant faith. Indeed, from Walters' point of view, all Orangemen 'must stand together to make sure that all Protestants vote "No". But why this *religious* imperative? My suggestion is that many of my Orange informants regarded campaigning against Scottish independence as part of their religious duty because they believed the proponents of independence to be motivated by an equally religious (if nefarious) aim – to sever Scotland from the UK as a route to transforming it into a Catholic colony. As such, Orange campaigning against Scottish independence came to be regarded by my informants (sometimes metaphorically, sometimes more literally) as, in Forsyth's words, a kind of 'second reformation', that is, as a valiant battle against an evil apostasy waged by God's chosen few. Importantly, I want to suggest that the latter (Protestantism) only makes sense, and can only be regarded as *good* by Orangemen, when placed under the dark shadow of the former (Roman Catholicism). And it is here where we must return to Orange historicity and Orange conspiracism.

A few months after beginning fieldwork in Glencruix, a good rapport had developed between myself and Dennis, helped not only by our shared interest in politics and religion, but also by my keenness to ask questions, as well as Dennis's love of answering them. As expected, then, in addition to being a chance to meet his family, visiting Dennis's house for dinner one evening was also an opportunity to hear more about his views on the upcoming referendum, and why he felt the outcome mattered for Scotland's Protestants. Dennis and his son John, who looked to be in his thirties, met me off the train, and the three of us chatted as we walked to their house in Chapelgeddie. It was mid-February, and the dim street lighting cast long shadows across the estate. The town, Dennis explained, was evenly split between Catholics and Protestants, whereas neighbouring Glencruix was still predominantly Protestant. As we talked, Dennis and I walked side-by-side, with John following behind. Nearing the house, Dennis mentioned that the Orange Juveniles were meeting in Glencruix that evening, describing the youth wing as a key way of recruiting younger members into the Order's adult lodges. 'Having said that, I've got four kids and *none* of them is in the Orange!' he admitted with a laugh, throwing a backwards glance at John. The house itself was ex-council, a modest semi-detached dwelling typical of the area. Inside it was comfortable and homely, with large sofas and an even larger television, as well as several porcelain ornaments belonging to Dennis's wife Margaret. To my surprise, given Dennis's penchant for displaying loyalist iconography, the decor gave away little about his Orange member-ship, with the exception of a small decorative plate displaying various symbols from the Royal Arch Purple.

Margaret had clearly gone to considerable effort in preparing the meal, with three courses served at the dinner table – complete with good china and a tablecloth – much to Dennis and John's amusement. 'What's wrong with dinner on our laps? Why don't I get a tablecloth when I come over? Do I get pavlova if I bring a scholar to tea?' John teased, causing his mother to blush with embarrassment. Before long, the conversation turned to politics, and to the referendum. Wanting to know what Dennis thought about the motivations of 'Yes' voters, I asked if lots of people would vote to separate from the UK if they believed that's what a proud Scot should do. Possibly misinterpreting my question as an *opinion* (rather than a hypothetical, as intended), Dennis responded by forcefully repeating the slogan of the Orange Order's 'No' campaign, and adding a few sentiments of his own. 'I'm proud to be Scottish and proud to be British, but if I had to choose – *which I don't* – I'm sorry, but I would choose British!'

Later that evening I asked Dennis how he thought Catholics in Chapelgeddie would vote in the referendum. Dennis's answer, which was even blunter than my question, was nonetheless insightful: 'It's an old saying, but it's true, that Home Rule is Rome Rule'. This phrase, originally used in the late nineteenth century by unionists fearful that the Home Rule movement would Catholicise Ireland by bringing it under the political and spiritual influence of the papacy (Jackson 2003: 59. See also O'Day 1998), was one I heard used by several of my Orange informants in relation to the 2014 independence referendum. Extrapolating out from this bygone political slogan, Dennis expanded his answer by repeating his often-made claims that Catholics across Scotland would vote 'in their own interest' and 'however it suits them'. Crucially, Dennis's assertion here was not only that Scottish Catholics were driven by narrow selfish interests, but that, as a result, they had no loyalty to the British State, of which they were citizens. Worse still, according to Dennis, was the fact that this disloyal self-interest was not, in reality, self-interest at all. This was because most Catholics would choose to vote 'however their priest tells them'. For Dennis, this was crucial, because it meant that Scotland's Catholics would not only vote as a bloc, but would do so according to the diktat of a foreign power. Dennis's logic was nothing if not consistent; because of their loyalty to the Pope, Roman Catholics, he explained, would vote 'whatever way they can to rebel against Britain'. In this sense, while Dennis was supportive of Orangemen voting as a bloc according to the pro-union instructions of the Orange hierarchy, this represented no double standard, for their doing so maintained (quintessentially Protestant) personal freedom and national sovereignty against the evil empire of Rome.

Before I had a chance to verbalise my growing scepticism, Dennis patiently connected the dots for me. The Roman Catholic Church wanted to destroy Britain, and particularly the monarchy and the Church of England, in order to re-establish Catholicism as the official religion of the United Kingdom. The Scottish independence referendum, which attempted to cleave Scotland from the UK, was part of that larger plot to eradicate Britain's Reformation heritage. Intriguingly, Dennis argued that seeking to undermine the Church of Scotland's Protestant foundations (by first undermining Scotland's place within the UK) was a relatively minor goal of the Roman Catholic Church. Their primary target, he asserted, was the Church of England, and particularly its links to the British monarch as 'Defender of the Faith', a faith which was, up to now, both singular and Protestant. Dennis ended the conversation by stating that as a 'pseudo-political organisation' the Catholic Church sought to 'dominate the entire world'. According to Dennis, the pattern was clear for all to see, namely that the Roman Catholic Church sought to exert its power 'where there would be *most* opportunity and *least* resistance' by expanding into areas of the world that were politically weak and economically unstable. 'I'm sorry to sound like a broken record, but Rome has stayed the same for 800 years, and it willna change – it's the "Holy Roman Faith" as they see it. The presentation may have changed, but the principles have not!' For Orangemen such as Dennis, such was the threat that Scotland was believed to be facing, and Scotland's Protestants most of all.

That Dennis's words were more than just the idiosyncratic assertions of an Orangeman enthralled by the 'paranoid style' (Hofstadter 1964) is evidenced by the fact that several of my other informants shared his views that the independence referendum was more than what it seemed. Andy Cooper, for example, described to me in great detail how the leaderships of the SNP and Catholic Church had formed an unholy alliance against Scots who identified as British and Protestant. The SNP, Andy explained, had gone to enormous lengths to court the Catholic vote, with Alex Salmond publicly supporting Cardinal Keith O'Brien in the wake of the sex scandal which had ultimately led to O'Brien's resignation. What made matters worse, from Andy's perspective, was the fact that the SNP's appeasement of the Catholic Church was matched by the Scottish Catholic Church's support for Scottish independence. Questioning Andy on whether this was really the case, Andy correctly pointed out that Cardinal O'Brien, who in 2012 was Scotland's most senior Catholic, was on record as stating that he would be 'happy' if Scotland became independent. 'I have it in black and white!' Andy insisted, pointing to his notebook. Andy's interpretation of the Cardinal's controversial intervention in the referendum debate was that the Catholic Church supported separation from Britain because the Vatican calculated it could achieve more influence within an independent Scotland. For Andy and Dennis, then, the truth was as obvious as it was appalling; the SNP and the Roman Catholic Church were conspiring to cleave Scotland from its Protestant union with Britain by transforming it into an independent, and increasingly Catholic, country.

Importantly, an interview with Grand Lodge Chaplain the Rev. Pete Singh confirmed that such sentiments were also found among the Order's leading hierarchy. Reflecting on the contemporary relevance of the phrase 'Home Rule is Rome Rule' within the context of the Scottish independence referendum, Singh stated:

> I'm very concerned about the place of the Christian faith within an independent Scotland. [Protestant Christianity is] enshrined in the Act of Union 1707, the Prelacy Act, the Protestant Religion and Presbyterian Church Act, [and] the act against papal supremacy.[1] There are many acts which are enshrined in that 1707 Act which allow the Christian faith to be promoted openly. So I would say that [Scottish independence] is a very big concern, [which might also mean] potentially losing the monarchy. Alex Salmond is very much cosying up to the Church of Rome, saying that it is 'one of the great institutions' in a recent speech. The SNP almost is a parrot of the Roman Church, and are very quick to silence people who do not agree with their views, and it does indicate a dictatorial state. Rome insists on segregated schooling, and it's not being challenged at all. The SNP are very keen to just let things be, and let Rome basically take our money and fund these schools [which] personally makes me rather angry. The SNP want to keep the status quo and let Rome prevail.

Singh's comments here are complex, but offer a strikingly similar critique to that offered by Dennis and Andy about the imagined interconnections between the SNP, the Catholic Church, and their shared plans for Scottish independence. For Singh, separation from Britain would imperil Scotland's ability to adhere to the one true faith of reformed Protestant Christianity – an adherence which, he states, has been protected by British constitutional law since 1707. In this view, if Scotland were no longer British, a domino effect might well follow, with the Protestant religion and the monarchy replaced by 'the Church of Rome' and the papacy. That this replacement would be facilitated by the SNP, who were said to be 'a parrot of the Roman Church', was evidenced, according to Singh, by Alex Salmond's courting of the Catholic electorate, and the SNP's deliberate failure to challenge Scotland's Catholic schooling system. Worse still, a future independent Scotland would not only be Catholic in substance but dictatorial in style, a prediction Singh makes by drawing on wider Orange ideas about Catholic complicity in the history of fascism (see also Chapters 2 and 4). Importantly, this is a claim that has been extended to include members of the SNP more generally, who Orangemen frequently referred to in my presence as the 'Yestapo'.

Yet, it would be wrong to suggest that Orange claims about the religious imperative of Scotland remaining as part of the UK was expressed in wholly negative terms. Perhaps the clearest positive Orange expression of religiously inspired unionist politics could be seen in worship services held in Glasgow Evangelical Church – affectionately referred to by my informants as the 'Orange Kirk'. Decorated with stained glass commemorating the Reformers, the Covenanters, and the bicentenary of the Orange Institution in Scotland, Glasgow Evangelical Church is led and attended by Orangemen and women, with Orange chaplains regularly providing pulpit supply in the absence of a permanent minister. As well as hosting Grand Lodge's annual divine service and other Orange-focused special events, regular Sunday services at Glasgow Evangelical Church have a distinctly 'Orange feel'. Congregants typically greet each other with Orange grips, copies of *The Orange Torch* are distributed before the service, the Bible is read from a lectern sculpted in the form of William atop his rearing white horse, sermons are delivered from a pulpit draped in the cross and crown symbol shared by the Royal Black Institution, and a portrait of the Queen which hangs in Orange Lodges also hangs in the church hall. In addition, the church's doctrinal statement on Protestantism notes that it is among other churches 'which reject the claim of the Pope to be the head of the Church, dispute the Roman Catholic theory of the Papacy generally, and disagree profoundly with the doctrine of transubstantiation' and it strongly echoes Orange degree initiation vows, where candidates must promise 'to give no coun-tenance to the unscriptural, superstitious and idolatrous worship of the Church of Rome'. Such were the hallmarks of this very 'Orange Kirk'.

Attending a service at Glasgow Evangelical Church early on in my fieldwork, on 'Reformation Sunday' no less, left quite an impression for me, most especially because of the way proceedings blended Protestantism and unionism. Easily a third of the congregation were wearing Orange collarettes. The service opened with a Bible being carried to the front platform by a church office bearer, overseen by the minister, a Grand Lodge Chaplain, who stood at the front of the platform. Next, six flag-bearing Orangemen in collarettes appeared at the back of the church, processing forward in two groups. One group turned left, carrying the Union flag and their Lodge Bible, while the other group turned right, carrying the Scottish Saltire emblazoned with the words 'We Will Maintain' – a reference to William III's 1688 mythical declaration 'the Protestant religion I will maintain'. Arriving at the front of the platform, the church office bearer received the flags from the Orangemen, placing them into upright holders at either side of the communion table, while their Lodge Bible was placed at the centre of the table. At the end of the service, after the benediction, the flags were lifted and handed back to their respective bearers, who then turned to face the congregation. The first two verses of *God Save the Queen* were then sung by the entire congregation, who all stood to attention, with arms held rigidly at their sides. During this singing, the Saltire was dipped, while the Union flag remained held at a more elevated angle, to symbolise the greater honour accorded to Britain. At the end of the anthem, the Saltire was raised in line with the Union flag, whereupon the flags and Bibles were processed out while the congregation sang Elgar's *Land of Hope and Glory*.

The religious patriotism of that Sunday service, and especially its deification of Britishness, was more than matched by other worship services I attended at Glasgow Evangelical Church. Indeed, the first service I attended there, in September 2012, was a special event to commemorate the centenary of the signing of the Ulster Covenant against Irish Home Rule. A banner hanging across the front of the church had been printed to mark the occasion, and simply read 'NO HOME RULE'. Below it, a smaller sign read 'The Orange Order at the HEART of Scotland', the words being flanked by a Union flag and a Saltire. In addition to prayers and hymns, the service was taken up by several speakers offering their thoughts on Ulster's Solemn League and Covenant, as well as their reflections on its contemporary relevance to the Scottish independence debate. Jonathan Henderson was first to speak, and he did so by giving a passionate call for Orangemen to defend the Union:

> The Union Jack is all about the *union*! The ties that bind Scotland and Ulster are deep! The ties that bind us to the people of Northern Ireland, these are ties that should not be broken. But here we are – the neo-Jacobites of the SNP want to end the union. We owe it to our Grand Lodge to put all of our time and talents to defend the integrity of our way of life. The call has come to us! The Loyal Orange Institution is the Protestant voice of the people of Scotland. We will always take on that responsibility!

Other speakers that evening were just as forthright in forging connections between the religious motives of the signatories of the Ulster Covenant and those who, in 2012, were campaigning against Scottish independence. A senior Orangeman visiting from Northern Ireland stated:

> The unionists [in 1912] opposed Home Rule, which in today's terms would be called devolution. They were right that Home Rule was Rome Rule. They held the flame of freedom high, and they passed it on! A century on, who would have thought that the issue we would be facing would be [Scottish] independence? We will stand by you, as you stood by us! That is what kinship is all about! We should not confuse patriotism with nationalism, and there will be an attempt to do that in [the] 2014 [independence referendum].

At the end of the service, *Land of Hope and Glory* was sung, but on this occasion the assembled congregation waved small plastic Union flags which had been distributed at the beginning of the service. Watching over a hundred miniature flags flutter as the chorus was sung – *Wider still and wider shall thy bounds be set; God, who made thee mighty, make thee mightier yet* – felt deeply foreign to me, especially in a church setting. Indeed, where fieldwork among the Exclusive Brethren in Scotland (Webster 2013) had taught me that this sacralisation of Britishness and Empire was a kind of blasphemy, these early observations among Scots-Orangemen pushed me to unlearn such assumptions by understanding how the politics of unionism could be experienced as a mark of divine election.

Other ethnographic observations within Glasgow Evangelical Church reveal more about this blending of ultra-Protestantism and ultra-Britishness. Just three months before the independence referendum, for example, Grand Lodge held their annual divine service in the 'Orange Kirk', with Grand Chaplain the Rev. Forsyth giving the sermon:

> These are the days when we are called to stand firm in the Word of God, our Protestant Biblical theology, Calvary's message of salvation through the Lord Jesus Christ, the example and the sacrifice of the Reformers, Covenanters, and martyrs, and we must, as an Order, stay faithful to Great Britain as one United Kingdom. We need to remain conscientiously Protestant, proud Scots, and passionately British. We have reached that crucial time when you must be a man or woman of your word. Yes, but even more than that, as an Orangeman or Orangewoman, there is a higher calling to be a man or woman of God.

That following this 'higher calling' required all Orange members to vote 'No' in the referendum was also made clear by the Grand Master, who stated during the same worship service that Protestantism and civil and religious liberty depended on maintaining the union between Scotland and the rest of the UK. More than this, Forsyth was clear that the fight to preserve British Protestantism was a divine battle, stating in a different service at Glasgow Evangelical Church that 'it doesn't matter who comes against us, because they aren't coming against us – they are coming against God'. Echoing Forsyth's invocations of divine backing, on the Sunday after the referendum result was announced, the Rev. Tom Greig stood to pray:

> Heavenly Father, we come before you this morning, and we think of our nation, and what has happened over this last week. We think of what our electorate, our population, has done – remaining true to the Union. And Lord we give You thanks for the vote. And Lord, while we are here today, we reflect on some of the political arguments that were fought over. We think of the Word of God, the Scripture, and some of the principles that scripture has taught us, like a threefold cord isn't easily broken. We are thankful of the words of Christ, that a house divided against itself will fall. And so we think not only about the political arguments, but the Biblical arguments. And so Lord we're thankful for what has happened politically. And Lord we now pray that a unity would come back to our nation.

In sum, the Scottish independence referendum was understood by my informants to be a Roman Catholic plot to destroy British Protestantism and that, as such, it could only be thwarted by a concomitant uprising of loyal Protestants dedicated to enacting Scotland's second Reformation. Here, Union flags and Saltires processed into church, or pictures of the Queen hung in church halls become symbols of divine favour and icons of divine power. Sermons that conflate the Bible and salvation with unionism, or equate Britain and Scotland to Israel do the same, as do prayers of thanksgiving which liken the referendum result to the teachings of Christ. Equally, anti-Home Rule banners and anti 'Rome Rule' slogans, when combined with critical commentary on the SNP, make this same point, but in reverse, by equating early twentieth-century Irish republicanism with twenty-first-century

Scottish nationalism, both of which, as a result, come to be regarded as (Catholic) enemies of true (Protestant) religion. For those of my informants most invested in this construction of referendum-as-reformation, the result was that their Orange membership positioned themselves and their fellow brethren as latter-day Covenanters. Indeed, just as the Scottish Covenanters were motivated by fears of Anglicanism-as-Romanism-in-disguise, so too did Scots-Orangemen pit themselves against what they claimed was Scottish nationalism as the 'back door' to 'Rome Rule'.

That this emic framing of Scottish-independence-as-papal-plot represents, from a sociological and political science perspective, a series of 'tall tales' (Rosie 2014) is surely something of an understatement. Importantly, Rosie (2004) is also correct to point out that expressions of religious bigotry in Scotland do not equate to the structural realities of sectarianism in Northern Ireland that continue to profoundly impact the life chances of many communities there. Equally, recent media reports about 'the Ulsterisation of Scottish politics', which paint the constitutional disagreement between the SNP and the Scottish Conservatives as somehow comparable to that which stands between Sinn Fein and the DUP, seem very wide of the mark. Unlike in Scotland, for example, while Northern Ireland had no functioning government from January 2017 to January 2020, it still has armed dissident republican and loyalist paramilitaries, as well as functioning peace walls to keep the communities in which they operate apart. Yet, as I describe below, while my informants' claims may well seem like 'tall tales' when compared against the findings of recent Scottish social attitudes surveys, to dismiss the content of their moral commitments on that basis is to miss what may be learned both *about* and *from* the Orange ethical projects which fill their lives.

'No surrender! No separation!': Scots-Orange unionism as ultra-British ethno-nationalism

Importantly, Orange claims about the Catholicism of Scottish nationalism and the Protestantism of Scottish–British unionism were not always expressed in religious terms, at least not to the exclusion of other framings. As my Orange informants continued to discuss the perils of Scottish independence, ethnicity often took centre stage. Here, Catholicism was sometimes displaced by (or conflated with) Irishness and Irish republicanism, most especially when Orangemen imagined what their lives would be like in an independent Scotland. Equally, it was not unusual to observe the categories of 'Protestant' and 'Protestantism' shifting emphasis from religious ideation to embodied practice. Here, fighting Scottish independence had little to do with resisting the papacy's encroachment on Presbyterian theological freedoms, as was the Covenanter's ultimate concern, and more to do with preserving visible symbols of British patriotism as a route to defending Orange 'heritage and culture'. Put another way, for those of my Orange informants most concerned with the ethno-nationalism of Scottish independence, the real threat was not the Catholic doctrine of transubstantiation but the politics of republicanism. As such, parades and protests replaced church services as the most effective weapons against the

SNP. Such views were stressed by the then Grand Lodge Executive Officer Scot Symon during an interview:

> If we go independent, on 19 September, there'll be no picture of the Queen on the wall [in Orange Lodges], that's for sure! There'll be no Union flag flying on the Orange hall. And let's be honest, [the SNP] will try and eradicate anything British. Orange Order parades would then be attacked. The facts are, in the last ten years, we have had nine court cases [against] local councils to defend our right to parade in various towns and villages throughout Scotland. And the nine local authorities were all SNP-controlled. If that's happened at local level, you can bet your boots that it will happen at national government level! An SNP MSP said to me in this very room, they have nothing to fear from the Orange Order, because we don't vote for them anyway. The SNP are basically republican, through and through, they are nationalist republican. I think that's how Alex Salmond gets on quite well with Martin McGuinness, and I think the two of them see that if Scotland was independent, Northern Ireland is going independent. Martin McGuinness and Sinn Fein will be pushing for a referendum again – you can see it coming, and it will be the break-up of the United Kingdom if Scotland goes. I think the fight is that Scotland must remain.

Importantly, as Grand Lodge Executive Officer, Symon represented the public face of Orangeism in Scotland, a role he fulfilled, in part, by fielding enquiries from journalists and academics. Indeed, Symon was the key gatekeeper with whom I negotiated access when first embarking on my studies, and it was he who was quoted in the Scottish media whenever the Order found itself at the centre of controversy, generally as a result of an incident of disorder at the fringes of an Orange parade. As such, his claims about the SNP as a 'nationalist republican' party with direct ideological and strategic links to Sinn Fein cannot be dismissed as somehow out of step with the Order's 'official line'. More importantly still, Symon's assertions that the Orange Order would find its symbolic displays banned and its parades under attack in an independent Scotland was a view I also heard frequently aired by grass-roots Orangemen. While Dennis was typically strident in this view, stating as part of a discussion about recent conflicts with local authorities about parading rights that an independent Scotland 'would be Armageddon for the Orange Order', others agreed, albeit in less dramatic terms. Norrie Brand, an Orangeman and bandsman explained to me in an interview that:

> We are Scottish but British; we don't want to be independent. If Scotland did break away, it would be the worst thing ever. We support Queen and country, [and] we hope we are going to get a King Billy – Prince William! The SNP don't believe in the Crown; they don't believe in anything we believe in. If Scotland do break away, it would be difficult for the Orange Institution and for the bands. There would be a campaign to stop us parading. Glasgow City Council are trying to do everything in their power to stop us.

Others echoed Symon's fears that Scottish independence would lead to a rising tide of Irish republicanism within Scotland. Eric Caldow, for example, explained that the 'culture war' he had observed between nationalists and unionists in Northern Ireland, was now coming to Scotland.

There has been an absolutely deliberate attempt to undermine the unionist population in Northern Ireland, and to vilify the Loyal Orders. I'm beginning to think, has there been a deal done behind the scenes? You hear about children's playparks being named after IRA terrorists. It's a deliberate attempt to deny any sign of Britishness. It's even come to Scotland. We had a dissident republican march through Scotland on 13 July, in Glencruix! [That has] never, ever been known! They were here deliberately seeking trouble, to stoke up tensions. I fear it may well be a growing trend. There has been a strategy set out by republicans; I think they are deliberately having parades in an attempt to get Orange parades stopped [because] I don't think they have a genuine parading culture.

Crucially, Caldow saw the SNP as part of this 'growing trend' of republicanism in Scotland, and as such, described the party as 'a threat to everything I believe in, and everything the Orange Institution believes in'. As was the case for other Orangemen, the Scottish independence referendum brought such concerns into sharp focus. Yet, unlike Forsyth and those most involved in Glasgow Evangelical Church, the specifically *republican* nature of the threat Caldow believed Scotland to be facing led him to focus his energies on political activism as opposed to religious supplication. More specifically still, Caldow's activism seemed to have been shaped, in part, by a Northern Irish style ethnicisation of constitutional politics. Here, Caldow's identification of dissident Irish republicanism as having 'come to Scotland' appeared inextricably linked to his efforts to form an opposing loyalist organisation, with direct links to Ulster, to campaign for a 'No' vote in the independence referendum. The group that was eventually formed, called 'Maintain the Union', was chaired by Caldow, and canvassed across Western and Central Scotland. Yet the group's innocuous-sounding name hid its targeting of a rather more 'fringe' section of the unionist electorate, a fact which Caldow openly admitted to. Indeed, Caldow was very clear that 'Maintain the Union' had been set up to target young Scottish loyalists, particularly those in the band scene, who, despite being instinctively anti-SNP and anti-nationalist, were generally disengaged from electoral politics, and tended not to turn out in large numbers on polling day.

In an attempt to galvanise this disenfranchised population of young bandsmen and other loyalists, 'Maintain the Union' forged links with two controversial loyalist groups in Northern Ireland – the Rangers FC supporters club the Vanguard Bears, and the Progressive Unionist Party (PUP), widely recognised as the political wing of the Ulster Volunteer Force and Red Hand Commando paramilitaries. Doing so, Caldow told me candidly, was a calculated move. '"Maintain the Union" won't attract mainstream voters, but we have our own community – bands, loyalists, Rangers supporters, and even paramilitary sympathisers'. Importantly, while the Grand Orange Lodge of Scotland did send a senior representative from their 'British Together' campaign to give a presentation to a 'Maintain the Union' meeting, Caldow was clear that 'Maintain the Union' 'are attempting to get to the people the Orange Institution may not be able to get to'. Whether Grand Lodge was not able to reach these individuals, or simply chose not to target them (because of their firm disavowal of loyalist paramilitarism) is difficult to answer. Regardless, that 'Maintain the Union' sought to re-enfranchise young Scottish loyalists by associating the independence referendum with the constitutional question (and ethnic conflict) in Northern Ireland by forging links to the Vanguard Bears and the PUP seems beyond reasonable doubt. That 'Maintain the Union' also donated money to Belfast's Twaddell Avenue loyalist protest camp (established in 2013 to demand the return of a banned Orange parade along the predominantly nationalist Ardoyne) further supports such a conclusion.

As such, to the extent that 'British Together' represented a hard-line unionist version of 'Better Together', it also seems true that 'Maintain the Union' represented a hard-line loyalist version of 'British Together'. Here, the metaphorical 'Mark of Cain' discussed earlier becomes something of a spectrum, and one that did not end with 'Maintain the Union'. At a protest staged outside the Scottish Parliament on 18 September 2013 (exactly a year before the referendum), Caldow and other 'Maintain the Union' activists made the journey to Edinburgh by sharing the cost of a private hire coach with a different loyalist group called the Commonwealth Unionist Party (CUP). Unbeknown to Caldow, the presence of the CUP – who formed in the wake of the flag dispute in Northern Ireland (Nolan et al. 2014) to demand that the Union flag fly over every public and civic building in Scotland – had also attracted supporters from UKIP, as well as the far-right Scottish Defence League (see Pilkington 2016). The presence of intoxicated SDL supporters wearing black face masks and chanting 'Ten German Bombers' was clearly too much for Caldow, who quickly decided to move the 'Maintain the Union' protest fifty yards from this larger and noisier group. Whether or not relocating their protest was enough to disassociate 'Maintain the Union' from those they had travelled with, Caldow's real frustration, he admitted, was that they had lost their opportunity to get their message out because the CUP and SDL had monopolised the attention of the few journalists who were present.

Equally, while Caldow did not want to share a platform with the Scottish Defence League on account of their far-right connections, Maintain the Union's social media content contained its own hard-line message – a message which used loyalist symbols and ideas to conflate the SNP and 'Yes' campaigners with Roman Catholicism, Celtic fans, and the IRA (referred to by one contributor as the Irish Roman Assassins). In the main, such content took the form of outraged comments tacked onto reposted photos from Celtic-supporting 'Yes' campaigners, including images of the hunger striker Bobby Sands, and banners showing the Union flag being thrown in the bin. In addition, anti-SNP content included a letter purporting to be from Alex Salmond's office stating 'there would be no Scotland without the RC Church', and rhetorical questions such as 'Do you really want Republican Roseanna Cunningham lording it over you? Scotland would be a cold place for Unionists'. Importantly, Maintain the Union's opposition to republicanism was mirrored by support for symbols of Britishness and loyalism. A Twitter image adapted from a 1900 edition of *Army and Navy* magazine, for example, showed two bulldogs standing atop a Union flag and guarding the coastline of British-controlled South Africa with the slogan 'what we've got, we'll hold'. As well as drawing on the history of Boer-era British imperialism, Maintain the Union's campaign materials also repurposed the famous First World War recruitment poster of a pointing Lord

Kitchener, complete with the slogan 'Your country needs you'. In addition, their campaign badge motto, 'the union we will maintain', intentionally echoed the Williamite maxim 'The Protestant religion we will maintain'. More generally, Maintain the Union's campaign leaflets contained copious Union flag symbolism, combining this with images of the British crown and the Saltire.

Given the evidence above, understanding Scots-Orange unionism as creative of (and emerging from) a kind of ultra-British ethno-nationalism does not seem to require much interpretative imagination. Perhaps a more interesting observation would be that entering into this ethnicised ultra-Britishness allowed Scots-Orange 'No' voters to transform themselves into latter-day loyalists, just as the ultra-Protestantism of Glasgow Evangelical Church transformed Orangemen into latter-day Covenanters. Here, supporters of 'British Together' and 'Maintain the Union' came to regard the Scottish independence referendum not as a fight for Scotland's soul, but as a fight for the constitutional destiny of the entire United Kingdom. By deploying a certain historical imagination, Scots-Orange unionists could place themselves within a long lineage of patriotic defenders of Great Britain – as loyal troops called by Kitchener in a time of national crisis, and as loyal subjects of the Queen and her empire. Of even greater importance, however, was a more con-temporary imagination of 'Ulster's cause', in the recent past and in the present, and the bearing Scottish independence would have on this conflict. Here, Orangemen and Orange sympathisers could experience themselves as literal maintainers of the Union, that is, as the frontline resistance against republican incursions into Scotland, and, by extension, Northern Ireland. In the words of Grand Lodge Executive Officer Scot Symon: 'I think that's how Alex Salmond gets on quite well with Martin McGuinness. If Scotland was independent, Northern Ireland is going independent, and it will be the break-up of the United Kingdom'.

In this view, efforts to safeguard local Orange parade routes, or demands that the Union flag fly over every public building in Scotland (which find their mirror image in objections to new republican parades, and fears about the removal of the Union flag in an independent Scotland) can be understood as entering into the ethnicised constitutional 'culture wars' of post-Troubles Northern Ireland. In more literal terms, Orangemen like Caldow, who not only canvas for a 'No' vote among Scotland's loyalist bands and Rangers supporters, but do so by forging links with Belfast-based Rangers Ultras, as well as the political wing of the UVF, actually *enact* this conflation of Scottish unionism and Northern Irish loyalism. Stepping beyond the usual Scots-Orange forays into 'Ulster's cause' undertaken by many of my informants via annual 12 July pilgrimages to the Shankill Road, Caldow's ethnicisation of the Scottish independence referendum deliberately transformed the Order's 'Mark of Cain' into a badge of honour. Here, Grand Lodge's taboo against associating with paramilitarism came to be strategically transgressed in a way that carefully balanced the spectre of loyalist violence designed to excite young bandsmen, with an at-arms-length plausible deniability afforded by forging links with radical groups based across the Irish Sea. That this 'Ulsterisation' of Scottish unionism had a strong appeal among some was neatly encapsulated by the reaction of a young Scots-Orange informant of mine who, decrying what he saw as republican attacks against symbols of Britishness, told me in a hushed but excited tone how loyalist paramilitaries 'are thinking about bringing out the toys again, and not just over there, over here too!'

Using 'toys' as a euphemism for guns, the 'here too' of a constitutionally turbulent Scotland came to be imaginatively reconfigured by this loyalist minority as a body-politic defined, in its most extreme form, not only by blood, but also by the shedding of blood – a British Protestant 'race apart' who claim willingness to use violence to preserve Scotland's place within the Union. For the vast majority of my informants, such statements were rhetorical; I only ever met one Scottish Orangeman who had served time in prison for involvement in paramilitarism. Seen in aspirational terms, however, such statements become more than pure bluster, existing instead as a way to signal an Orange yearning for Scotland's present and future to be marked, as in its mythical past, by an ethnic Protestant triumphalism totemically represented by, variously, King Billy, the UVF, and Rangers Football Club, to name only a few. Importantly, having aspirations to see Scottish politics dominated by the adoration of such totems (and the ethno-national group they collectively represent) did not preclude those of my Orange informants who identified as loyalist from engaging in more 'ordinary' acts of campaigning. Yet, even these ordinary acts – leafleting, phoning community leaders to ensure they were 'getting the vote out' – frequently came to be experienced as yet another facet of the ethnicisation of the Scottish independence question.

On 17 September, just a day before the vote, I was invited to go out leafleting with a group of Orangemen and bandsmen in Livingstone and Broxburn. Unsure of what to expect, I asked the group of men, ranging from those in their late teens, to those in their sixties, what to expect. One man responded by telling me how, on more than one occasion, they had been spat on by 'Yes' supporters, an experience that others in the group confirmed with angry nods and disgusted expressions. Stories of this kind, of being abused and discriminated against for, in their view, simply having the courage of their unionist and loyalist convictions, were repeatedly shared with me that afternoon and evening as the men went from house to house putting leaflets through letter boxes. Andy, for example, explained to me how the referendum had hardened anti-British attitudes within his nationalist-dominated workplace. Whenever colleagues became aware of his unionist and Rangers tattoos they ostracised him, he said. With building resentment, he explained how his boss had gone even further, publicly outing him as a unionist in a meeting by declaring to all those around the table: 'I've never employed a Rangers season ticket holder before!' His boss's comment, I was told, which took for granted the conflation of Rangers fans with 'No' voters, was a jibe designed to signal to fellow nationalists that he would never have offered Andy the job had he known he was a Protestant unionist. 'He's a fucking mickey bastard' Andy concluded. Another Orange campaigner echoed Andy's suggestion that ethnic prejudice was at the heart of Scottish nationalism by offering his own story about someone who had switched to being a 'No' supporter because of the level of anti-English abuse her husband had received from Scots 'Yes'-supporting workmates. All the Orangemen present agreed that this was typical of the 'anti-English racism' that they said was endemic within the SNP.

As we moved through the streets of Broxburn, I asked the group of Orangemen I was with why the leaflets they were handing out listed their organisation as 'Independent Unionists' – why not campaign under the banner of the Orange Order and use the Order's own 'British Together' leaflets? Sam answered candidly that if they openly campaigned as part of the Orange Order, they would be labelled 'bigots' by those who received their material, meaning that the vast majority of their leaflets would be put straight in the bin. Another Orangeman, James, offered a slightly different perspective, stating that they chose not to leaflet as the Orange Order 'because it's not a religious vote'. Without any sense of contradiction, James continued: 'We need Catholics to vote "No" or we are going to lose our country. We need to use people to our own ends'. What both answers had in common, then, was a clear sense that, when it came to their unionist ethno-religious identity, honesty was not the best policy. For Sam, this was because Orange expressions of unionism were never given a fair hearing by the majority of Scots, who were instinctively (and in his view, bigotedly) anti-Orange. While James clearly agreed with Sam on this point, his own explanation went further, stating that by obscuring their Orange identity, Orangemen could 'use' Catholics to their own Orange ends by attempting to persuade them to vote for a constitutional arrangement which, in effect, would safeguard Scotland's status as a British Protestant nation.

From the perspective of these Orangemen, then, the independence referendum was 'not a religious vote' because it was ethnicity and not religion which primarily influenced whether someone was a 'Yes' or a 'No' supporter. Indeed, even the statement 'we need Catholics to vote "No"' can be seen as a comment on ethnicity and not religion, since, in this context, 'Catholic' functions as a shorthand for anti-unionist and pro-nationalist, anti-Rangers and pro-Celtic, anti-British and pro-Irish, which, in Andy's summary, can be reduced down even further to the moniker 'fucking mickey bastard'. While other Orangemen I spent time with that day chose other labels – 'Tim' being the most common – the intended meaning of such language remained the same, namely that while 'Catholic' was a reliable and largely discrete category of persons, the category was not necessarily, in and of itself, a religious one. Here, the religion of Orange politics became racialised through the identification of a Scots-Irish sub-electorate who might be persuaded (that is, 'used') to vote against their own ethno-national proclivities. This would be achievable, however, only if the Orange source of such a message was sufficiently disguised for, regardless of the extent to which the referendum was 'not religious', it was assumed that the mere mention of the colour Orange would be enough to close the minds of the Order's many Scots-Irish detractors.

Importantly, these ethno-national entrenchments and hostilities cut both ways, a fact that was particularly obvious on referendum day, which I spent in Glencruix. The day's events began in the social club with Eric and Dennis. Unsurprisingly, however, the atmosphere was markedly different to a normal Thursday of drinking and banter. Instead of their usual pints and whiskies, Eric, Dennis, and a few of the other regulars, sat with mugs of tea, mobile phones in hand, ticking off names on a list, or highlighting those who had, as yet, not taken their calls (see Figure 5.1). The aim was simple: to contact every Orangeman, as well as every loyalist bandsman

5.1 Getting the unionist vote out in Glencruix.

in the surrounding area to ensure that they voted. This was no small task, as the enormous lists of names in tiny print demonstrated. Sitting for what felt like several hours watching Dennis and the others coax and cajole scores of Orangemen and Orange sympathisers into early voting, inhabiting this ethno-nationalist bubble it was easy to conclude that 'No' would win the day, and nowhere more so than in North Lanarkshire. But any of my questions about what they thought the outcome would be were batted away, either to show that they were 'not taking anything for granted', or else out of a fear of 'jinxing' the result.

In between phone calls, the men swapped gossip about a brawl that had occurred the night before in Glencruix town square between 'Yes' and 'No' supporters, with both groups trying to monopolise the public space in order to hand out campaign leaflets. The same had happened in Glasgow another man said, with violence erupting when nationalist supporters had started covering the George Square war memorial in 'Yes' stickers. The men spoke excitedly about how, in both instances, police were drafted in to restore order. About two hours into this canvassing marathon, a local Orangeman named Jonny entered the bar to announce that he was in a dilemma. He was planning on helping an elderly neighbour to get to her local polling station so she could cast her 'No' vote. However, after already agreeing to help, this same neighbour had since asked for additional help with casting her son's proxy vote. The problem, he explained, was that he knew for a fact that the son was a 'Yes' supporter. Jonny looked genuinely conflicted. Holding a piece of paper with a telephone number on it, Jonny further explained that a local councillor had given him the necessary contact details to enquire about how to properly cast a proxy vote. Without hesitation, Eric bounced out of his seat, grabbed the piece of paper and tore it into small pieces. After a moment of shock had passed from his expression, Jonny said 'well, that's my dilemma solved!' as he and the other Orangemen in the room chuckled with laughter.

As afternoon approached, it was decided that Dennis would continue to organise operations from within the social club, while Eric would visit several local polling stations, both to leaflet outside their perimeter, and to monitor goings-on to ensure that 'Yes' campaigners were not playing any 'dirty tricks'. Driving through Caldercosh with Eric, it was clear that other loyalists had been doing some campaigning of their own, most likely late the previous night. On two separate sections of road we saw council workers busily using power washers to remove large red letters spray-painted onto the tarmac. The clean-up had seemingly just begun, with both slogans still visible. One read 'CALDERCOSH SAYS NO!' while another, echoing the famous loyalist slogan of Troubles-era Northern Ireland read 'NO SURRENDER!' Also notable was the fact that several lamp posts had Union flags tied to them, another key symbolic demarcation of sectarian territory in Northern Ireland that loyalists in Caldercosh had repurposed for the occasion of polling day. Nodding at the flags, Eric said that many more had been put up around the surrounding villages but that most had been taken down by the council early that morning, a fact he planned to make a formal complaint about, as he viewed their being erected as entirely legal.

As we moved from one polling station to another, Eric scrutinised every visible aspect of the 'Yes' campaign's materials, explaining how he wanted to ensure that not a single 'Yes' poster was too close to any polling station, and that none were covering any 'No' posters. 'Yes' campaigners routinely took down opposition placards, Eric explained, which, despite being illegal, was not acted against by local politicians who were generally of a nationalist persuasion themselves. In between these informal checks, I stood with Eric as he talked nervously with a few Labour councillors who were also out campaigning for a 'No' vote, albeit for non-Orange reasons. Snatches of local information about voter turnout were exchanged, with Eric occasionally turning to me to contextualise the relevance of one place or another by stating whether or not it was a Catholic-nationalist area. As afternoon turned to evening and voting began to slow, I travelled with Eric and his family to their own local polling station as they cast their votes, and then returned with Eric to the social club. With their phone calls all made, Dennis and a few others were now sipping pints while they waited for polling to close at 10 p.m. Later still, I was invited by Dennis and Eric to a meal at a local curry house with Todd Walters, the Grand Master of the Orange Order in Scotland. As we ate, the mood was jovial and, while the men were all clearly nervous, they began to congratulate themselves on their long efforts of campaigning. A few of the men present even began to allow themselves to predict that '"No" would win the day'.

It was not until the next morning, after a long night of drinking at Eric's house with Dennis and several other social club regulars as we watched the live TV coverage, that the announcement came that 'No' had indeed won, with the eventual figure being 55.3 per cent voting against independence. While Eric was clearly relieved that Scotland would remain part of the Union, I was surprised to see just how aggrieved he was by the fact that his own home district, the local authority of North Lanarkshire, had narrowly voted 'Yes' by a margin of 2.9 per cent. His mood echoed that of the Orangemen I had been leafleting with on the eve of the referendum, who all agreed that voting 'Yes' was tantamount to 'stabbing your country in the back'. Eric's anger at this local result was, in part, then, because he felt betrayed by so many of those living in his local authority, an area which in the past he had run for as a Labour councillor, and which he still felt a real affinity for and loyalty towards. With Glencruix being such a historic centre of Orangeism, Eric had hoped that he and his fellow brethren would carry the day for the Union; that they had not was clearly a bitter disappointment.

I was less surprised, however, by Eric's explanation for the local result in North Lanarkshire, which he put down to the numbers of Catholic republicans in the areas surrounding Glencruix. According to Eric, this same explanation could also be applied to the other two local authorities which had voted 'Yes', namely Dundee and Glasgow, which, he said, were well known for containing significant populations of Catholic Scottish nationalists. His logic fit with the views of other Orangemen I talked to about the referendum result, who frequently commented that Glencruix, like Bridgeton in Glasgow's East End where Grand Lodge had its headquarters, was a bastion of loyalism surrounded by disloyal nationalists and republicans who identified as Scots-Irish instead of British. Keen to understand more about Eric's reading of the local specificities of the 'Yes' result in North Lanarkshire, I asked him what he thought the result would have been in Dennis's hometown of Chapel-geddie, which, despite being less than three miles from 'loyalist Glencruix', was commonly held to be politically and demographically dominated by Catholic nationalists and republicans. While Eric was in no doubt that those in Chapelgeddie would have contributed significantly to North Lanarkshire's 'Yes' vote, my question still prompted him to seek out evidence to substantiate his suspicions. Having made the request, Eric was told by the council that no such localised polling data would ever be released. Ultimately, this didn't seem to matter for, in his mind and in the minds of many of my Orange informants, the simple truth was that Glasgow and North Lanarkshire had voted 'Yes' because 'the green element' had turned out in force to try and permanently sever Scotland from its British Protestant heritage. Of course, what mattered more for Eric was that these 'enemies within' had ultimately failed.

In the context of this lack of local polling data, my Orange informants' post-referendum suspicions about the hostility of this 'green element' were confirmed in a different and more immediate way, as opposing crowds of loyalists and nationalists gathered in Glasgow's George Square the night after the referendum. Foreseeing what was to come, Eric had spent much of that Friday afternoon on his phone, calling and texting various Glencruix loyalist youth to dissuade those he suspected might be tempted to travel to Glasgow to join the building fracas. Eric's view, he explained, was that any such gathering could only lead to trouble, and as it turned out, he was correct. Breaking through lines of police separating the two groups, a sizeable number of young loyalists, many draped in Union flags, sang *Rule Britannia* and brawled with groups of 'Yes' supporters who were determined to stand their ground. Over thirty arrests were made during and after the disturbances. Media coverage the following day was quick to link these loyalists to far-right supporters and football hooligans, some of whom were reported to have given Nazi salutes during the ensuing violence. Andy Cooper, who had spent some of that evening in George Square celebrating the victory of the 'No' campaign, was outraged by what he saw as the pro-nationalist bias of the media coverage, which he said was 'full of lies'. All he had witnessed, he explained, was a good-natured group of young men singing patriotic songs to celebrate their British identity and the referendum result:

> There were no sectarian songs sung, only *Rule Britannia* and the national anthem! And there were only Union flags, and only *one* of these said 'No Surrender' – what's sectarian about that? The 'Yes' supporters had been there [in George Square] for two days! All we wanted to do was celebrate! The 'Yes' side provoked us – they were calling it 'Independence Square'.

While Eric and Andy took different views about whether or not to travel to George Square that evening, they were united in their condemnation of what they viewed as nationalist provocation and republican aggression following the failure of the 'Yes' campaign. Crucially, according to many of my Orange informants, the actions of these nationalists revealed what had really motivated 'Yes' voters in Glasgow and North Lanarkshire all along, namely a hatred of Britishness, and a concomitant desire to see Scotland turned into a Scots-Irish ethnic enclave in which the Orange Order would be persecuted out of existence.

In the immediate aftermath of the referendum result, however, such fears about recalcitrant Scots-Catholic nationalists and republicans 'not taking "No" for an answer' did not completely dominate the sentiments of my Orange and Orange-sympathising informants, for the vote also stimulated among them a renewed sense of British-Protestant triumphalism. Such feelings were strongly on display two days after the referendum, during a parade by the Pride of Govan Flute Band entitled 'Celebrating the Union'. Attending the parade so soon after the referendum result, the emotions of relief mixed with residual concern were palpable among loyalist marchers and spectators alike, made all the more noticeable as the procession made its way through a Scots-Irish identifying area of Govan.

Just yards from where the band began to assemble stood the 'Tall Cranes', a windowless-fronted emerald-green Celtic bar. Bedecked in Saltire bunting, silver tinsel shamrocks, and a large 'Vote Yes' poster, there was no mistaking the 'Tall Cranes' as a site of both Scottish nationalism and Scots-Irish identity (see Figure 5.2). As if to reinforce this symbolic display, a few doors down from the bar stood a building, the doors of which had been scrawled with the words 'REPUBLICAN GOVAN' (Figure 5.3) written in two-foot-high letters. In striking contrast, as The Pride of Govan, accompanied by other bands from across the Central Belt, readied to march off, a large banner about ten feet across was unfurled, which read 'We Maintained The Union'. The banner was decorated with the Saltire, the crown, and the Union flag, and was framed with the dates 1707 and 2014 (Figure 5.4). By laying claim to both the Scottish and British flags, and by deliberately conflating the

5.2 The Tall Cranes.

5.3 Republican Govan.

5.4 'Celebrating the Union' loyalist band parade.

histories of the eighteenth-century Acts of Union and the present-day independence referendum, the marchers that day enacted (and re-enacted) what they regarded to be the past and present triumphs of British-Protestant patriotism over Scots-Irish nationalism.

Yet, these loyalists also seemed to remain wary of what they saw as the threat of this disloyal nationalism, which many of my informants suspected still lurked close to the surface of Glasgow society. Echoing the band's defiance of their decidedly un-loyalist symbolic surroundings, a street hawker wandered among the crowds of spectators selling large Union flags which had been overlaid with the words 'RULE BRITTANIA' and 'GOD SAVE OUR QUEEN', as well as the letters RFC, for Rangers Football Club. The spectators' mood, like the band's music, was celebratory, as both those marching and those following basked in the unionist glory of the referendum result. At times, this revelling in the moment of victory became rather pointed, as parade spectators, for example, repeatedly poked small Union flags through the window-grills of an Irish pub along the route. Later, an act of remembrance at the Govan war memorial offered a more sedate, if no less loyalist, expression of victorious Britishness, as wreaths were laid and a minute's silence observed by representatives from the bands and the local Somme Association. The crowds of spectators were particularly appreciative as the parade made its way past the 'Louden Tavern', the self-styled 'quintessential Rangers Supporters Pub' with its bold 'WE ARE THE PEOPLE' sign (Figure 5.5) serving as a further reminder, if one was needed two days after the referendum result, of loyalist claims to ethno-religious constitutional triumph. Moments later, the skies opened with rain falling

5.5 The Louden Tavern.

so hard and so fast that everyone was soaked to the skin within seconds. Undeterred, a stocky man wearing a Rangers FC jacket held aloft a Union flag with arms stretched high and wide in a gesture of patriotic conquest (Figure 5.6). As the rain began to ease and the parade finally reached its conclusion, the crowds dispersed as dripping bandsmen hurried into the Govan Orange Hall for shelter and drinks.

Conclusions: Orange reifications

In the 1998 preface to *Ethnic Groups and Boundaries* Barth reflects on 'a few of its central ideas … in a debate with our contemporaries of thirty years ago'. Now fifty years on from its original 1969 publication, Barth's famous volume is still highly relevant, both in relation to my own analysis of Scots-Orangeism and within a broader contemporary social and political context where populist concerns about the ethnic 'other' appear to have taken centre stage once again. But what, in this contemporary context, are we to make of Barth's warning against viewing 'the world as a discontinuous array of entities called societies, each with its internally shared culture' (1998: 5)? Was Barth right to critique this socio-centrism as the dominant position across the social sciences due to a tendency of these scholars to reproduce 'commonsense reifications of people's own discourse and experience' (ibid.)? While I find Barth's central thesis compelling, these later reflective comments seem to present something of a challenge to the very idea of 'the ethnographic stance' (Laidlaw 2014), whereby the anthropologist seeks to learn about the social and moral world they are investigating by simultaneously learning from it. Barth's

5.6 Loyalist spectator celebrating the referendum result.

challenge becomes all the more pointed when we realise that the Orange Order do, in effect, reify their own discourse and experience, a process, I have argued, that takes place semiotically, through realist assertions about the connections they draw between, for example, lines of school buses, overgrown weeds, referendum campaigns, and papal plots to overthrow the British monarchy and undo the Reformation (see Ball 2014).

Of course, depending on one's theoretical approach, reification can either be used critically, as Barth does above, to suggest a *misplaced* concretisation of something abstract, or it can be used descriptively, and in the transitive sense, as simply meaning to make something abstract real. Through my adoption of the ethnographic stance, I have, as a result, partly stepped away from Barth by deliberately stepping into my informants' reifications of their own experience by seeking to learn from their semiotic realism, their connecting of historical, ritual, fraternal, and consti-tutional dots, and thereby learn about (and from) Orange claims about the moral worth of triumphalism, secrecy, hate, and ultra-unionism. Clearly, then, where Scots-Orangemen engage in what Barth calls reification, they do so unapologetically, and with no sense that what they are doing is misplaced or illogical, for the con-nections they forge to make sense of their own experience posit no clear distinction between the abstract and the real.

In this reading, reifications of Orange 'discourse and experience', reifications which my own informants engaged in more or less constantly, and which I have sought to ethnographically inhabit and then redeploy as anthropological theory, worked hard to close the gap between claims about reality and observable political outcomes. That both Glasgow and North Lanarkshire voted 'Yes' to Scottish independence, for example, is not disputed but is regarded as fact. Yet my Orange informants also regarded the undue influence of 'the Church of Rome' to be a key fact in explaining these localised referendum results. Seen from this perspective, reification is not a fallacy – it is not wrongly positing an abstraction as something real – but is a clear-eyed assessment of how hidden forces and abstract powers *become* real, in this case through observing and participating in a constitutional referendum.

Clearly, Orangemen do what Barth says anthropologists should not do, namely they view 'the world as a discontinuous array of entities called societies, each with its internally shared culture' (1998: 5). That I have sought to follow my informants into their self-essentialism, is, I am sure, something that Barth would warn against, eroding, as it does, the distinction between emic observation and etic scholarly analysis. But in this instance, I am convinced that just such erosion is required to learn about Orange unionism 'from the inside of a set of ethical concepts' (Laidlaw 2014: 45). Seen from this 'inside' perspective, for Orangemen, British Protestant unionism and Scots-Irish Catholic nationalism are indeed discontinuous, with each having its own distinct and ethnically bounded culture. In a way, by adopting a different approach to Barth regarding the intellectual worth of reification, I have (at least partly) followed my informants in doing what Barth says anthropologists should not do. Indeed, instead of seeking to expose what many will regard as a fallacious connecting of religious, political and ethnic dots, my aim has been to trace out how these dots have been connected in a way that is semiotically and morally generative, and thus deeply realist. As such, I have not sought to step away from reifications of Orange morality, but have sought to step into them, and in so doing, to explain what my informants regarded to be the hidden reality of Catholic and republican plots against Britishness in Scotland. Understood thus, I have sought to make sense of how Orangemen reify not only their ethno-political and ethno-religious morality, but also how they reify themselves. Celebrated as latter-day Covenanters and latter-day loyalists, Orangemen, I have argued, come to regard themselves and their fellow brethren as religious and constitutional guardians of British Protestant unionism.

That such guardianship takes place through gossip, storytelling, and the circulation of conspiracy beliefs highlights another element of Barth's argument that appears to be at odds with how my Orange informants experienced life within the Order. Where Barth states that 'people's categories are for acting, and are significantly affected by interaction rather than contemplation' (Barth, 1998: 29), I have sought to show how acts of moral contemplation are central to Orangeism. This is true not only for the Masonic-style Orange initiation rituals described in Chapter 3 (which, as in Freemasonry, are imagined to work their magic *after the fact*, through contemplative reflection), but can also be seen within Orange campaigns for a 'No' vote. Here, much of my informants' energy was spent reflecting on the meaning of the phrase 'Home Rule is Rome Rule', and, more specifically, by contemplating the threat of Scottish nationalism with its imagined links to Roman Catholicism and Irish republicanism. More positively, Orangemen also contemplated, variously, what it meant to be British, a loyalist, a Presbyterian from the Covenanting tradition, a Rangers FC supporter, and a monarchist. In this sense, acts of political activism were also acts of contemplation. Handing out 'Independent Unionist' leaflets, rallying outside the Scottish Parliament, making speeches from Orange platforms, scrutinising the placement of SNP posters outside polling stations – all of these acts existed as social, political, and religious interactions that were simultaneously contemplations of constitutional change, and thus of existential threat and hoped-for victory.

Seen in this way, one conclusion we might draw about Scots-Orangeism, both in the midst of its referendum battle and more generally, is that it is, or at least strives to be, a discontinuous entity with an internally shared culture that does what it does, socially, politically, and religiously, in and through acts of moral contemplation. This is, in essence, what I will argue next, in the Conclusion of this book. More specifically, I want to argue that Orange moral contemplation produces Orange apophatic exceptionalism – a carefully thought out (and lived out) sense of ethno-religious and ethno-national chosenness, coupled with a (no less carefully thought out and lived out) rejection of what is seen to be 'green', in all its imagined 'popishness' and 'disloyalty'.

Note

1   Act of Supremacy 1534 and Act of Supremacy 1558.

Conclusion: 'The Good' of Orange exceptionalism

And to the Reubenites, and to the Gadites, and to half the tribe of Manasseh, spake Joshua, saying, Remember the word which Moses the servant of the Lord commanded you, saying, ye shall pass before your brethren armed, all the mighty men of valour, and help them; Until they also have possessed the land which the Lord your God giveth them. And they answered Joshua, saying, All that thou commandest us we will do, and whithersoever thou sendest us, we will go. [...] And the children of Reuben, and the children of Gad, and half the tribe of Manasseh, passed over armed before the children of Israel, as Moses spake unto them. (Joshua 1: 12–16; 4: 12)

What does it mean to be special? For my Orange informants, this question has several answers, all of which are necessary, but none of which are sufficient, if taken alone, to encapsulate what makes British Protestants, and Orangemen most of all, a truly exceptional 'race apart'. Within the Orange Order, the concept of 'specialness' is often made sense of with reference to the Old Testament. The narrative above, for example, taken from the book of Joshua about the 'two-and-a-half tribes' who led Ancient Israel into the Promised Land, stands as a key element of the founding mythos of the Orange Institution. What these Orange appropriations of Israel's exodus offer us, then, is a distillation of how Orangemen see themselves not only within the context of formal ritual, but also in the daily round of their lives inside and outside the Order. Given both the salience of these Old Testament narratives for my informants, and the wider anthropological insights they offer interpreters of Orangeism, I want to take the rather unusual step of beginning this concluding chapter not with a summary of my arguments thus far, but by offering something new.

What I want to offer, then, is an account of the astonishing and sometimes disorientating claims of British Israelite theology, as connected, in part, to American ideas about manifest destiny, before applying these more directly to Orange ideas about divine queenship, and finally, to Orange ideas about British Protestant exceptionalism. Yet, in an important sense, nothing I am about to describe will be entirely new to the reader, for 'British-Israel Truth', as it is known by those who follow it, stands as the theological foundation not only of Orange ritual, but also of Orange morality. What comes to be constructed on top of this foundation,

I shall go on to argue, is a form of exceptionalism which defines Orange specialness apophatically, producing a version of moral personhood that is said to apply to some, but crucially is also said not to apply to all. I want to begin setting out this argument by returning to the mystical number of the Orange Order – the 2½ – and to its connection to the biblical passage from Joshua quoted above.

Reuben, Gad, and the half-tribe of Manasseh were an elite subsection of God's Chosen People, selected to lead the vanguard across the Jordan and into the land God had given them. Not only did they commune with their patriarchs Moses and Joshua, but also with God Himself, receiving and following His divine commands. More than this, they were 'mighty men of valour', strong and brave soldiers, armed and ready to battle those who would oppose the expansion of God's 'special possession'. While several of my Orange informants followed British Israelite theology to draw these parallels in a very literal manner (believing themselves to be the historical and thus biological descendants of the 2½), most Orangemen I met likened themselves to Israel in a more metaphorical sense. Importantly, this is not to suggest that British Israelite theology was only of peripheral importance to Orangemen. Indeed, as I demonstrate below, the moral logic of 'British-Israel Truth' permeated both Orange and wider Protestant-unionist-loyalist culture via its provision of a constellation of Protestant-Zionist signs and symbols, including everything from flags, to coronation liturgies, to national anthems, to football chants, which could be connected up in diverse ways to produce a wide range of different images and imaginations of (decidedly non-metaphorical) Orange exceptionalism.

The importance of the language of chosenness for Orangemen has also been noted by Buckley (1985), whose analysis of the biblical stories on which Orange, Royal Arch Purple, and Royal Black Institution regalia are based states that 'the texts provide a set of metaphors which allow Ulster Protestants … to see themselves as similar in certain respects to the Israelites and Jews described in the Bible (1985: 5). Buckley also notes the ways in which biblical metaphor and allegory – which position Orangemen and Sir Knights as 'the chosen few' – can simultaneously be imbued, from both a Calvinist and British-Israel perspective (ibid.: 23), with more literal claims. Commenting on the Exodus narrative, the story of Reuben, Gad, and Manasseh, and several other biblical passages important to Orange and its sister Purple and Black Institutions, Buckley concludes that while it is true that 'if one were to ask a Blackman directly whether he believed himself to be one of God's chosen people, he would probably respond with appropriate embarrassment' (ibid.), it is also true that 'the idea of having been 'chosen' by God … is one which has some significance in Protestant thought in Ulster' (ibid.). As such:

> It would indeed be difficult for a Protestant unionist who encountered these stories … not to recognise the similarity between the situation of the Ulster Protestant and that of the heroes of the various stories. Like the people of Israel in Canaan, Ulster Protestants have been given, and now occupy, an alien land. The foreigners whose land they occupy are, like the Canaanites, the Midianites, the Philistines, and all others, adherents of an alien religion. Like Jacob, they steadfastly avoid marrying the daughters of their enemies. Like the heroes of the stories, they lay great stress on loyalty, whether to their religion or to the crown. (ibid.)

For Buckley, ritual re-enactments of these stories further reinforce these Ulster Protestant claims to chosenness:

> At its mildest, individuals will frequently maintain that when they do God's work, they do so by the grace of God and hence they may say they have been chosen by God to do His work ... [while] a stronger form of this logic ... express[es] more explicitly that they are of the 'elect' and hence they are members of God's chosen people. There is also a small but influential number of individuals in Ulster who hold that the people of the British Isles are descendants of the peoples of the Northern Kingdom of Israel. They hold that Queen Elizabeth is rightful queen because of her direct descent from King David. For these, the people of Britain, and especially those who are loyal both to Queen and to the Protestant faith are, in a peculiarly Old Testament sense, God's chosen people. (ibid.)

As I detail below, what Buckley describes of members of the Royal Black Institution in Ulster more than thirty years ago is also strongly present among Scottish Orangemen today. And as Buckley rightly points out, the importance of such exceptionalist logic does not depend on whether it was taken to offer historical or allegorical truths, but rather depends upon how it provides 'object lessons' (ibid.: 24) about 'a fixed relationship ... between Catholicism and Protestantism' (ibid.: 14) via stories about 'the difficulties faced by God's chosen people when dealing with heathens, foreigners and other villains' (ibid.). Indeed, whether or not one took the claim that British Protestants were the biological descendants of the 'Lost Tribes' literally or metaphorically, the effect was broadly the same, producing a narrative and experience of chosenness which allowed Orangemen make sense of how and why they were special.

Consider the following. Like their ancient Hebrew forebears, Orangemen stand as an elite subsection of an already special nation, leading British Protestants (God's chosen nation and people) to secure their place within their 'land of hope and glory', their 'New Jerusalem'. Despite papal resistance, they do so, moreover, by communing with God through the open Bible and through God's chosen monarchs, past and present, in their commemoration of King Billy 'Prince of Orange', and in their service to Queen Elizabeth II, 'Defender of the Faith'. As such, like Reuben, Gad, and the half-tribe of Manasseh, Orangemen stand as mighty men of valour, ready to resist those who resist their expansion, as they march through the highways and byways of Scotland, Northern Ireland, England and Wales. More than this, a select few – especially in Northern Ireland in the pre-Good Friday era – stood ready to do battle, armed against their Catholic and Irish Republican enemies, supplementing Orange banners (and sometimes Israeli flags) with actual weapons of war. While I encountered few contemporary Scots-Orangemen who claimed active links to loyalist paramilitarism, many more had links to the British army – links which were often celebrated as part of an Orangeman's patriotic and sacred duty to protect the nation. Crucially, while such battles were framed as a struggle, like their Williamite and Hebrew forebears, any such hardship was thought to be endured with the sure knowledge that God's purposes were being worked out for the good of all his elect.

In this context, being special means being chosen, while being chosen means being united to God – spiritually, semiotically, and thus materially – through the unfolding of history and through the securing of territory, be it Canaan, Ulster, or Scotland. Of course, Orangemen are not the only ones to think of themselves as somehow exceptional, indeed, such claims to uniqueness appear as the foundational assumption of nearly all forms of nationalism, for even in the civic nationalism of liberal democracies they see themselves as especially excellent, precisely on the basis of their liberal values (see Fukuyama 1992). More than this, Orangemen are not the only Protestants to deploy Old Testament accounts of the Hebrew Exodus as a route to giving weight to exceptionalist claims. Stephanson's analysis of the English Puritan roots of nineteenth-century American ideas about 'manifest destiny' is illuminating on this point:

> English Protestantism, early on, had developed a notion of England as not only spatially but also spiritually separate from the European continent, as the bastion of true religion and chief source of its expansion: a place divinely singled out for higher missions. The [Puritan] Separatists who crossed the Atlantic were part of this tradition, only more radical. Old England, in their eyes, had not broken in the end with the satanic ways of popery. Divine purposes would have to be worked out elsewhere, in some new and uncorrupted land. (1995: 3–4)

What Stephanson says about New World Puritans' fear and loathing of Anglican compromise with Rome was (and is) precisely the same fear expressed by the Scottish Covenanters and their contemporary Orange champions, with one exception. For Orangemen, while continental Europe was indeed thought of as the hell's mouth of popery, England (and Britain generally) was not thought to be lost. Indeed, while under perpetual threat from a potentially resurgent ultramontane papacy, Ulster and Scottish Orangemen who dedicated themselves to keeping the Williamite tradition alive continued to see Britain as the rightful home of true religion, as guaranteed not by the expansionism of an American Protestant free-for-all, but by the consolidation of a British Protestant constitutional monarchy led by the king or queen of God's choosing. Regardless of this difference, the Exodus story still provided an invaluable wellspring of inspiration for ultra-Protestants in both the Old and New worlds:

> When 'manifest destiny' was coined in the 1840s, apocalyptic Protestantism and utopian mobalization had actually reached a level unmatched since early colonial times. So it is no surprise that the expression should have been heavily suffused with religious overtones. Its origins, in fact, lay directly in the old biblical notions, recharged through the Reformation, of the predestined, redemptive role of God's chosen people in the Promised Land: providential destiny revealed … Yet it was more than an expression: it was a whole *matrix*, a manner of interpreting the time and space of 'America'. […] This, then, was the New Canaan, a land promised, to be reconquered and reworked for the glory of God by His select forces, the saving remnant in the wilderness. (Stephanson 1995: 5–6)

The fact that this notion of a 'land promised' could be used (to good effect) to refer to Co. Armagh, the West of Scotland, *and* North America indicates not only

the malleability of such a narrative, but also its power, allowing all Protestants in
those places, if so inclined, to claim to be citizens of a this-worldly Zion, with all
the privileges such a moral status would afford. Indeed:

> The Puritan re-enactment of the Exodus narrative revolved around the powerful
> theology of chosenness [and thereby] ... inherited and reworked the Hebrew
> tradition of divine election as consecrated through the covenant with God... 'Ye
> shall be unto me a kingdom of priests, and a holy nation' (Exodus 19:6). [Applying
> this theology to themselves] through the Reformation ... the Puritans emerged
> as the truest of the true Christians, hence assuming teleological responsibility for
> righteousness and journeying alike in the exodus to the New Israel. (ibid.: 6–8)

During the mid-nineteenth century, while Protestant colonisers from New England
continued to journey west into the proffered American wilderness, Orangemen
from Ulster journeyed east to Scotland, moving into the urban slums of Glasgow.
For both sets of migrants, despite inhabiting radically different physical environments
on either side of the Atlantic, imagining their common historical origins, their
analogous present realities, and their shared future destinies as akin to that of
Ancient Israel seemed not only apt, but deeply logical. The lands they entered were
rich with opportunity, and yet strewn with hostile enemies – Indian 'heathens'
and Irish papists – who, like the Hittites and Amorites, knew not God's ways.
Despite suffering expected opposition, as new Protestant arrivals they flourished,
clearing and claiming land and building industry wherever they went. Guided and
enlightened not only by the spirit of capitalism, but also by the spirit of God,
American and Ulster-Scots Protestants of this era, with lineages which traced back
to Britain, could now also trace their lineage and lived experience (sometimes
literally, sometimes figuratively) to Father Abraham.

Among those of a more literal persuasion was W. T. F. Jarrold, a leading British-
Israel writer, whose 1927 book *Our Great Heritage* confidently declared that:

> With the British Israel *Master-Key* it has been brought home ... that God's promises
> to Abraham some four thousand years ago are being literally fulfilled in our time
> in the British Nation, her Dominions, and the American people ... The heritage
> is great, and with it our responsibilities as a Nation are equally so, and it behoves
> every one living under the Union Jack to do their upmost to further the coming
> of God's Kingdom. (Jarrold 1927: xiii–xiv)

While old-fashioned, Jarrold's Union-flag-draped language and sentiments could
hardly be more Orange. Importantly, the passage quoted above is far from a rhetorical
outlier, with much of the argument and evidence contained within *Our Great
Heritage* touching upon similar ethno-religious and ethno-national themes. Indeed,
for Jarrold, 'a careful study of God's Word reveals ... the history of a *family* which
has been *chosen of God* to carry out His Divine purposes in and for the world at
large' (ibid.: 1), thereby proving 'the origin of the British people and their lineal
descent from the *Ten Tribes* and *House of Israel*' (ibid.: 5). As such, the etymology
of the word 'British' is said to be 'formed of two Hebrew words, "*Brith*" and "*Ish*",
meaning in Hebrew "*Covenant People*"' (ibid.: xx). As a nation of 'special advantages'
(ibid.: 2), the Protestant people of Britain are said to be 'a literal and not a mere

mythical race, having been chosen by Him out of the rest of mankind as His own inheritance (ibid.: 59).

For Jarrold and other followers of British Israelite theology, evidence for this special status abounds. Union flag colour symbolism, for example, is said to be foreshadowed 'in the curtains and coverings of the Tabernacle in the Wilderness' (ibid.: 97), while the Royal Standard is said to be 'made up of the Lion of Judah and the Unicorn of Ephraim' (ibid.: 110–111). Equally, the British national anthem is said to date 'back to the day when *King Saul* was chosen *King of Israel*: "And all the people shouted, and said, *God Save the King*" (1 Sam. X, 24)' (ibid.: 110). To add to such claims, the Stone of Destiny, also known as the Coronation Stone, historically used by Scottish monarchs but last used in the coronation of Elizabeth II, is said to be the pillow used by Jacob as he dreamed of the heavenly ladder described in Genesis 28 (ibid.: 168). So, too, is the language of Britain said to have sacred origin, 'the English tongue [being] … so Hebraic that the Bible can be literally translated into English better … than into any other known tongue' (ibid.: 100–101). Even Scotland's most famous poem, Burns' 'Auld Lang Syne', is said to reveal 'a looking backward of our Saxon fathers to the old days and times in Palestine of old and a further Waymark of our Ancient Race' (ibid.: 102). Here, the 'old acquaintance be forgot' is that between Britain and Israel – a kinship to be remembered and reclaimed through the promulgation of 'British-Israel Truth' (ibid.: passim). So clear is the evidence, according to Jarrold, that 'any reasonable and reflecting man' (ibid.: 328) will come to agree that British Protestants stand as the 'outward, visible, and earthly … "Kingdom of God"' (ibid.: 189). Indeed:

> No more remarkable manifestations of the exact fulfilment of the Divine Decrees as shown in the Bible have ever been recorded in history than those displayed in the Almighty's providential dealings with the peoples dwelling in Great Britain and Ireland – these *'isles which are beyond the sea'* (Jer. xxv, 22). In every phase of British history, and especially in the marvellous perpetuation of the *Royal Line of our Sovereigns* … we can trace unmistakable evidences showing 'The good Hand of God upon Us' (Ezra vii, 9), ordering and directing National affairs, according to His Will and Pleasure, in pursuance of His vast designs concerning *'The remnant of His people'*, the *'Outcasts of Israel'* and the *'Dispersed of Judah'*. (ibid.: 129–130)

While all of the above is self-evidently true for convinced British Israelites, much of it also rang true for my Orange informants. Indeed, while uncovering the literal Hebrew origins of the British monarchy or the English language was a niche interest of some Orangemen, the broader claim that there was something deeply (and even literally) sacred about Britishness was affirmed by every Orangeman I met. More than this, Orange framings of the sacrality of Britishness shared many hallmarks of British Israelite theology, rendering the connection far more than one of mere elective affinity. In order to make sense of these ethnographic observations, their cultural salience within Scots-Orangeism, and their wider theoretical importance for anthropological understandings of exceptionalism, I have chosen to group them under three interrelated themes, namely: (i) Britishness and divine queenship; (ii) British light and Romish darkness and; (iii) Football rivalry and British-Protestant chosenness. These themes have been selected not only because they help make ethnographic sense out of disparate Orange expressions of 'British-Israel Truth' and thereby the divine specialness of Britain as a Protestant nation, but because they also speak to the wider empirical and conceptual content of this book – to imaginations of Catholic conspiracy and the history of Protestant triumph, to the ritualisation of secrecy and secretly crafted identities, to the sectarian curation of loving fraternity and hateful enmity, and to the preservation of British unionism as a political and religious imperative. I want to consider each theme in turn, allowing each set of reflections to build on the next, before concluding with a final argument about the challenge Orange exceptionalism poses to both the anthropology of Christianity and the anthropology of morality.

Britishness and divine queenship

Orange claims about the divine status and mission of the British monarchy emerge from a number of different quarters. At its simplest, the British monarch was valorised by my Orange informants as a Protestant bulwark against Roman Catholicism. Such an assertion was often made without recourse to specific historical events, but was stated flatly, as a simple and self-evident truth, which, to Orangemen, it certainly was. When a diachronic narrative account was offered, such comments often referred to the Act of Settlement 1701, which, following the Glorious Revolution of 1688, legislated to prevent a Roman Catholic from sitting on the throne. In this post-Williamite context, as acute sectarian panic gave way to chronic religious suspicion, the British monarch was transformed from a short-term deliverer to a long-term protector – a literal *Fidei Defensor* or 'Defender of the Faith'. Under this guise, the current Queen may be formally referred to as 'Elizabeth the Second, by the Grace of God, of the United Kingdom of Great Britain and Northern Ireland and of Her other Realms and Territories Queen, Head of the Commonwealth, Defender of the Faith'.

While this last element of the designation is a specifically Anglican one, establishing the British monarch as Supreme Governor of the Church of England, this specificity mattered little to my Scots-Orange informants, who were clear in their minds that, while Presbyterian was probably (but not universally) preferable, what was of ultimate importance was the apophatic content of Anglicanism, for to be Anglican was, in essence, to be a 'not Catholic' who defended Protestantism primarily by defending *against* Catholicism. According to one Grand Lodge staff member I interviewed, such royal defence was still needed today:

> She [the Queen] is the one constant. She's still at the front. Still unwavering. She doesna hide her beliefs. She is a Christian lady. The Roman Catholic Church were the only religious body that pushed for the removal of the Act of Settlement. Why? [Because] if we have a Roman Catholic monarch, the monarch is no longer the Head of State – the Pope is.

I encountered similarly fervent attitudes whenever my Orange informants spoke of Prince Charles, whom they accused not only of wanting to pluralise this element of the royal designation – to 'Defender of the Faiths' – but to do so to please his second wife Camilla Duchess of Cornwall, whom many believed to be a secret Catholic, having been brought up in the faith, along with her still practising Catholic siblings, by their Catholic father. Some of my informants went further, suggesting that Charles' real plan was to pave the way for the removal of the Act of Settlement, allowing Camilla to reign as a future Catholic Queen, returning the throne, and therefore Britain, to papal control. Such was the sacred importance of Queen Elizabeth II's role as the (indefectibly singular) Defender of the Faith.

While Prince Charles was viewed with considerable contempt within Orange circles (with several of my informants admitting to me that they wished he would somehow miss out on being King, allowing his son William, a latter-day 'King Billy', to take the throne), Elizabeth II was universally revered by Orangemen. In addition to everyday acts of royalism – singing the national anthem, offering a 'loyal toast' to the Queen's portrait, praying for the Royal Family, claiming all British streets as 'the Queen's highway', expressing love for 'Queen and Country' – I also encountered Orangemen who spoke of the Queen in terms that gave her an almost divine status. Reflecting on such attitudes, Bill, a leading Orangeman in the East of Scotland told me how, within the Order, the Queen functioned as 'Protestant iconography'. Having noticed my surprise, given that what he was claiming appeared so strikingly un-Protestant, far from qualifying it, Bill made his claim stronger still, explaining that to many Orangemen, the Queen was 'a plaster-cast saint'.

While deliberately provocative, Bill's Marian-inspired descriptions were still insightful, helping me to see how, in a semiotic sense, the Queen was indeed a religious icon. This is because, for Orangemen, she physically resembled and offered a real connection to the divinity of British Protestantism. As Head of State and Head of the Church of England, she was thought of by Orangemen as the guarantor (and personification) of both the Union and the Reformation. Indeed, the primary symbol of the Order – the open Bible topped with the crown – was held by my Orange informants to bear a literal truth, namely that a British Protestant monarch was the only thing preventing the Bible from being snapped shut by a papacy who feared that mass biblical literacy would expose its heresy and thereby thwart its ultramontane ambitions (see also Webster 2015). As an icon, as a 'plaster-cast saint', the person and institution of the Queen was thus believed to rest upon solidly Protestant-biblical foundations, as in Orange symbolism, where her crown rested atop (and was thus founded upon) the open Bible. For my Orange informants, then, piety was a kind of patriotism, just as patriotism was a kind of piety, with the result that the very idea of British Protestant ethno-religious nationalism became a tautology, a surplus-to-requirement qualifier on the self-evidently valid conflation of the religion and politics of Orangeism.

Yet, Britain remained as God's 'special possession', I was assured, only and insofar as this biblical foundation lay secure. On more than one occasion, the historical proof for such a claim was given in the form of a story told about Queen Victoria, as she presided over the might of the British Empire. In the Orange retelling of this story, Victoria was said to have been asked by a foreign ruler (sometimes Indian, sometimes African) what the secret of Britain's greatness was.

How and why was it so prosperous and so militarily superior? Victoria's response, my informants explained, came in the form of an answer that was as simple as it was humble – 'the secret of Britain's greatness is the open Bible'. It seems very likely that the source of this Orange myth can be found in a painting by Thomas Jones Barker entitled *The Secret of England's Greatness* (*c*.1862–63) which depicts a nearly identical scene. That, in Barker's depiction, the Bible being handed by Victoria to the East African ambassador is actually closed matters little, for Orangemen find their symbolic sentiment amply reinforced by a prominent carving of an open Bible placed centrally at the bottom of the frame, which, in case the meaning were lost on any viewer, is also inscribed with two verses from Psalm 119: Thy word is a lamp unto my feet, and a light unto my path/I love thy commandments above gold; yea above fine gold (National Portrait Gallery (NPG 4969). See also Nead 2014). With 'England' functioning here as shorthand for Britain and the Empire, and indeed for monarchy and for Reformed biblicism – a series of conflations my Orange informants would be untroubled by – the Queen, be it Victoria or Elizabeth II, stands as a British Protestant icon, a manifestation of God's divine favour, built upon the Bible, and conditional on it remaining open.

As such, not only did this imagined Victorian encounter exist as a popular anecdote during Barker's own day, but his depiction of it found a new audience (and thus an expanded interpretation and significance) among contemporary Orange and loyalist communities in Scotland and Northern Ireland, where the image was recirculated in storytelling and in banner painting (Loftus 1994). Of course, such recirculations were deeply ideological, with the trope of the open Bible remaining open being deployed not simply as a positive claim about Protestantism, but also (perhaps even more fundamentally) as a negative claim about Catholicism. The Orange call to 'keep the Bible open', then, while founded upon support for the Reformed principle of *sola scriptura*, was also a critical call made in the firm belief that this divinely revealed doctrine was one which the Roman Catholic Church decisively (and blasphemously) rejected in favour of priestcraft and papal infallibility. Such blasphemy, I was told, had lethal consequences, culminating in the murder of many Protestant martyrs during the Counter-Reformation, as depicted on many Orange banners, and in the contemporary stained glass of Glasgow Evangelical Church. In this framing, keeping the Bible open was equated with more than merely maintaining 'Britain's greatness', for it also came to be equated with Britain's very survival (both physical and spiritual) as a Protestant nation.

It is difficult to overstate the importance contemporary Scots-Orangemen attach to the Queen's role in this regard. I first came to realise how literal was the identification made by Orangemen between the British monarchy as a Protestant institution and the British nation as a divine community when attending a Grand Lodge annual divine service at Glasgow Evangelical Church in June 2013. Standing to deliver the sermon, Grand Lodge Chaplain the Rev. Alex Forsyth commenced his address with a thinly veiled critique of Prince Charles as heir apparent, and his assumed predilection for religious pluralism, before proceeding to contrast this with the singularity and exceptionalism of the Old Testament origins of the British coronation ceremony. Importantly, much of what he said emphasised the blessings this coronation ritual continued to afford Britain as a Protestant nation, a point he made particularly emphatic by placing great emphasis on the word 'Protestant' each time he used it:

> It would be very encouraging this afternoon to believe that the next monarch would swear allegiance to the *Protestant* throne of the United Kingdom. But unless he does, God will cry '*Ichabod!*' and His Spirit will depart from the British *Protestant* throne, ending 1,000 years of blessing on a little island that has been used by God to do great and mighty things – that His will might be done on earth as it is in heaven. The coronation litany has the full weight of God's authority, and was produced by a revelation from God to use the same spiritual rites that applied to the consecration of a Jewish High Priest. There is no Biblical rite higher, and there is none that is greater. We have, then, a sacred trust, placed by Almighty God in our monarchy at the coronation of the kings and queens of Great Britain. There is this holiness attached to it. They are not only crowned and enthroned, but like the Ancient Priesthood of God, they are set apart and they are anointed. Thus God's anointing and God's appointing are upon them. This places God as Sovereign King over this nation of the United Kingdom, and we become His people. Nowhere but in Israel itself are there a people like the British. So for a thousand years the British people have been blessed with an anointed monarchy who have been faithful to the Word of God.

What Forsyth helps us see here is how, for many within the Order, the British crown did not merely rest on top of the Bible, but was drawn directly from its pages. Indeed, for Forsyth, such a claim was historical fact, as Elizabeth II was made Queen using 'the same spiritual rites that applied to the consecration of a Jewish High Priest'. As such, like the Kings of Ancient Israel, Britain's monarchs were (and still are) holy, set apart, anointed, being bearers of God's sacred trust. Today, such a literally sacred monarchy confers a special blessing onto God's subjects, who are also Elizabeth II's subjects. The result is a monarchical exceptionalism which can only but spill over onto those who are ruled, assuming all parties remain 'faithful to the Word of God', and thus, by definition, the Protestant religion. For Forsyth and my other Orange informants, the consequence of such faithfulness is the 'greatness' of Great Britain, marking this nation, and her people, as specially blessed with a vicarious anointing which has lasted for a thousand years – for 'nowhere but in Israel are there a people like the British'.

Yet, according to these same informants, a thousand-year precedent was by no means unbreakable. Just as popular loyalty to the monarch was conditional on that monarch remaining Protestant (hence, in this narrative, the downfall of James II), so too, I was told, was God's loyalty to Britain conditional on its people remaining Protestant. Here we see how a narrative of exceptionalism can also be a narrative of betrayal. Indeed, it was notable that Orange retellings of Victoria's meeting with the East African ambassador were often followed by an account of national failure, whereby Victoria's British Empire was said to have entered terminal decline once, as a nation, it had begun to secularise, and thus 'close its Bibles'. On this point, Derek, a key informant of mine, was emphatic if also more specific, claiming that

Britain's loss of greatness had accelerated when, in the contemporary period post-Balfour Declaration, the UK had adopted a more critical foreign policy stance towards Israel. 'Britain turned its back on Israel' Derek said, shaking his head, a situation he blamed on what he saw as the logically prior decision taken by the country as a whole to 'turn its back on the Bible' and thus the biblical truth of British Israelite theology.

Forsyth and Derek were not alone in making such claims. Bill Paterson, for example, a well-known Orangeman in the East of Scotland, was also clear that Britain, and particularly Scotland, had, like Israel, enjoyed an especially close relationship with God, a relationship that was now foundering due to a betrayal by apostates in the national Kirk, and in Scottish society at large. Consider, for example, this extract from a speech Paterson gave at an open-air Orange service at the Covenanters' Memorial in Edinburgh's Grassmarket, the themes of which Paterson also frequently discussed in other more informal settings:

> It is hard, at times, my friends, to believe that we were like Enoch and Elijah of old, and walked so close to God – this land of the Book, this land of the Reformation – making Scotland second only to Israel in spiritual and religious significance. With liberalism and ecumenism destroying the church, we are very much like Ancient Israel, far from faith, far from belief in Jehovah God. It is imperative then that we maintain our Protestant ideals and Christian faith that made this small island a jewel in Christ's crown, which was used mightily by God as a means of spirituality, and practically blessing the world in education, science, industry, art, literature, and in sharing the gospel message of our Lord Jesus Christ – Glory to His Name.

For Paterson, Scotland was once utterly exceptional. As citizens of 'the land of The Book', early Scots-Protestants 'were like Enoch and Elijah of old', being patriarchs and prophets whose greatness rested upon their unwavering loyalty (even unto death) to the God of the Reformation. Such Scots were, in spiritual significance, 'second only to Israel', being an adorning possession of Christ, who used them to bring blessing to the world, most powerfully in martyrdom, as they were burned at the stake by the Catholic establishment. Yet, subsequent to the latter-day betrayal shown by liberal and ecumenical churchmen who sought conciliation with Rome, such whoring after other gods had taken Scotland far from Jehovah, just as it had for Israel during their long exodus. United by their idolatrous compromise with false religion (be it papal or Philistine), modern Scotland and Ancient Israel found themselves estranged from their Hebrew-Protestant Heavenly Father and from his unbroken line of chosen monarchs – from David and Solomon, to the Prince of Orange, to Queen Victoria, to Elizabeth II. Such was the specialness of British Protestantism, that it found itself united to Israel not just in good times, but also in bad.

British light and Romish darkness

Of course, from a British Israelite perspective, significant elements of which all three of the Orangemen quoted above share, the irony of such a betrayal was that it stood as a self-inflicted injury, for a Protestant who turns his back on Israel, also, by definition, turns his back on himself. This was the case not only because all Orangemen ritually identify with the Ancient Israelites of the Exodus, but because, much more broadly, Orange claims about Protestant exceptionalism identify all British Protestants as in some sense part of Israel, in and through the divine chosenness of the British Protestant monarch, whose High Priestly coronation and defence of 'True Religion' renders them part of God's 'special possession' and thus a part of His 'chosen race'. In case it is thought that such claims were restricted to the rarefied discourse of formal Orange speeches and Grand Lodge archive deliberations, it should also be noted that I witnessed such debates about British Israelite identity within the Glencruix Social Club. Consider the following ethno-graphic example, drawn from an encounter between the club's regular drinkers and an elderly (non-Orange) visitor called Ralph who walked into the bar from the street and struck up an animated conversation about the true identity of British Protestants.

To my ears – relatively untrained, at that time, in British Israelite theology – Ralph's opening gambit was more than a little bold. Ralph explained how Britons were actually Hebrews, and that Scottish Gaelic was the closest language to Ancient Hebrew still spoken today. To my surprise, Dennis and the others did not appear surprised. Indeed, Dennis's agreement was vocal: 'there is truth in that!' he said confidently, nodding seriously as Ralph spoke of Britain's Israelite origins. Perhaps noting my confusion, Ralph patiently explained that the Ancient Israelites had travelled to Britain, and that modern Scots, in particular, were living descendants of a Hebrew princess who first landed in Ireland. 'If we never had a west wind, we would never have had Britain!' he insisted. Drawing on what I later learned to be a classic British-Israel trope, Ralph also insisted that the word 'British' (*Bris Ish*) meant 'Covenant Man', and that this Hebrew etymology was crucial in pointing to the covenant God had made with Ancient Israel, and thus still held out to Britain today. '*Modern* Israel' Ralph scoffed, 'that's a name they invented to take the name away from *us*!' he insisted with a real sense of anger. As the conversation developed, it quickly became clear that the 'they' Ralph was referring to was Catholics, as well as other 'enemies'.

Elaborating, Ralph went on to warn of similar attempts at historical revisionism, most especially regarding the publication of modern Bible translations, which he said were a 'popish' plot to undermine the Hebrew-English accuracy of the King James version. Several of the Orangemen around the table nodded in agreement. At one point, in response to Ralph's description of the enemies facing God's people, Dennis offered a sudden interjection: 'Roman Catholicism has *always* been evil, *intrinsically evil!*' Listening with considered seriousness, it was Ralph who was now nodding in agreement with Dennis's most vociferously sectarian statements. After a wider discussion about a communist takeover within Glasgow City Council, as well as the godlessness of space exploration and the Edinburgh Tram project, the conversation eventually drew to a close with Ralph speaking a warning about the dangers of change, a warning which offered strikingly similar sentiments about historical exceptionalism and contemporary decline to those already discussed above:

> The Covenanters gave us our freedom. They stood for the Covenant and wouldn't change [even while] the papacy controlled all of Europe. Lots of people call

themselves Christians, but a good way to tell is to ask them where Israel is, and they will normally say 'somewhere in the Middle East'. But it is not! *Israel is all over the world!* It has all changed now; people have been blinded by technology, and they are getting it all muddled up. The masses are caught up with television and the internet. It is difficult to get such books [about British Israelite theology]; no one is interested in such truth. Only elderly people have such books, from before such knowledge was restricted. This world system will creep into everything, but once you have the Bible, you can see all the knowledge spinning out of it.

Interestingly, my internally incredulous reaction to Ralph's claims were not at all matched by the reactions of the club regulars, most of whom seemed to agree not only with his anti-Catholic propositions, but also with his general claims about the Hebrew origins of Britain. Indeed, once Ralph had left, allowing the Orangemen a chance to debrief among themselves, the strongest objection to emerge was Dennis's dislike of Ralph's coat, which he said looked as if it hadn't been taken off since the 1970s. In contrast to this sartorial faux pas, Ralph's claims about Hebrew princesses and local government communist takeovers (see also Chapter 4) seemed, to my Orange informants in Glencruix at least, to raise few eyebrows. Such claims were, it appeared, both familiar to and in broad agreement with wider Orange claims about the specialness of British Protestants as a (literal) race apart.

More than this, in the context of my other interactions among the social club regulars, what seemed to ring most true was Ralph's narrative about the rise and fall of British-Protestant national greatness, a narrative also shared by Paterson and other leading Orangemen. 'It has all changed now' Ralph explained, because 'people ... are getting it all muddled up'. Crucially, as in Orange narratives, for Ralph, unwelcome social change and the ignorance of the British masses emerged from two sources, namely the failing of Protestants who should know better, and the enmity shown to them by Catholics and other enemies. Thus, while the Covenanters were said to have offered Britain freedom, the Protestant masses of today had exchanged this gift for enslavement to modern technology, choosing to become 'caught up with television and the internet'. Perhaps even more insidiously, the attractiveness of such entertainment had allowed the carrying out of a bait-and-switch manoeuvre, a deliberate hiding of knowledge about the true Hebrew identity of British Protestants. 'No one is interested in such truth. Only elderly people have such books, from before such knowledge was restricted'. Yet, for Ralph and for my Orange informants, while the masses remained blinded to the 'popish' plot to deny their divine specialness, as part of the 'Chosen Few' of fully enlightened followers of the Reformed faith, they remained 'in the know' about the real reasons for the past heights and present decline of Britain's greatness.

Here again we see how the fetishisation of the British loyalist historical mythos, as well as the mourning of its partial loss in the Orange present, acts to equip Orangemen with a strong sense of the peaks and troughs of their own exceptionalism. Looking backwards through British history, all of my Orange informants (bar none) confidently asserted to me that British Protestantism had 'invented democracy', as well as the dual principle of 'civil and religious liberty'. Such peaks in national Protestant achievement, often founded upon ideas about how Henry VIII 'stood up to the Pope' or how the Glorious Revolution secured the 'Protestant will of the people', were also seen in more general terms to be demonstrative of the 'greatness of Great Britain'. Britain's role in the Second World War stood as a more recent example of the same, whereby, according to Orange interpretations, the Protestant democracy of Churchill battled victoriously against the Catholic fascism of Hitler and Mussolini.

Yet, there were also troughs, just as there were for Ancient Israel in the wilderness. If the mass appeal of the papal visit in 1982 was Protestant Scotland's most memorable golden calf moment, a more recent low point for Scots-Orangeism occurred as a result of the 2011 Scottish Parliament election, which returned a majority SNP government, despite the vote occurring under a version of proportional representation specifically designed to prevent single-party majorities. Taken together, both cases represent a 'turning away' from Scots-Protestantism and Scots-unionism, as (divinely) personified in the God of the Reformation and in His chosen monarch and the United Kingdom's anointed sovereign, Elizabeth II. As such, for Orangemen watching the 'masses' fall in love with Roman Catholicism and Scottish nationalism, Ralph's words of warning: 'it has all changed now, people ... are getting it all muddled up' seemed particularly apt.

Nonetheless, the majority of my informants still regarded their present, and indeed their future, as guided by the kind of manifest destiny Stephanson (1995) describes of the expansionist American West, albeit one with its own uniquely Orange colouring. From this vantage point, while the peaks of Protestant exceptionalist triumphalism are loudly celebrated in referendum victories and Boyne demonstrations, the troughs of Scots-Protestant experience, too, call Orangemen to affirm and defend 'The Good' of the Reformation and of unionism. 'I'm still fighting the good fight' was a popular Pauline refrain among my informants, and was offered as a statement that one was fulfilling one's Orange vows 'to bear true allegiance to Her Majesty the Queen' and 'to resist by all lawful means, the extension and encroachment' of 'the Church of Rome'. Here, positive support for monarchism and negative critique of 'Romanism' co-constituted one another, just as fraternal love and sectarian hate did so within the context of the Orange social club.

Expressed positively, Britain – as a union of nations, as a constitutional monarchy, and as a democracy – was held up to be the contemporary manifestation (or perhaps, *continuation*) of Thomas Jones Barker's icon of national self-congratulation. As such, England's (that is, Britain's) Victorian-era 'greatness' was held to be an unimpeachable fact, being as true in the contemporary period as it was at the height of the Empire. On this point my Orange informants were emphatic. In response to my asking about the status of the armed forces within contemporary Orange culture, Chuck, for example, was clear that the British colonial impulse of the past was still justified today: 'Britain *is* great, and being great, we have to do our part to support the world in cutting oppression' he explained. Chuck was not alone in basing his sense of duty to extend Britain's civilising mission on the logic of exceptionalism. For Derek, too, the greatness of Great Britain was visible in the realm of comparative international politics. Explaining how he would persuade an undecided voter to support Scotland remaining part of the UK, Derek's answer, given to me as part of an informal recorded interview, was detailed and wide-ranging, yet entirely dependent upon an exceptionalist reading of the highs and lows of Britain's past, present, and future:

> As a United Kingdom, we have the greatest organisation in this world. That's including all the Americans and all the big people. There is nobody like Britain. We have a great system in Britain. Everyone is treated equally, everyone has the right to work, the right to worship, the right to do as they want. The countries that are keeping the world free at present is America, Britain, Australia, and Canada. All the rest of the countries, if you look at them, they are ruled by the church. The church does nae rule in Britain; the church belongs to the people of Britain. Our church system is simple; you can worship God in freedom of choice. There is no need for holy water, statues, eucharist, and all these things. They're not mentioned [or] permitted in the Bible.
>
> Countries have tried for years to break Britain, especially the Roman Empire. Everybody talks about Armageddon. At the end of the day, Christ will rule supreme – it tells you that in the Bible. When the last days come on this earth, there are going to be terrible scenes. If you read and follow scripture, you'll find that all the signs that Christ talked about and promised are all coming to pass. If you take the tribulations that's in the world today, flooding and fire, these things are all related to God and the times.
>
> Britain has lost [its] place in the Christian world; they are gradually losing the Christian system. There are people who are full of hypocrisy in this country, and they're running our country. And one of the biggest traitors we had was Tony Blair. He tried to turn his religion to Roman Catholicism, and he said it was because of his wife. Tony Blair thought he was walking on as the President of the EU, but God had other ideas. [The EU] is Roman Catholic orientated; it was them that started it, and most of the countries that were in it to start with were made up with Roman Catholicism. If you take Southern Ireland as an example, they are the worst country. They have been put in liquidation, and Britain gave them millions of pounds to clear their European debt, and they are still trying to override and change the British constitution. We have a constitution that is second to none, and anyone that understands the constitution [knows that] America comes from the British constitution. All the Free World comes from the British constitution. And now [there is a] Free World that is built around that British constitution.

Derek's comments are worth quoting at length here because they capture something of the complexity and diversity of Orange ideas about 'The Good' of their own exceptionalism, yet do so in a way that also crystallises a number of common themes already touched upon above. First and most obviously is the flatly exceptionalist claim that 'there is nobody like Britain' which is said to be 'the greatest organisation in this world'. In this reading, not only is Britain free, but it gave freedom to the whole world, since 'all the Free World comes from the British constitution'. Second, and connected to this first claim, is the idea while Britain offers all of its citizens freedom of religion, true Christianity (namely British Protestantism), is uniquely biblical, and therefore simple, unmediated, and unadorned. 'There is no need for holy water, statues, eucharist, and all these things. They're not mentioned [or] permitted in the Bible'. Third, the explicit (negative) comparison here is with Roman Catholicism, which not only insists on 'all these things', but does so with a nefarious political agenda in mind, namely to 'rule' every country where it is found.

Fourth, then, as long as it resists subjection to Rome, Britain finds itself under attack by Catholic forces from without and from within – from *foreign* powers like the Republic of Ireland, who, having taken British financial bailouts, sought to 'override' its constitution, and from *domestic* politicians like Tony Blair, who, having betrayed his own Protestant upbringing, sought to turn Britain back to papal rule as a shortcut to achieving his own European political ambitions. Fifth and finally, while Britain is still great in this exceptionalist imaginary, it is not as great as it once was, for as a Protestant nation it is 'gradually losing the Christian system'. Thus, from an Orange perspective, while Britain may remain the pre-eminent bearer of 'the light of the gospel', its grip on this spiritual torch, once held so proudly aloft, appears to be weakening, for Scots-Orangemen and their Queen can only do so much in the face of the increasing apostasy of the masses.

In the meantime, Orangemen seek to spread both 'the light of the gospel' and the light of British imperial sentiment as far and as wide as they are able. Importantly, however, as I argued in Chapter 3, this is not the universal pan-humanist light of Freemasonry; it retains a remarkably specific Protestant quality, which, certain Ghanaian and Mohawk Orange Lodges notwithstanding (Kaufmann 2007: 3), is almost entirely made up of ethnically white populations drawn from the UK and the Commonwealth (ibid.: 9–10). While Britain as the 'light to the nations' may not be burning quite as brightly as my Orange informants believed it once did, this multifaceted metaphor of standing as 'light in a dark place' was still powerfully present within Orange imaginations of itself as an Institution, even where it had receded somewhat from Orange claims about the modern British nation as a whole. Here again, the apophatic quality of such claims is hard to miss, with a few Orangemen even praying that Catholics would 'see the light' exactly because such Orange light was imagined to *not* be darkness, bondage, or defeat, just as being Protestant was tantamount to being a 'not-Catholic'. Of course, the reverse was also true, namely that, in the context of Scots-Orangeism, being a Catholic was largely defined in terms of its enmity to British unionism, and thus to Orangeism.

For Derek, the interplay between this doubled apophasis was clear, for Scottish iterations of British Protestantism and European Catholicism were in opposition to each other, and were thus negatively defined by each other:

> The Roman Catholic Church, if you go back and read early history, they have tried to take over Britain from the first day they ever settled. There are good Roman Catholics, but there's another crowd called the *fenian* who would destroy everything that is British. The fenian wants to destroy everything that is British. They have decided they want the Union Jack down because it is an offensive emblem to them! Wherever the Union Jack flies there is freedom. Popery hates everything that is British. And the Union flag flies over the Free World – wherever you see a Union Jack flying, you know there is a free people there. The aim of

Roman Catholicism is to destroy Britain – to destroy the monarchy in Britain, and the constitution of Britain. [Then] the Roman Catholic Church will move in. The Pope rules supreme over most of the countries that are Roman Catholic: Poland, Italy, France. If you take the European Union flag, with all the stars round about it – all those stars are Roman Catholic, all papish countries, ruled by the Pope.

To the extent that G. E. R. Lloyd is correct that 'antithesis is an element in any classification, and the primary form of antithesis … is division into *two* groups' (1966: 80. Emphasis original), then one conclusion to be drawn here is that Protestant-Orange exceptionalism is significantly defined by *what it is not*. Crucially, this group-formation-by-antithesis also carried with it strong aesthetic, and thus moral, judgements, a process which, as Bourdieu points out, are shown (yet again) to be deeply apophatic, for 'tastes are first and foremost distastes, disgust provoked by horror or visceral intolerance of the tastes of others' (1984: 56). Most fundamentally, then, as above, Protestantism is *good*, it is morally *tasteful*, insofar as it remains separate from its moral antithesis, namely the horrors of Roman Catholicism. Protestantism, then, as a *dis*-taste, may be defined in this purview as 'not-Catholicism'.

But, as Derek makes abundantly clear, many other apophatic dualisms are also at play, negatively defining the contents of exceptionalism, always with reference to its moral antithesis – to that which it is disgusted by, and thus opposes. A British loyalist is the antithesis of an Irish 'fenian', or, more simply, a loyalist is a 'not-fenian'. In the same way, the Union Jack is the not-European-flag (all the more so post-Brexit), just as Protestant freedom is not-Catholic-bondage, and constitutional monarchy is not-papal-supremacy. Other apophatic claims abounded among my informants: Orange was 'not-green', unionist was 'not-nationalist', Rangers was 'not-Celtic', and so on. To develop an example already discussed above, the *true* 'secret of England's greatness' was not simply the Bible, or even an open Bible, but a Bible that *did not remain closed*, and this in spite of all the anti-biblical efforts of the Counter-Reformation to (literally) chain and padlock it shut (see Webster 2015: 22–24). The open Bible carried at the front of every Orange lodge on parade in Scotland is thus fundamentally a 'not-Catholic' Bible, insofar as a Catholic Bible is 'not-open' and thus 'not-Protestant'.

Even the stand-alone concept of exceptionalism (temporarily severed, for our purposes, from any Scots-Orange truth claim) can be seen as a product of this positively generative outworking of the negative (see also Chapter 4), for being exceptional means being '*out of* the ordinary' or '*un*usual' (OED). Importantly, a third definition of the word 'exceptional' is offered by the Oxford English Dictionary, namely 'special'. We find ourselves returning, here, to the question I asked at the very beginning of this Conclusion, namely, what does it mean to be special? To say that being special means being exceptional is surely true, but the tautology it presents seems analytically limiting, at least in the first instance. Equally, while it is true to say that being special may be defined apophatically as being 'not-ordinary' or 'not-usual', this too seems to stop short of where we need to be to gain a better sense of the precise nature of the intellectual challenge that Orange models of 'The Good' pose to the anthropology of morality.

One possible way ahead is to take a brief diversion away from the Orange Institution proper to examine the apophatic qualities of a separate loyalist 'institution', that of Rangers FC. Rangers is Scotland's pre-eminent British 'Protestant' football club and arch-rival of Celtic FC, Glasgow's other top division team, whose fan base is widely associated with Scotland's Irish Catholic community. As already described in Chapter 4, together Rangers and Celtic form the 'Old Firm', Scotland's most infamous football derby, recognised as such because of its role in providing an outlet for public and semi-public expression of (sometimes serious) sectarian disorder. What Rangers offers us, then, is a chance to examine the social life of Orange exceptionalism as it occurs partially outside the confines of the Order by placing ethno-nationalist religion squarely within the context of sporting fandom and 'antifandom' (Theodoropoulou 2007).

Football rivalry and British-Protestant chosenness

While it would be wrong to say that all Orangemen are Rangers fans, a great many *are*, and as a result the links between the Institution and the club are strong, if informal, even well outside of Glasgow. In Glencruix, for example, the Orange social club had a large collection of Rangers memorabilia displayed on the wall, and was host to a local Rangers supporters club who met there on match days to drink and socialise before taking coaches to Ibrox. Live screenings of Old Firm matches were good for business, as they always packed out the Glencruix Social Club, with local Orangemen and other Rangers supporters embracing the fraternal opportunity to drink, cheer together, and then to sing loyalist anthems long into the night. More generally, it was common to see Orangemen with RFC tattoos and rings, and even more common to see spectators at Orange marches wearing Rangers tops. Furthermore, loyalist fancy-goods stalls at Orange marches were always stocked with a plethora of RFC merchandise, while unofficial Orange Order merchandise could also be purchased outside Ibrox on match days. Seemingly out of a desire to affirm such informal links, a prominent Rangers fan group during my fieldwork operated under the deliberately unsubtle name 'The Blue Order'.

Yet, more formal links between Rangers FC and the Orange Order also existed, all the way up to Grand Lodge level. In 2004, for example, as a way to raise money for both organisations, Grand Lodge purchased shares in Rangers Football Club to resell to their own Orange membership. The scheme, which resold the shares with an accompanying Grand Lodge certificate signed by the Grand Master, was marketed as an ideal gift for Rangers-supporting Orangemen, allowing them to become part-owners of the club. It seems justified to conclude that Grand Lodge launched such a joint fundraising initiative, not only because they knew that a ready market existed for such shares within the Institution's rank and file, but because leading members within the Orange hierarchy (including the then Executive Officer) were themselves active Rangers fans. The scheme certainly had some uptake in Glencruix, with one Orangewoman describing to me how she had bought the shares for her husband, an Orangeman, several years in a row 'for his Christmases'. Of course, as Rangers went into liquidation in 2012, these shares are now worth rather less than their original purchase price, even with the addition of the Grand Lodge certificate. Indeed, in the assessment of the Orangewoman quoted above, 'now they aren't worth the paper they're printed on!'

Despite these recent financial difficulties, according to Rangers fans, their football club is special. And while most football fans would surely claim the same about the club they happen to support, Rangers fans, many of my Orange informants included, appeared to make their case on rather different grounds. Indeed, by drawing on quasi-Calvinist notions of chosenness, Rangers fans embraced forms of exceptionalism which closely mirrored those at the centre of Orange experience, doing so in ways that were deeply reliant on apophatic logic. For example, many Rangers supporters clubs took the name 'Chosen Few' as part of their name – Bridgeton Chosen Few, Bellshill Chosen Few, St Andrews Chosen Few, and so on. When I asked a close Orange informant about the meaning of this designation, his answer made no reference to Gideon's chosen men in Judges 7 (see Buckley 1985: 24) but instead quoted what many regard to be a key biblical proof-text for the doctrine of predestination – a move which helped clarify the wider salience of Rangers fans' claims not only to being elite but also *elect*: 'It's biblical language. Jesus' followers were few – he only had twelve disciples. "Many are called but few are chosen". I believe that's where it comes from'. Here, fewness and chosenness co-constitute each other, as per the Gideon story, making the 'chosen few' a special group by virtue of being numerically small *and* deliberately selected. Rangers fans, then, are a faithful remnant, who, like the 2½ tribes of the exodus and their Orange contemporaries, form a vanguard to lead the elect into the Promised Land. It is perhaps unsurprising, then, given the popularity of such tropes, that one of Northern Ireland's most infamous Rangers supporters clubs named itself 'The Vanguard Bears', with this designation and its associated Ulster six-pointed star emblem (coloured blue with a V-insert, echoing the Star of David) being drawn from the Ulster Vanguard movement, a loyalist political grouping active in the 1970s. Such is the narrative of chosenness among Rangers fans.

Other examples abound, such as Rangers' most famous slogan, 'We Are The People', which reveals further details about the logic and narrative force of exceptionalism. For our purposes, this slogan is particularly important because it stands as an assertion not simply of being special, chosen, or elect, but does so in a way that is both totalising and singularising. To be one voice among thousands in the stands of Ibrox chanting 'We Are The People!' is to claim a monopoly over moral personhood. To say 'we are *the* people', is thus to say we are the *only* people, or at least the only 'full' and 'proper' people. Yet, it also seems important to note that Rangers fans are not alone in making such a claim, as the ethnographic and historical record, as well as common idiom, make clear.

Three brief (and intentionally unrelated) examples seem enough to indicate this. First, consider not only the well-known translation of 'The Inuit' as meaning 'The People', but also, more specifically, Yup'ik considerations of themselves as 'the real people' (Fienup-Riordan 1991), a model of personhood which renders all non-Inuit (that is, non-people) as 'ethnically (and racially) distinct' (Searles 2008: 240), and subject to 'repudiation' (ibid.) on that basis. Second, note the historical designation of early Christianity as 'The Way' (as recorded in the Book of Acts, Chapters 9 and 19), a name thought to reference Jesus' unavoidably exceptionalist self-identification as 'the way and the truth and the life' – a self-identification, moreover, which is immediately followed (and thus constituted) by a negative statement, namely, 'no one comes to the Father except through me' (John 14: 6). Third, consider the use of the term 'The City' to refer to various parts of various metropolises, including London's financial district, as well as Manhattan, New York, as if those parts somehow constituted the whole of that city (and indeed all cities), allowing all other urban areas to be somehow erased from one's geographical consciousness. *The* Inuit, *The* Way, *The* City – all become both singularising and totalising, claiming a monopoly over the whole of, variously, peoples, religions, and geographies.

Crucially, as is the case for the above examples, for Rangers fans to say 'We Are The People' is not to stand guilty of the fallacy of composition; it, rather, stands as a true emic reflection of the way in which a specific part legitimately comes to define every (proper) part of the whole, and thus the whole itself. So:

1   We Are The People.
2   We are Protestant-unionist-loyalists.
3   Therefore all (proper) people are Protestant-unionist-loyalists.
4   Therefore all non-Protestant-unionist-loyalists are not (proper) people.

That such a narrative is rarely stated so explicitly, at least not by following it to its logical conclusion in this way, is not evidence of the absence of the kind of exceptionalism I have been describing. Indeed, as discussed below, there is important evidence to the contrary. Furthermore, Rangers fans do not need to be students of philosophical logic in order to dispute the applicability of the fallacy of composition as it might readily be levelled at them. Indeed, all that Rangers fans need do is assert a different (namely a non-universal) moral model of personhood in order for points three and four above to be broadly logical conclusions of points one and two. It is in considering how and why such conclusions might be reached, moreover, that we see the return of apophasis.

As such, not only are Rangers 'Simply the Best', as proclaimed by the club's official Tina Turner anthem, but Celtic are, according to the popular football chant, 'scum, scum, scum'. (Notably, in this context, Turner's anthem is also sung with the additional line 'Fuck the Pope and the IRA' repeatedly inserted). In the same way, where the slogan 'We Are The People' circulates widely in loyalist communities as the graffitied acronym 'WATP', its apophatic inversion may be posited as 'Kill All Taigs', with 'KAT' being inscribed just as commonly, if not more so, on the walls and bus shelters of these same neighbourhoods. Other similar statements of religious and ethno-nationalist antifandom abound within the Rangers scene, with 'No Pope of Rome' and 'No Surrender' being particularly prominent tropes, often chanted in the same supporters club context as the song 'We hate Catholics, Everybody hates Roman Catholics' (see also Chapter 4). Taken together, what such sentiments represent is merely one facet of Protestant-unionist-loyalist exceptionalism – an exceptionalism which, being deeply apophatic, is just as concerned with *what it is not* as with what it *is*.

In this sense, the window onto exceptionalism that Rangers fans open for us via their performances of fandom and antifandom show it to be co-constituted by the inseparability of inclusion and exclusion, love and hate, and ultimately, moral personhood and non-moral personhood. Consider finally, then, this popular Rangers mantra, which combines and conflates positive claims about chosenness with negative claims of dismissal:

> Bluenoses are born, not manufactured
> We do not choose, we are chosen
> Those that don't understand don't matter
> Those who understand need no explanation!
> WE ARE THE PEOPLE

That this same mantra offers a near-perfect encapsulation of the kind of Orange exceptionalism I witnessed over the course of five years in Glencruix and across Scotland's Central Belt seems worthy of further reflection. With a few small word changes, the phrase accurately summarises my central theoretical claim about exceptionalism, namely that it revolves around attributions of specialness that are deeply apophatic, and, as such, produces monopolistic claims about moral person-hood. Indeed, in the daily and deliberative experiences of my informants, Orangemen are born, not manufactured; they do not choose, they are chosen; Catholics who don't understand, don't matter; Protestants who understand need no explanation. They are *The* People.

These sentiments are true for my Orange informants for all of the reasons described in this book. Orangemen are born, their Protestantism being a literal birthright – an inherited and thus inalienable substance that resides 'in the blood', just as much (if not more so) as it resides in any act of volition. It is for this reason that failure to regularly attend a Protestant place of worship will not lead one to being expelled from the Order, while marrying a Catholic certainly will; engaging in such miscegenation with 'the daughters of their enemies' (Buckley 1985: 23) is to sin against the chosenness of the Chosen Race, and thereby to invite 'the menace of Rome' into one's family and fraternity. More than this, as a 'race apart', Orangemen are not manufactured, not even by any initiation ritual, for such rituals act not to confer but to confirm and elucidate the mystical existence of the substance and faith that previously resided within the heart of the neophyte, and who thus *already* stands as 'a true and faithful Protestant, and a loyal subject' (GOLS 1983: 25).

Being a 'race apart', British Protestants also stand as a 'Chosen Race' – as ritual enactors (and, for some, literal descendants) of the Ancient Israelites whose Exodus wanderings took them into the Promised Land, as led by the vanguard of the 2½ tribes, and later, by God's chosen and anointed monarchs. Importantly, such Orange chosenness means being (initially passive) recipients of God's favour, as opposed to agentive producers of divine merit. In this sense, the Orange claim that British Protestants are also God's 'special possession' can be seen as deliberately and unproblematically objectifying, for to be chosen is to be acted upon and selected, or even worn, like so much jewellery – a strikingly similar experience to that described by Simmel in his analysis of secrecy as an 'adorning possession' (1950: 337). As such, to be born and chosen is only fully comprehendible with reference to their apophatic qualities, for Orangemen are also not-manufactured and do-not-choose.

The apophasis of Orange exceptionalism and its monopolistic claim over moral personhood is perhaps most clearly expressed in the second half of the mantra quoted above, namely that 'those that don't understand don't matter', while 'those who understand need no explanation'. Given the context, it should, I hope, be clear that those who neither 'understand' nor 'matter' are, variously, Catholics, nationalists, republicans, and Celtic fans. Importantly, the link here between not understanding and not mattering should be taken as sequential. This is because the Rangers slogan 'We Are The People' (also included at the end of the 'Bluenoses' mantra) is something of a shibboleth, allowing Orangemen and other 'loyal Protestant friends' to readily determine who is *not* a friend, and thus who does *not* matter, on the (prior) basis of their lack of tacit understanding of the meaning and significance of the phrase. Put simply, those who don't understand don't matter precisely because they don't understand, and are therefore 'not-The-People'.

That this shibboleth was frequently deployed as a call-and-response type catechism by a Grand Lodge Chaplain during Orange services in Glasgow Evangelical Church (Chaplain: 'Who are the people?' Congregation: 'We Are The People!') is helpfully clarifying, for it further demonstrates the way in which apophasis and exceptionalism co-constitute each other. Here, not understanding and not mattering are a sequential pair, but they are also constituted by their opposition to the pair which follows them, namely understanding and needing no explanation. Inverting the summary above, here we find that those who understand *do matter* precisely because they need no explanation, and are therefore included within 'The People'. Just as the first and second halves of the shibboleth act in concert to complete the phrase and thus reveal the shared identity of the questioner and answerer, so too with understanding and not-explaining, which, acting in concert, reveal to the Rangers-supporting Orangeman who is a loyal Protestant friend, and thus who truly 'matters'.

'The Good' of apophatic exceptionalism

Of course, for Dennis, and Andy, and Derek, as well as for all my other Orange informants 'who profess hostility to the distinctive despotism of the Church of Rome' (GOLS 1986: 2) – to say that Catholics 'don't matter' is to make a claim about *moral worth*, not a claim about political power or eschatological prominence.[1] Indeed, to say that an ideology or a person is not worthy of being *valued* is not the same as saying they are not worthy of *critical attention*. Indeed, it should be abundantly clear by this point that Orangemen spend a huge amount of time giving critical attention to Roman Catholicism, which they regard as being deserving of hostility, and, for some, outright enmity. From this perspective, for my Orange informants, 'Rome' mattered a great deal, not because it understood the glorious mysteries of British Protestant exceptionalism, but because it hated the very idea of British Protestantism, and as such, in Derek's assessment, sought to 'destroy it'.

What, then, does a good Protestant life look like? Phrased more specifically, what is 'The Good' of Scots-Orangeism? My suggestion throughout this book has been that, for my Orange informants, a good Protestant life is a life that affirms, maintains, and extends 'The Good' of British Protestant exceptionalism, and does so in a way that also remains eternally vigilant against what we might want to call 'The Bad' of Roman Catholic despotism. Looking to history, Orangemen affirm this good by maintaining and extending memories of past Protestant triumph, primarily the victory at the Battle of the Boyne in 1690, but also the resilience of Presbyterianism during 'The Killing Time' of the Scottish Covenanters in the decade immediately preceding it, as well as the rapid expansion of Orangeism in the late eighteenth and early nineteenth centuries, and, much more recently, the maintenance of British rule in Northern Ireland during 'The Troubles'.

Yet, embedded within these exceptional victories were the machinations of Rome, which, according to those in the Grand Lodge archive and the Glencruix Social Club, were plain for all to see. Secret papal directing of Anglican violence against the Scottish Covenanters; James II's ultimate goal to undo the Reformation in England, Scotland, and Ireland; plots to use mobs of armed Catholic peasants in mid-Ulster to challenge the Penal Laws as a route to ending Protestant ascendancy and; the support of Catholic priests for physical force in Irish republicanism during 'the Troubles' – such was the long history of 'the menace of Rome'. Here, the history of victorious Protestant exceptionalism was unavoidably marked by apophasis, with 'The Good' coming to be defined as not-Anglo-Catholic-betrayal, not-British-papal-theocracy, not-Catholic-ascendancy, and not-Irish-reunification. Such was the 'The Bad' of Catholicism that demanded the vigilance of Orangemen in order to protect the memory of the Protestant 'Good'.

If the Orange past was protected as a way to safeguard 'The Good' of Protestantism, so too was the present, not least because it stood as the foundation of the Orange future, and thus the foundation of the future of British unionism, constitutional monarchy, and the Reformed faith. Orange parades, in this view, were a crucial exercising of the hard-won freedoms secured at the Battle of the Boyne, namely civil and religious liberty. To parade through the streets of Edinburgh carrying a huge Orange banner bearing the inscription 'No popery' was thereby an apophatic act which (re)secured the right to free assembly, the right to protest, and the right to witness. That Glasgow City Council and the SNP government had banned a series of loyalist parades in Glasgow in September 2019, and was considering legal options for extending the ban indefinitely, thus came as no surprise to my Orange informants, who told me that any such ban was blatant anti-Protestant and anti-unionist discrimination, and political punishment for campaigning against Scottish independence. It is also no accident that Orange parades are referred to as 'marches' and 'demonstrations'. In terms of the former, to march behind such a banner backed by a military-style loyalist flute band is to march on parade as any army would, engaging in a public show of strength designed to buoy one's supporters and to intimidate one's enemies. Regarding the latter, to engage in a demonstration is not only to protest *against* something, but also to offer up an alternative, to *positively* demonstrate (or witness to) what a good Protestant life looks like, that life being a life of exceptionalism. Of course, according to my informants, the exceptional goodness of such parades, and indeed the *necessity* of such parades, was further demonstrated, as above, by the opposition they attracted, for 'popery', being the ultimate enemy of civil and religious liberty (and the ultimate ally of the SNP), did not want itself to be marched, demonstrated, and witnessed against. To parade against Roman Catholicism then, was to transform apophasis into a kind of *walking* – to parade against those who sought to abolish Orange parades and thereby abolish the exceptionalist freedoms and truths that only the 'No popery' of Protestantism could provide.

If Orange parades show how exceptionalism and apophasis can be co-constituted as a type of walking, then my time within the Glencruix Social Club appears to show how this co-constitution can also occur in and through talk. In Glencruix, 'The Good' of Protestantism came to be defined, in part, as an experience of fraternity that revolved around communal drinking, storytelling, gossip, joking, and banter. Where every such speech act contributed to the love my informants had for the Orange brotherhood, taken together, they formed an exceptionalism borne of language. Here, the 'collective joy' (Turner 2012) of belonging to a special group – the 'Chosen Few' – was positively affirmed by sharing memories about being on parade, by telling stories about drunken escapades in loyalist bars abroad, by cheering on Rangers during televised matches, and by singing loyalist songs during social club music nights. Such 'talk', such words and language, made the Protestant life of Orangemen good. Yet it was not the only thing to make such lives good, for of equal importance was the way in which the goodness and love of fraternal exceptionalism was also constituted by a hatred of that which it was not.

Again, apophasis comes to the fore, with words and language deployed in the negative as a way to create 'The Good' of a 'hateful love', whereby hating Roman Catholicism and Roman Catholics became inextricable from (and even a constituent part of) expressions and experiences of love for Protestantism and fellow Protestants. From this perspective, Orangemen who recount stories about street brawls with Catholics, who yell 'dirty fucking fenian bastard' at Celtic players on television, or who boast about writing 'No Catholics allowed' on the back of their organ donor card are doing something good; they are showing love for their Protestant brethren by performing hatred for Catholics and Catholicism. That this should be so may seem less surprising, moreover, when we realise that Protestantism itself may be defined apophatically as 'not-Catholicism'.

That not everyone agreed with these emic claims was a fact of which my inform-ants were well aware. Indeed, so aware were they of such disagreement that the criticisms they frequently received (generally in the form of pointed accusations of being sectarian) came to be incorporated into their apophatic exceptionalism, and thus into their model of 'The Good'. Dennis's assertion that it was right and good to hate Catholics because Catholics hated the Orange Order is merely one such example. Being hated by one's enemies because they believed you to be hateful was the very thing that justified showing hatred to one's enemies. Such logic, for my Orange informants, was as irrefutable as it was tautological. Other examples included hating Glasgow City Council because of its supposed Catholic-Labour hatred of Orange parades, as well as, more abstractly, hating the colour green because of the way in which those who loved the colour green were imagined to hate the colour Orange. The recently repealed Offensive Behaviour at Football and Threatening Communications (Scotland) Act 2012, which criminalised the performance of certain proscribed football chants on the basis of their purported offensive content stands as another such example. In this case, Rangers-supporting Orangemen who felt unfairly targeted by the Act described to me how they were right to hate it because those who passed the legislation – Scottish National Party MSPs – did so out of a hatred of Rangers, Britishness, and loyalism. Hating those who hated Orangemen merely for speaking the truth of their own Protestant exceptionalism, was, for my informants, part of what made their lives good, for in doing so, they were yet again defending a constituent part of their specialness, namely their apophatic identity as not-Catholics.

As with Scots-Orange accounts of history, parading, and fraternalism, so too with Orange unionism, which gave further expression to the apophatic exceptionalism of my informants, but in this case within the uniquely charged political context of the Scottish independence referendum. To campaign for Scotland to remain part of the United Kingdom, then, was to campaign for Scotland to remain Protestant – and thus *good* – as ruled over by the Defender of the Faith, Queen Elizabeth II, God's chosen and anointed monarch. By definition, then, what the Order's 'British Together' campaign also fought for was the preservation of the greatness of Great Britain, for Britain would remain great, as in Barker's painting, only if the Bible remained open throughout all of its Empire. Importantly, for the Orangemen I followed during the months leading up to polling day, such aspirations were not a backward-looking nostalgia, but were primarily directed towards the future. Safeguarding Scotland's place within the UK meant safeguarding everything Orangemen held sacred, not just the monarchy, but the Union flag, their British citizenship, their freedom to parade as Orangemen, and ultimately, their freedom to worship as Protestants. Without the Union, Scots-Orangemen would no longer be British, which, at its most severe, would entail being left 'outside the camp', cleaved from their rightful place within the 2½ tribes, and thereby divorced from God's elect. Such was the urgency of Scotland's constitutional question, and thus the religion of Orange politics.

As an emergent feature of the exceptionalism described above, the apophatic qualities of Orange unionism are hard to miss. Perhaps the simplest example of this came, albeit from a non-Orange source, as a result of the question on the ballot paper, namely 'Should Scotland be an independent country?' which forced all unionists to pursue a campaign defined almost entirely by the word 'No'. With widespread concerns about the electoral consequences of this negative framing, both the mainstream cross-party campaign and the Orange Order campaign sought a positive reframing of unionism by working under the names 'Better Together' and 'British Together'. Regardless, both campaigns made liberal use of the word 'NO' on their posters and leaflets, and always did so in block capitals – a fact moderated only slightly by 'Better Together's late decision to use the slogan 'NO THANKS'. In this context, unionism came to be defined as 'anti-nationalism' and 'anti-independence', despite unionist efforts to label the SNP and 'Yes Scotland' as 'separatists'.

Among my Orange informants, however, the apophasis of their unionist constitutional commitments extended far beyond that which was prompted by the wording of the question on the ballot paper. Indeed, Orangemen I observed during the months and days leading up to the referendum spoke far more readily, both to me and to each other, about who and what they were fighting *against*, than what they were fighting *for*. In informal conversations and formal campaign speeches, words such as enemy, tyranny, betrayal, deception, threat, treachery, and unforgivable were common. Importantly, that this 'divisive and evil enemy' the Order saw itself facing down was not just the Scottish National Party but also the Catholic Church can be seen in the phrase 'Home Rule is Rome Rule', a slogan I heard repeatedly in Grand Lodge, in Glencruix, and among those Orangemen I observed campaigning door-to-door. As was often the case, Dennis provided the most forthright summary of this aspect of Orange ideology, explaining to me that priests were instructing their parishioners to vote 'Yes' as a way to destabilise British Protestantism in Scotland. Many of my other informants agreed, suggesting that independence would give the Roman Catholic Church more influence in Scotland, and could even lead to a compounding of the dictatorial tendencies of the SNP and the Catholic Church, allowing these institutions to join forces in attacking the civil and religious liberties of Protestants.

As such, the Orange solution to the problem of Scottish nationalism was not 'unionism' per se, but, in Alex Forsyth's framing, 'No Surrender!' and 'No Separation!' It was this distinctly apophatic quality of unionism, then, which mattered so greatly to my informants, for unionism was not-Rome-Rule in exactly the same way that an SNP government – and, all the more so, an SNP-led independent Scotland – was imagined to be Rome Rule. Beyond the referendum, that one consequence of this apophatic commitment to vote for whoever was most likely to 'stop the SNP' was Orangemen choosing to vote for pro-union Catholic Labour candidates over pro-independence Protestant Scottish nationalists was an irony not lost on my informants. Yet, even here, Orangemen felt themselves to be voting with a clear conscience, for just as they had sought to 'use people to our own ends' by persuading Catholics to vote 'No' in the referendum, so too were Orangemen willing to use politicians to their own ends, by tactically voting for Catholic candidates who were believed to be defying their own church hierarchy by supporting Scotland's place within the union. To vote 'No' in the referendum, then, was to protect and maintain a good Protestant life marked by apophatic exceptionalism, that is, a life marked, in Forsyth's words, by 'no surrender to this evil enemy!'

Moral personhood: dualism, monism, and the absence of good

Much of this book, it seems, has been about dualism: Protestants and Catholics; unionists and nationalists; loyalists and republicans; British and Irish; orange and green; Rangers and Celtic; the initiated and the uninitiated; revelation and concealment; fraternity and enmity; love and hate. Drawing inspiration from Joel Robbins' suggestion that it might be anthropologically productive to treat 'the understandings of others as potentially theoretical' (Robbins 2018: n.p.), I hope to have shown not only how these dualisms become real in the lives of my Orange informants – variously, in how they narrate history, undertake ritual, worship, socialise, and engage in political activism – but also how this very duality might be used to better theorise what makes Orangemen's lives good. More than this, by using Orange dualisms to theorise the Orange good, I have also sought to try and clear the ground for a wider re-theorisation of what anthropology means by 'The Good', primarily by seeking to question what might legitimately be included within this category. On this point, I have argued that Orange constructions of apophatic exceptionalism – which assert that a defining feature of the specialness of Protestant- ism is found within its status as 'not-Catholicism' – allow for hate to be included within human experiences of 'The Good', because to hate what one *is not*, by virtue of the logic of apophasis, is to simultaneously love what one *is*.

It also needs to be recognised, how, whenever Orange exceptionalism and apophasis come to the fore, the classificatory impetus of dualism insists upon an emic evaluation, whereby dichotomous pairs are placed in moral opposition, with one (and only one) deemed appropriate for selection. One cannot be deemed a 'good' Orangeman *and* a Scottish nationalist, for example, as the case of Andrew Watson amply demonstrated, neither can one be an Orangeman ('good', or otherwise) *and* choose to marry a Catholic, for such a marriage would trigger one's expulsion from the Order. Other such examples – being an Orangeman and a Celtic fan, being an Orangeman and an Irish republican – seem equally unimaginable. Crucially, the issue is not lack of imagination, but a moral claim about entity and non-entity, presence and absence, abundance and privation. What we see here, then, is the transformation of dualism into monism, whereby 'The Good' of Protestantism comes to form a totality of existence, and thus, as argued above, may claim a monopoly over moral personhood.

Perhaps the best-known example of this kind of claim about entity and non-entity is found in Augustine's theology of evil as *privatio boni*, or the absence of good, an argument he constructs, in part, using the metaphor of a diseased and wounded animal:

> For what is that which we call evil but the absence of good? In the bodies of animals, disease and wounds mean nothing but the absence of health; for when a cure is effected, that does not mean that the evils which were present – namely, the diseases and wounds – go away from the body and dwell elsewhere: they altogether cease to exist; *for the wound or disease is not a substance, but a defect in the fleshly substance* – the flesh itself being a substance, and therefore something good, of which those evils – that is, privations of the good which we call health – are *accidents*. (Augustine in Bourke 1974: 65. Emphasis added)

For Augustine, just as darkness is the absence of light, and disease is the absence of health, so is evil the absence of good – it has no substance in and of itself. It is not an entity, but a non-entity. While there is a certain irony in using the work of a pre-Reformation theologian to theorise Orange experience, and to do so by sug- gesting that Orange definitions of Protestantism depend upon positioning Catholicism as the absence of good, this is precisely what I want to do. Consider the following.

For Orangemen and Orange-sympathisers, being a Protestant-unionist-loyalist means being able to say with confidence 'We Are The People!', and, moreover, to say these words and live them out in a way that goes far beyond the rhetorical. As with Yup'ik considerations of themselves as 'the real people' (Fienup-Riordan 1991), and, more generally, Inuit assessments of non-Inuit as (culturally and racially) non-people (Searles 2008), Orange claims to being *The* People similarly render non-Orange others as non-persons, at least in the sense that they are not full moral persons in the way that God's 'Chosen Few' are. From this perspective, Catholic-nationalist-republicans, as explicitly *not*-The-People, stand apophatically as an 'absence of good'. Indeed, using the logic of Augustine's theology of evil as *privatio boni*, Orangemen view the 'distinctive despotism of the Church of Rome' as a 'wound' inflicted upon the body-Protestant, a spiritual 'disease' that the Reformation sought to cure, and a historical 'accident' put right by King Billy at the Boyne.

How, then, does this relate to my suggestion that Protestantism may be defined apophatically as 'not-Catholicism'? Can Protestantism be 'not-Catholicism' if Catholicism is itself a non-entity? The answer, which I have contended for throughout this book, is that Protestantism can still be defined as 'not-Catholicism' via the invocation of a simple double negative. Consider, for example, the biblical statement 'God is light, and in him is no darkness at all' (1 John 1: 5). Here, the positive statement 'God is light', is, in the very same verse, reformulated apophatically as a double negative, for God also contains 'no darkness', that is, (in the Augustinian sense), he contains no not-light. So too for Orange Protestants, who understand themselves (apophatically) as containing 'no Catholicism', a double negative insofar as Catholicism is regarded as a kind of darkness, and thus as a kind of 'not-light'. The result is a moral monism where Protestantism becomes *all that there really is* – a state of being which stands as a near-perfect example of exceptionalism, Orange or otherwise. This is the case because, in the religiously dualist imaginary of my Orange informants (where one is either a Protestant or a Catholic), Catholicism, as a metonym for everything that deviates from and opposes Protestantism, comes to be understood as the absence of good, being populated by those who are not only 'not-*The*-People', but more fundamentally, not even full moral persons. So also was 'The Good' of Scots-Orange Protestantism – a 'good' which defined and defended its exceptionalism in and through an apophatic claim to being '*The* People', and thus *not*-Catholic, and, in the end, the only *moral* people that could really be said to exist at all.

Having thus adopted the ethnographic stance, what is it, precisely, that anthropology may learn from the exceptionalism and apophasis of Orange morality? One answer is surely that moral personhood cannot be taken as a human universal, for to do so would be to miss the point of Orange claims to being special. As Alex Forsyth proclaimed from the pulpit of Glasgow Evangelical Church to a congregation of Orangemen:

> We are a people who are of God. The principles and expectations of the Orange Order are extremely demanding, and we are called to faithfulness to God's Word and to His doctrine. There are very few people like us, and we need to be faithful to every tenet and every principle.

Edging towards the oxymoronic, another answer would be to widen the scope of non-universal moral personhood to such a degree that its exclusivism is shown to include almost all persons, and to do so in such a way that allows Forsyth's words quoted above not only to be *comprehended by* but also *made applicable to* the kind of self-exceptionalism tacitly claimed by so many peoples and cultures who regard themselves as having a special status in negative relation to those they find somehow distasteful. There are, in this sense, very few people who are *not* like Orangemen, for a good Protestant life, like nearly any life, is deemed to be good to the extent that it can sustain a convincing claim to being exceptional. Learning from exceptionalism in this way allows anthropology to confront aspects of Orange morality that many find unsettling – no more so, surely, than assertions about 'The Good' of religious bigotry and hate – and to see them as having long been a part of 'our' morality, and thus part of 'our' good, even if our ethical gag reflex only becomes visible when we find ourselves in the presence of 'non-liberals' (Fader 2009: passim) whom we (ironically or not) regard with disgust and treat with visceral intolerance. Put simply, learning from the morality of Orangeism seems to involve learning that we are not so very different from them, nor are they so very different from us, for both Orange and non-Orange moralities seem built upon a logic of apophatic exceptionalism that defines 'The Good' of us in relation to 'the Bad' of them, whoever happens to be selected to fulfil those roles.

Note

1 Nor is it to suggest that Orangemen view Catholics as 'not persons' or not human. Clearly, the ethnographic record is replete with (now canonical) accounts of personhood and its limits (see, for example, Read 1955 and Fortes 1973), some of which document very strong demarcations of personhood and non-personhood. It is not my intention to intervene in these debates, most especially because members of the Orange Order *do* regard Catholics as persons, and thus as human beings. My claim should thus be read as a more limited one about the nature of 'proper' and fully moral personhood as informed by Orange ideas about 'The Good' of British-Protestant exceptionalism and 'the Bad' of Catholicism.

Bibliography

Babcock, B. 1978. *The Reversible World: Symbolic Inversion in Art and Society*. New York, NY: Cornell University Press.

Ball, Christopher. 2014. 'On Dicentization' in *Journal of Linguistic Anthropology* 24(2): 151–173.

Barker, Thomas. 1862. 'The Secret of England's Greatness' (Queen Victoria presenting a Bible in the Audience Chamber at Windsor) in *National Portrait Gallery*. NPG 4969. www.npg.org.uk/collections/search/portraitLarge/mw00071/The-Secret-of-Englands-Greatness-Queen-Victoria-presenting-a-Bible-in-the-Audience-Chamber-at-Windsor (accessed 23 September 2019).

Barkun, Michael. 1997. *Religion and the Racist Right: The Origins of the Christian Identity Movement*. Chapel Hill, NC: University of North Carolina Press.

Barkun, Michael. 2003. *A Culture of Conspiracy: Apocalyptic Visions in Contemporary America*. Berkeley, CA: University of California Press.

Barth, Fredrik. [1969] 1998. *Ethnic Groups and Boundaries: The Social Organization of Culture Difference*. Long Grove, IL: Waveland.

Berger, John. 1972. *Ways of Seeing*. London: Penguin.

Blanning, Tim. 2017. *George I: The Lucky King*. London: Penguin.

Blom Hansen, Thomas. 2000. 'Predicaments of Secularism: Muslim Identities and Politics in Mumbai' in *Journal of the Royal Anthropological Institute* 6(2): 255–272.

Bourdieu, Pierre. 1984. *Distinction: A Social Critique of the Judgement of Taste*. London: Routledge.

Bourke, Vernon. 1974. *The Essential Augustine*. Indianapolis, IN: Hackett Publishing.

Bruce, Steve, 1985. *No Pope of Rome: Militant Protestantism in Modern Scotland*. Edinburgh: Mainstream Publishing Company.

Bruce, Steve. 1998. *Conservative Protestant Politics*. Oxford: Oxford University Press.

Bruce, Steve. 2009. *Paisley: Religion and Politics in Northern Ireland*. Oxford: Oxford University Press.

Bruce, Steve. 2012. *Religion and Politics in the United Kingdom*. London: Routledge.

Bryan, Dominic. 2000. *Orange Parades: The Politics of Ritual, Tradition, and Control*. London: Pluto Press.

Bryan, Dominic. 2016. 'Ritual, identity and nation: when the historian becomes the high priest of commemoration' in Grayson, Richard and McGarry, Fearghal (eds) *Remembering 1916: The Easter Rising The Somme and the Politics of Memory in Ireland*. Cambridge: Cambridge University Press.

Bryce, D. 2018. *The Irredeemable Papacy*. Privately published.

Buckley, Anthony. 1985. 'The Chosen Few: Biblical Texts in the Regalia of an Ulster Secret Society' in *Folk Life* 24(1): 5–24.

Buckley, Anthony. 1987. 'The Chosen Few: Biblical Texts in the Symbolism of an Ulster Secret Society' in *The Irish Review* 2: 31–40.

Burke, Kenneth. 1966. *Language as Symbolic Action: Essays on Life, Literature, and Method.* Berkeley, CA: University of California Press.

Burton, Frank. 1978. *The Politics of Legitimacy: Struggles in a Belfast Community.* London: Routledge & Kegan Paul.

Butcher, Deborah. 2014. *Ladies of the Lodge: A History of Scottish Orangewomen,* c. 1909–2013. Unpublished PhD thesis. London Metropolitan University.

Cairns, David and Smyth, Jim. 2002. 'Up off our Bellies and onto our Knees: Symbolic Effacement and the Orange Order in Northern Ireland' in *Social Identities* 8(1): 143–160.

Candea, Matei, Cook, Jo, Trundle, Catherine and Yarrow, Thomas. 2015. *Detachment: Essays on the Limits of Relational Thinking.* Manchester: Manchester University Press.

Cannell, Fenella. 2005. 'The Christianity of Anthropology' in *Journal of the Royal Anthropological Institute* 11(2): 335–356.

Cannell, Fenella. 2006. *The Anthropology of Christianity.* London: Duke University Press.

Cargo, David et al. 1993. *History of the Royal Arch Purple Order.* Belfast: Royal Arch Purple Order Research Group.

Childs, J. 1980. *The Army, James II and the Glorious Revolution.* Manchester: Manchester University Press.

Clawson, Mary Ann. 1989. *Constructing Brotherhood: Class, Gender, and Fraternalism.* Princeton, NJ: Princeton University Press.

Clough, Paul and Mitchell, Jon. 2001. *Powers of Good and Evil: Social Transformation and Popular Belief.* New York, NY: Berghahn Books.

Connolly, Sean. 2007. *The Oxford Companion to Irish History.* Oxford: Oxford University Press.

Cowan, Ian. 1968. 'The Covenanters: A Revision Article' in *The Scottish Historical Review* 47(143) Part 1: 35–52.

Cruickshanks, Eveline. 2000. *The Glorious Revolution.* London: Palgrave.

Csordas, Thomas. 2013. 'Morality as a Cultural System?' in *Current Anthropology* 54(5): 523–546.

Da Col, Giovanni and Graeber, David. 2011. 'Foreword: The Return of Ethnographic Theory' in *Hau: Journal of Ethnographic Theory* 1(1): vi–xxxv.

Dudley Edwards, Ruth. 1999. *The Faithful Tribe: An Intimate Portrait of the Lloyal Institutions.* London: Harper Collins.

Durkheim, Émile. [1912]. 1915. *The Elementary Forms of the Religious Life: A Study in Religious Sociology.* London: Allen and Unwin.

Esseveld, Johanna and Eyerman, Ron. 1992. 'Which side are you on? Reflections on methodological issues in the study of 'distasteful' social movements' in Diani, Mario and Eyerman, Ron (eds) *Studying Collective Action.* London: Sage.

Fader, Ayala. 2009. *Mitzvah Girls: Bringing Up the Next Generation of Hasidic Jews in Brooklyn.* Princeton, NJ: Princeton University Press.

Faubion, J. D. 2001. *The Shadows and Lights of Waco: Millennialism Today.* Princeton, NJ: Princeton University Press.

Festinger, Leon, Ricken, Henry and Schachter, Stanley. 1956. *When Prophecy Fails: A Social and Psychological Study of a Modern Group That Predicted the Destruction of the World.* New York, NY: Harper Torchbooks.

Fienup-Riordan, Ann. 1991. *The Real People and the Children of Thunder: The Yup'Ik Eskimo Encounter with Moravian Missionaries John and Edith Kilbuck*. Norman, OK: University of Oklahoma Press.

Finn, Gerry. 1991. 'Racism, Religion and Social Prejudice: Irish Catholic Clubs, Soccer and Scottish Society – II Social Identities and Conspiracy Theories' in *International Journal of the History of Sport* 8(3): 370–397.

Fortes, Meyer. 1973. 'On the Concept of the Person among the Tallensi' in *Colloques Internationaux du C. N. R. S.* No. 544. Paris: Centre National de la Recherche Scientifique.

Franke, William. 2007. *On What Cannot be Said: Apophatic Discourse in Philosophy, Religion, Literature, and the Arts*. Notre Dame, IN: University of Notre Dame Press.

Fukuyama, Francis. 1992. *The End of History and the Last Man*. New York, NY: Free Press.

Ganiel, Gladys. 2008. *Evangelicalism and Conflict in Northern Ireland*. New York, NY: Palgrave Macmillan.

Geertz, Clifford. 1984. 'Distinguished Lecture: Anti Anti-Relativism' in *American Anthropologist* 86(2): 263–278.

Gell, Alfred. 1998. *Art and Agency: An Anthropological Theory*. Oxford: Oxford University Press.

GOLS. 1983. *Manual of Ritual and Ceremony for Lodges*. Glasgow: Grand Orange Lodge of Scotland.

GOLS. 1986. *Laws and Constitutions of the Loyal Orange Institution of Scotland*. Glasgow: Grand Orange Lodge of Scotland.

Gray, Tony. 1972. *The Orange Order*. London: The Bodley Head.

Grice, Herbert Paul. 1975. 'Logic and conversation' in Cole, Peter and Morgan, Jerry L. (eds) *Syntax and Semantics Volume 3: Speech Acts*. New York, NY: Academic Press.

Haddick-Flynn, Kevin. 1999. *Orangeism: The Making of a Tradition*. Dublin: Wolfhound.

Hann, Chris. 2007. 'The Anthropology of Christianity *per se*' in *European Journal of Sociology* 48(3): 383–410.

Hastrup, Kirsten. 2004. 'Getting it Right: Knowledge and Evidence in Anthropology' in *Anthropological Theory* 4(4):455–472.

Harding, Susan. 1991. 'Representing Fundamentalism: The Problem of the Repugnant Cultural Other' in *Social Research* 58(2): 373–393.

Hertz, Robert. [1909] 2008. *Death and the Right Hand*. London: Routledge.

Hickman, Jacob. 2019. 'Culture and hermeneutic moral realism' in Slife, Brent and Yanchar, Stephen (eds) *Hermeneutic Moral Realism in Psychology: Theory and Practice*. New York, NY: Routledge.

Hickman, Jacob and Webster, Joseph (In Press). 'Millenarianism' in *The Oxford Handbook of the Anthropology of Religion*. Oxford: Oxford University Press.

Hofstadter. 1964. 'The Paranoid Style in American Politics' in *Harper's Magazine* November 1964. https://harpers.org/archive/1964/11/the-paranoid-style-in-american-politics/ (accessed 23 September 2019).

Imperial Grand Black Chapter. 2013. *Take Five! A New Look At Old Truths*. Loughgall: Imperial Grand Black Chapter.

Jackson, Alvin. 2003. *Home Rule: An Irish History, 1800–2000*. Oxford: Oxford University Press.

Jarrold, W. T. F. 1927. *Our Great Heritage with Its Responsibilities: How and Where to Find the Title-Deeds*. London: Simpkin, Marshall, Hamilton, Kent and Co. Ltd.

Jenkins, Timothy. 1994. 'Fieldwork and the Perception of Everyday Life' in *Man* 29(2): 433–455.

Jones, J. R. [1961] 1985. *The First Whigs: The Politics of the Exclusion Crisis, 1678–1683*. Westport, CT: Greenwood Press.

Kapferer, Bruce and Gold, Marina. 2018. *Moral Anthropology: A Critique*. New York, NY: Berghahn.

Kaufmann, Eric. 2007. *The Orange Order: A Contemporary Northern Irish History*. Oxford: Oxford University Press.

Keane, Webb. 2007. *Christian Moderns: Freedom and Fetish in the Mission Encounter*. London: University of California Press.

Keane, Webb. 2014. 'Freedom, Reflexivity, and the Sheer Everydayness of Ethics' in *Hau: Journal of Ethnographic Theory* 4(1): 443–457.

Keane, Webb. 2018. 'On Semiotic Ideology' in *Signs and Society* 6(1): 64–87.

Keates, Jonathan. 2015. *William III & Mary II: Partners in Revolution*. London: Penguin.

Kulick, Don. 1997. 'The Gender of Brazilian Transgendered Prostitutes' in *American Anthropologist* 99(3): 574–585.

Laidlaw, James. 2002. 'For an Anthropology of Ethics and Freedom' in *Journal of the Royal Anthropological Institute* 8(2): 311–332.

Laidlaw, James. 2014. *The Subject of Virtue*. Cambridge: Cambridge University Press.

Lambek, Michael. 2010. *Ordinary Ethics: Anthropology, Language, and Action*. New York, NY: Fordham University Press.

Landes, Richard. 2006. 'Millenarianism and the dynamics of apocalyptic time' in Newport, Kenneth and Gribben, Crawford (eds) *Expecting the End. Millennialism in Social and Historical Context*. Waco, TX: Baylor University Press.

Lebra, Takie. 1972. 'Millenarian Movements and Resocialization' in *American Behavioural Scientist* 16(2): 195–217.

Lévi-Strauss, Claude. 1952. *Race and History*. Paris: Unesco.

Lloyd, Geoffrey Ernest Richard. 1966. *Polarity and Analogy: Two Types of Argumentation in Early Greek Thought*. Cambridge: Cambridge University Press.

Loftus, Belinda. 1994. *Mirrors: Orange and Green*. Dundrum: Picture Press.

Loyal Orange Institution of Scotland. 1983. *Manual of Ritual and Ceremony for Lodges*. Glasgow: Grand Orange Lodge of Scotland.

McAuley, James, Tonge, Jon and Mycock, Andrew. 2011. *Loyal to the Core? Orangeism and Britishness in Northern Ireland*. Dublin: Irish Academic Press.

McDonald, Maryon. 1989. *'We are Not French!': Language, Culture and Identity in Brittany*. London: Routledge.

McFarland, Elaine. 1990. *Protestants First: Orangeism in Nineteenth Century Scotland*. Edinburgh: Edinburgh University Press.

McKittrick, David. 1999. *Lost Lives: The Stories of the Men, Women and Children Who Died as a Result of the Northern Ireland Troubles*. Edinburgh: Mainstream Publishing Company.

MacPherson, D. A. Jim. 2016. *Women and the Orange Order: Female Activism, Diaspora and Empire in the British World, 1850–1940*. Manchester: Manchester University Press.

MacRaild, Donald. 2005. *Faith, Fraternity and Fighting: The Orange Order and Irish Migrants in Northern England, c. 1850–1920*. Liverpool: Liverpool University Press.

Mahmud, Lilith. 2014. *The Brotherhood of Freemason Sisters: Gender, Secrecy, and Fraternity in Italian Masonic Lodges*. Chicago, IL: University of Chicago Press.

Malcomson, W. Peter. 1999. *Behind Closed Doors: The Hidden Structure Within the Orange Camp [the Royal Arch Purple Order] Examined from an Evangelical Perspective*. Banbridge: Evangelical Truth.

Malcomson, W. Peter. 2009. *Inside the Royal Black Institution: The Mysteries, Secrets and Rites Publicly Revealed for the First Time in History*. Londonderry: Evangelical Truth.

Manley, Gabriela. 2019. 'A Scottish Kind of Conspiracy' in *Anthropology News* 12 July 2019. www.anthropology-news.org/index.php/2019/07/12/a-scottish-kind-of-conspiracy/ (accessed 23 September 2019).

Marshall, W. S. 1996. '*The Billy Boys': A Concise History of Orangeism in Scotland*. Edinburgh: Mercat Press.

Mattingly, Cheryl and Throop, Jason. 2018. 'The Anthropology of Ethics and Morality' in *Annual Review of Anthropology* 47: 475–492.

Mead, Margaret. 1928. *Coming of Age in Samoa*. New York, NY: William Morrow.

Millar, Stephen. 2016. 'Let the People Sing? Irish Rebel Songs, Sectarianism, and Scotland's Offensive Behaviour Act' in *Popular Music* 35(3): 297–319.

Miller, John. 1977. *James II: A Study in Kingship*. London: Wayland Publishers.

Mitchell, Richard. 1993. *Secrecy and Fieldwork*. New York, NY: Sage.

Moore, Henrietta and Sanders, Todd. 2001. *Magical Interpretations, Material Realities: Modernity, Witchcraft and the Occult in Postcolonial Africa*. London: Routledge.

Murdie, Cecil, Cargo, William and Kilpatrick, Cecil. 1993. *History of the Royal Arch Purple Order*. Belfast: Order Research Group.

Nead, Lynda. 2014. 'The Secret of England's Greatness' in *Journal of Victorian Culture* 19(1): 161–182.

Needham, Rodney. 1983. *Against the Tranquility of Axioms*. Berkeley, CA: University of California Press.

Needham, Rodney. 1987. *Counterpoints*. Berkeley, CA: University of California Press.

Nenner, Howard. 1995. *The Right to be King: The Succession to the Crown of England. 1603–1714*. Chapel Hill, NC: University of North Carolina Press.

Nolan, Paul Bryan, Dominic, Dwyer, Clare, Hayward, Katy, Radford, Katy and Shirlow, Peter. 2014. *The Flag Dispute: Anatomy of a Protest*. Belfast: Queen's University Belfast.

O'Day, Alan. 1998. *Irish Home Rule, 1867–1921*. Manchester: Manchester University Press.

Olsen, William and Csordas, Thomas. 2019. *Engaging Evil: A Moral Anthropology*. New York, NY: Berghahn Books.

Omelchenko, Dimitri and Pilkington, Hilary. 2015. *Loud and Proud: Listening to the English Defence League*. International Visual Sociology Association. https://visualsociology. org/?p=579 (accessed 23 September 2019).

Önnerfors, Andreas. 2017. *Freemasonry: A Very Short Introduction*. Oxford: Oxford University Press.

Orr, John. 2005. *Review of Marches and Parades in Scotland*. Edinburgh: The Scottish Ministers.

Pilkington, Hilary. 2016. *Loud and Proud: Passion and Politics in the English Defence League*. Manchester: Manchester University Press.

Putnam, Robert. 2000. *Bowling Alone: The Collapse and Revival of American Community*. New York, NY: Simon and Schuster.

Read, Kenneth. 1955. 'Morality and the Concept of the Person among the Gahuku-Gama' in *Oceania* 25(4): 233–282.

Robbins, Joel. 2007. 'Between Reproduction and Freedom: Morality, Value, and Radical Cultural Change' in *Ethnos* 72(3): 293–314.

Robbins, Joel. 2012. 'On Becoming Ethical Subjects: Freedom, Constraint, and the Anthropology of Morality' in *Anthropology of this Century* 5. n.p.

Robbins, Joel. 2013. 'Beyond the Suffering Subject: Toward an Anthropology of the Good' in *Journal of the Royal Anthropological Institute* 19(3): 447–462.

Robbins, Joel. 2016. 'What is the Matter with Transcendence? On the Place of Religion in the New Anthropology of Ethics' in *Journal of the Royal Anthropological Institute* 22(4): 800–808.

Robbins, Joel. 2018. 'Theology and the Anthropology of Christian Life'. *Stanton Lectures 2018*. Faculty of Divinity, University of Cambridge. https://sms.cam.ac.uk/collection/2654114 (accessed 4 October 2018).

Robbins, Joel and Engelke, Matthew. 2010. 'Introduction' in *South Atlantic Quarterly* 109(4): 623–631.

Roberts, David. 1971. 'The Orange Order in Ireland: A Religious Institution?' in *The British Journal of Sociology* 22(3): 269–282.

Robertson, David. 2016. *UFOs, Conspiracy Theories and the New Age: Millennial Conspiracism.* London: Bloomsbury.

Rosaldo, Renato. 1989. 'Introduction: Grief and a Headhunter's Rage' in *Culture and Truth: The Remaking of Social Analysis.* Boston, MA: Beacon Press.

Rosie, Michael. 2004. *The Sectarian Myth in Scotland: Of Bitter Memory and Bigotry.* New York, NY: Palgrave Macmillan.

Rosie, Michael. 2014. 'Tall Tales: Understanding Religion and Scottish Independence' in *Scottish Affairs* 23(3): 332–341.

Sahlins, Marshall. 1966. 'The original affluent society' in Lee, Richard Borshay and DeVore, Irven (eds) *Man the Hunter.* New York, NY: Transaction Publishers.

Saul, Gwendolyn and Marsh, Diana. 2018. 'In Whose Honour? On Monuments, Public Spaces, Historical Narratives, and Memory' in *Museum Anthropology* 41(2): 117–120.

Scheper-Hughes, Nancy. 1995. 'The Primacy of the Ethical: Propositions for a Militant Anthropology' in *Current Anthropology* 36(3): 409–440.

Scott, Michael. 2007. *The Severed Snake: Matrilineages, Making Place, and a Melanesian Christianity in Southeast Solomon Islands.* Durham, NC: Carolina Academic Press.

Scott, Michael. 2014. 'To be a wonder: anthropology, cosmology, and alterity' in Abramson, Allen and Holbraad, Martin (eds) *Framing Cosmologies: The Anthropology of Worlds.* Manchester: University of Manchester Press.

Searles, Edmund. 2008. 'Inuit Identity in the Canadian Arctic' in *Ethnology* 47(4): 239–255.

Senior, Hereward. 1966. *Orangeism in Ireland and Britain, 1795–1836.* London: Routledge & Kegan Paul.

Shoshan, Nitzan. 2016. *The Management of Hate: Nation, Affect, and the Governance of Right-Wing Extremism in Germany.* Princeton, NJ: Princeton University Press.

Shweder, Richard. 2016. 'Channeling the Super-natural Aspects of the Ethical Life' in *Hau: Journal of Ethnographic Theory* 6(1): 477–483.

Simmel, Georg. 1950. 'The secret and the secret society' in Wolff, Kurt (ed.) *The Sociology of Georg Simmel.* New York, NY: The Free Press.

Smith, Alexander. 2011. *Devolution and the Scottish Conservatives: Banal Activism, Electioneering and the Politics of Irrelevance.* Manchester: Manchester University Press.

Smith, Katherine. 2012. *Fairness, Class and Belonging in Contemporary England.* New York, NY: Palgrave Macmillan.

Speck, William. 2002. *James II.* London: Longman.

Stasch, Rupert. 2003. 'Separateness as a Relation: The Iconicity, Univocality and Creativity of Korowai Mother-in-Law Avoidance' in *Journal of the Royal Anthropological Institute* 9(2): 317–337.

Strathern, Marilyn. 1996. 'Cutting the Network' in *Journal of the Royal Anthropological Institute* 2(3): 517–535.

Stephanson, Anders. 1995. *Manifest Destiny: American Expansionism and the Empire of Right.* New York, NY: Hill and Wang.

Theodoropoulou, V. (2007). 'The anti-fan within the fan: awe and envy in sports fandom' in Gray, Jonathan, Harrington, C. Lee and Sandvoss, Cornel (eds) *Fandom: Identities and Communities in a Mediated World.* New York, NY: New York University Press.

Troost, Wout. 2005. *William III, The Stadholder-King: A Political Biography.* Farnham: Ashgate Publishers.

Turner, Edith. 2012. *Communitas: The Anthropology of Collective Joy*. New York, NY: Palgrave Macmillan.

Uscinski, Joseph. 2018. *Conspiracy Theories and the People Who Believe Them*. Oxford: Oxford University Press.

Van Wyk, Ilana. 2013. 'Beyond Ethical Imperatives in South African Anthropology: Morally Repugnant and Unlikeable Subjects' in *Anthropology Southern Africa* 36 (1&2): 68–79.

Walker, Graham. 1995. *Intimate Strangers: Political and Cultural Interaction Between Scotland and Ulster in Modern Times*. Edinburgh: John Donald Publishers.

Walker, Graham. 2016. *The Labour Party in Scotland: Religion, the Union, and the Irish Dimension*. New York, NY: Palgrave Macmillan.

Webster, Joseph. 2013. *The Anthropology of Protestantism: Faith and Crisis among Scottish Fishermen*. New York, NY: Palgrave.

Webster, Joseph. 2015. 'Objects of transcendence: Scots Protestantism and an anthropology of things' in Jones, Timothy Willem and Matthews-Jones, Lucinda (eds) *Material Religion in Modern Britain: The Spirit of Things*. New York, NY: Palgrave.

Webster, Joseph. 2018. 'The Exclusive Brethren 'doctrine of separation': an anthropology of theology' in Lemons, Derrick (ed.) *Theologically Engaged Anthropology*. Oxford: Oxford University Press.

West, Harry. 2007. *Ethnographic Sorcery*. Chicago: University of Chicago Press.

West, Harry and Sanders, Todd. 2003. *Transparency and Conspiracy: Ethnographies of Suspicion in the New World Order*. Durham, NC: Duke University Press.

Index